Rosa Baughan

The influence of the stars

A book of old world lore

Rosa Baughan

The influence of the stars
A book of old world lore

ISBN/EAN: 9783742829139

Manufactured in Europe, USA, Canada, Australia, Japa

Cover: Foto ©Andreas Hilbeck / pixelio.de

Manufactured and distributed by brebook publishing software
(www.brebook.com)

Rosa Baughan

The influence of the stars

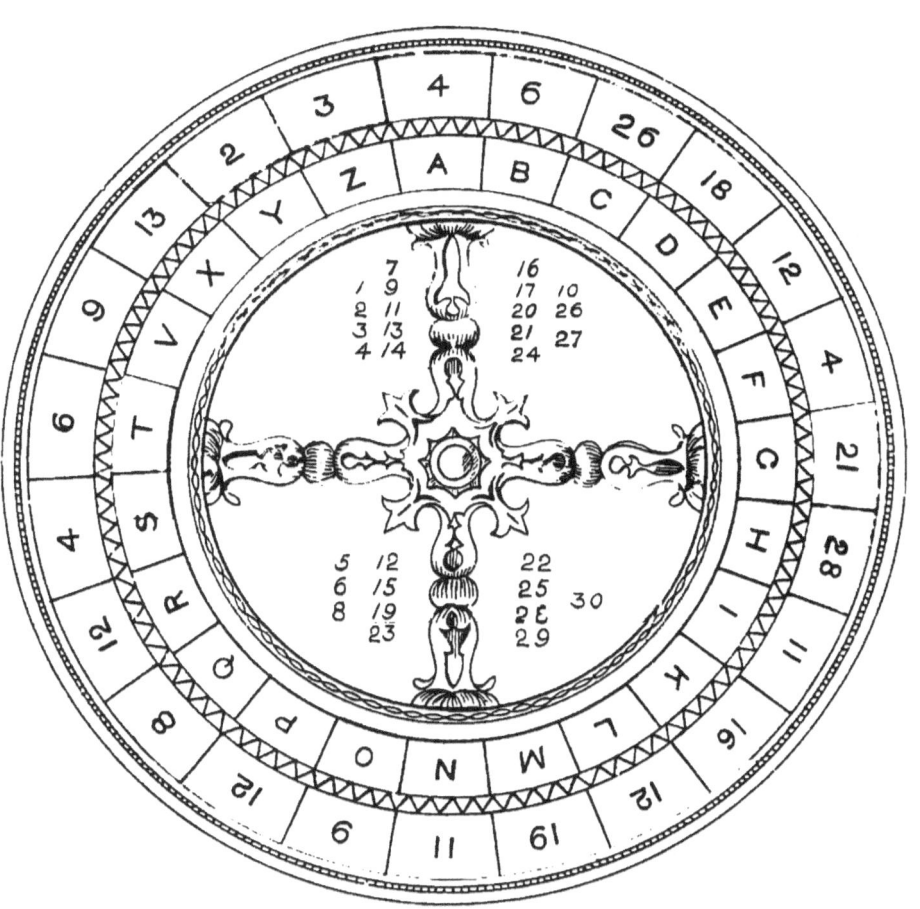

WHEEL OF PYTHAGORAS. FACSIMILE FROM AN OLD WOODCUT
DATE. 1657.

THE

INFLUENCE OF THE STARS:

A BOOK OF OLD WORLD LORE.

BY

ROSA BAUGHAN,

Author of " The Handbook of Palmistry," " Character in Handwriting," &c., &c.

" Ye stars which are the poetry of Heaven !
  If, in your bright leaves we read the fate
Of men and empires—'tis to be forgiven,
  That in our aspirations to be great,
Our destinies o'erleap this mortal state
  And claim a kindred with you ; for ye are
A beauty and a mystery, and create
  In us such love and reverence from afar,
That Life, Fame, Power, and Fortune have named
  themselves a star."   BYRON.

IN THREE PARTS.

Part I.—ASTROLOGY.   Part II.—CHIROMANCY.
Part III.—PHYSIOGNOMY.

To which are added Chapters on the Significance of the Moles of the Body astrologically considered, the Mystical Wheel of Pythagoras and the Methods of working it.

Illustrated with 9 Plates.

LONDON :

KEGAN PAUL, TRENCH, TRÜBNER & CO., LTD.

1891.

have followed in this track, thus rendering their works comparatively worthless, and one well-known writer, whilst producing a book full of the wisdom of the ancients, boldly disavows astrology in the following sentence: "The names assigned to the mounts, which are those of the principal seven planets, are not given them by reason of any astrological significations which they were supposed to bear, but because we have been accustomed to connect certain characteristics with certain gods of the pagan mythology." This is contrary to the views of every ancient writer,— Greek, Latin, German, Spanish, Italian, French, and English, —on this subject, who one and all base the whole theory of Chiromancy on planetary influences. Dr. Saunders, in the preface to his exhaustive work on Chiromancy and Physiognomy, published in 1671, and dedicated to his friend Lilly, the great astrologer, says: "For our more orderly proceeding with the body of this work, it is in the first place necessary to be observed that there are seven planets, named *Stellæ Errantes*,—wandering stars,—which have each of them its separate character as they are used in astrologie; the which stars have great power over inferior bodies, and do each of them govern some part or other of man's body, and they *especially have their material existence in the hand*, and without astrology Chiromancy could not subsist and be subservient to true wisdom." Now, why, in the face of this and many other equally forcible words among the old-world authorities, do the modern writers try to force their own crude theories upon us? To drag the time-honoured study of Chiromancy into the turmoil of nineteenth-century existence and—by robbing it of its mysticism—to strain it into unison with the realism of modern thought, strikes the earnest student with the same sense of incongruity as would the hanging of a carnival mask over the mystically calm features of an antique statue.

ROSA BAUGHAN.

March, 1889.

ASTROLOGY.

To deny the influence of the stars is to deny the wisdom and providence of God.—Tycho Brahe.

THE INFLUENCE OF THE STARS.

ASTROLOGY.

"To doubt the influence of the stars is to doubt the wisdom and providence of God."—TYCHO BRAHE.

CHAPTER I.

THAT a certain power, derived from æthereal nature, pervades the whole earth, is clearly evident to all. Fire and air are altered by the motions of the æther, and these elements, in their turn, encompassing all inferior matter, vary it, as they themselves are varied, acting equally on earth and water, on plants and animals. The Sun, not only by the change of the seasons, brings to perfection the embryo of animals, the buds of plants, and the springs of water, but also, by his daily movement, brings light, heat, moisture, dryness, and cold.

The Moon, being of all the heavenly bodies the nearest to earth, has also much influence, and things, animate and inanimate, sympathise and vary with her. By her changes rivers swell, or are reduced, the tides of the sea are ruled by her risings and settings, and animals and plants are influenced as she waxes or wanes. The stars also produce in the ambient* many impressions, causing heats, winds, and storms, to the influence of which earthly things are subjected. The force of the Sun, however, predominates, because it is more generally distributed; the others either

* The ambient means the heavens when spoken of in a general manner.

co-operate with his power or diminish its effects. The
Moon more frequently does this at her first and last quarter;
the stars act also in the same way, but at longer intervals,
and more obscurely than the Moon. From this it follows
that not only all bodies which may be already in existence
are subjected to the motion of the stars, but also that the
impregnation and growth of the seeds from which all bodies
proceed are moulded by the quality in the ambient at the
time of such impregnation and growth. When, therefore, a
person has acquired a thorough knowledge of the stars (not
of what they are composed, but of the *influences* they
possess), he will be able to predict the mental and physical
qualities and the future events in the existence of any one
whose actual moment of birth is accurately given to him.
But the science of astrology demands great study, a good
memory, constant attention to a multitude of different
points, and much power of deductive judgment; and those
persons who undertake to cast horoscopes without possessing
these qualities, must necessarily make frequent mistakes in
their judgments, which, perhaps, accounts for much of the
disbelief which exists as regards the power of astrology;
but it is unfair to blame the science for inaccuracies which
are only the result of the ignorance of its exponents. No
one should attempt to pronounce judgments on the influence
of the stars without having first given years of study to the
science; and even then, unless he should have been born
under certain influences,* he will never become a proficient
astrologer.

The practice of observing the stars began in Egypt in
the reign of Ammon (about a thousand years before the
Christian era), and was spread by conquest in the reign of
his successor into the other parts of Africa, Asia, and
Europe; but it appears to have been taught in the earliest
ages only by oral tradition, for there is no good evidence

* Saturn, Mercury, and the Moon.

of its having been reduced to written rules before some
years after the first century of the Christian era, when
Claudius Ptolemy (who was born and educated in Alex-
andria) produced a work called " Tetra-biblos," or Quadri-
partite, being four books of the influences of the stars. In
this treatise (translated into English by John Whalley—
professor of astrology—in the year of 1786) Ptolemy seems
to have collected all that which appeared to him of importance
in the science. Another translation of the " Tetra-biblos,"
rendered into English from the Greek paraphrase of that
work by Proclus, was made in 1822 by J. M. Ashmand, and
this is, by most people, preferred to the translation made
by Whalley. Somewhere between 1647 and 1657, Placidus
di Titus, a Spanish monk, published a system of astrology,
founded, to a great extent, upon Ptolemy's calculations.
This work was printed in Latin, and is called the " Primum
Mobile : or, First Mover," and was translated by John
Cooper in 1816 ; other translations have appeared, but this
is the best among them.

The planetary orbs, which the ancients recognised as
having the most powerful influence, were seven in number
(now known under the Latin names of the principal deities
of the heathen mythology), viz.: Jupiter, Saturn, Apollo
or Sol, Mercury, Venus, Mars, and Luna or the Moon.

It may be objected that science has long since revealed to
us many more planets than the seven known to the ancients ;
but in considering a study so mystical as that of astrology
it is better to adhere to the theories of the old-world
writers. In the earliest ages almost all the inhabitants of
the earth led pastoral lives,—were, in fact, merely shepherds,
—but amongst these shepherds there naturally arose, from
time to time, men of superior intelligence, whose imagina-
tions (purified and strengthened by solitude and the constant
communion with nature, which grew out of that solitude)
led them to the study of those distant lights which they
saw, night after night, appear and disappear in the wide

expanse of the heavens above them. Of purer lives and
more impressionable than we moderns, they were necessarily
more open to the influences of nature; and all their
thoughts being given to the study of the mysteries by
which they felt themselves surrounded, their intuitive perception is likely to be a safer guide on mystical subjects
than the scientific conjectures of our day. Besides, as the
results produced by their methods were astoundingly correct,
why should we imagine ourselves capable of bettering their
theories ? Jupiter, Saturn, Mars, and Mercury are *still* the
most important planets, whilst the Moon (though so small)
has a more subtle influence in consequence of her nearness to
us ; whilst of the Sun's power over us and the whole creation
there can, of course, be no question. Each of these seven
planets is in the ascendant once during the space of the
twenty-four hours forming the day and night; and according
to the junction of two or more planets, under which a person
is born, his outward appearance, character and fate, will
be influenced. The sign of the zodiac, too, under which a
child comes into the world, possesses a power to produce
a particular form of body and mental inclination, always
however, *subject to the influence* of the seven planets.

It must also be borne in mind that the planets dominating the lives of both parents would, to a certain extent,
have an influence not only during the pre-natal period of
our existence, but also in arresting or hurrying forward the
moment of our advent into life. The father's influence is
strong at the moment of conception; the mother's during
the whole period of pre-natal existence. In this way we
can account for the resemblance between parents and
children, and also for the physical and mental qualities
which we see constantly reproduced through a long line
of ancestry. It is rarely that one planet is the sole influence
of a life, for the child at birth may, and more generally
does, receive influences from several planets, and some not
those of the father or mother ; and thus we can account for

the innumerable differences of mind and body to be found among members of the same family.

For the benefit of those who object that there is too great a leaning to what they would call "the dangerous doctrine of fatalism" in these old-world beliefs, it may be well to quote a few reassuring words from a very able and voluminous writer on these subjects, Dr. Richard Saunders, who modestly styles himself on the title-page of his learned work (published in 1671) student in astrology and physic. "The stars," he says, "have such an influential power over us that we act by them, and though *they are but second causes*, their influences do so necessitate us that we cannot avoid their fatality, *unless* we have recourse to the First Cause which governs this all." In other words, though the stars influence us, God rules the stars.

CHAPTER II.

THE ALPHABET OF ASTROLOGY.

THE Science of Astrology consists of four branches, namely, *Mundane Astrology*, which is the art of foreseeing, by the aspect of the stars, at certain periods, the events likely to happen to nations, such as pestilences, wars, inundations, and earthquakes; *Atmospherical Astrology*, which is the art of foreseeing, by the positions of the heavenly bodies, the quality of the weather at any particular time or place; *the Casting of Nativities*, or the art of foretelling, from the position of the stars at the moment of birth, the fate and character of the native; and *Horary Astrology*, or the art of foreseeing, by the positions of the heavens at the moment, the result of any business or circumstance.

As the two former branches are treated in the astrological

almanacks issued every year by Zadkiel, Raphael, Orion, and
others, it is needless to go into them ; but as the casting
of nativities and the answering of horary questions require
individual treatment, the working of these two branches of
astrology (after the ancient methods) shall be described as
clearly as possible.

Before the student can do anything in astrology he
must master its alphabet,—that is, he must make himself
thoroughly acquainted with the symbols used to represent
the planets, the signs of the zodiac, and the aspects.

The planets recognised by the ancient astrologers are, as
we have seen, seven in number, and are as follows, with
their symbols :—Saturn, ♄ ; Jupiter, ♃ ; Mars, ♂ ; Sol, ☉ ;
Venus, ♀ ; Mercury, ☿ ; Luna, ☽ .

There are also the Dragon's Head, thus symbolised, ☊ ;
and the Dragon's Tail, ☋. These are neither planets nor
signs of the zodiac, nor constellations, but are only the
nodes or points where the ecliptic is crossed by the Moon.
One of these points looks northward, where the Moon
begins her northern latitude, and the other points south-
ward, where she commences her south latitude. The head
of the Dragon is considered of a benevolent nature ; the
tail of the Dragon is of evil tendency.

There is also the Part of Fortune thus symbolised, ⊕.
This is merely a position affecting the judgments in a
nativity, and its effects will be explained in their proper
place.

There are also the twelve signs of the zodiac, which are
as follows, with their symbols :—

NORTHERN.	SOUTHERN.
♈ Aries	♎ Libra
♉ Taurus	♏ Scorpio
♊ Gemini	♐ Sagittarius
♋ Cancer	♑ Capricorn
♌ Leo	♒ Aquarius
♍ Virgo	♓ Pisces

Through these twelve signs the planets continually move and are ever in one or other of them.

They are divided into *north* and *south*. The first six, from Aries to Virgo, are *northern*; the latter six, from Libra to Pisces, are *southern*: this is because the Sun and planets when in the first six are north of the equator, and when in the last six they are south of that line.

Each point of the zodiac rises and sets once every twenty-four hours, occasioned by the earth's revolution on its axis once every day; therefore, when any given point is *rising*, the opposite point must be *setting*.*

As the zodiac consists of 360 degrees from the first point of Aries until we come to that point again, and as these are divided into twelve portions or signs, they must consist of 30 degrees each.

The aspects are five in number; they represent certain positions which the planets bear to each other as they move through the signs of the zodiac; they are as follows, with their symbols :—

    ♂ Conjunction, when two planets are in the same place : viz., in same degree of the same sign.

    ✳ Sextile, when they are 60 degrees or two signs apart.

    □ Square, when they are 90 degrees or three signs apart.

    △ Trine, when they are 120 degrees or four signs apart.

    ☍ Opposition, when they are 180 degrees or six signs asunder.

The Conjunction (♂) is rather a position than an aspect, as planets can hardly be said to *aspect* each other when they are in the same place. When Saturn is in the first degree of Aries, and any planet in the same degree of that sign, they are said to be in conjunction; this is good or evil, according to the nature of the planets thus posited.

---

* Aries is always opposite to Libra; Taurus to Scorpio; and so on of all the rest, as shown by the table given (p. 6).

The Trine ($\triangle$) is the most powerful of all the good aspects.

The Sextile ($*$) is favourable.

The Square ($\square$) is evil.

The Opposition ($\mathcal{S}$) is also very evil.

There are several other aspects (sometimes called the " modern aspects ") invented by Kepler; but as they only appear to complicate what is at best a very intricate study, it is best to ignore them, and adhere in this, as in the matter of the planets, to the old methods.

CHAPTER III.

CONCERNING THE SIGNS OF THE ZODIAC.

THE zodiac is a band or belt, measuring about 14 degrees in breadth, but, as Venus sometimes appears to have more than her real latitude, it is more correctly considered to be 18 degrees in breadth. The *ecliptic*, or path of the Sun, passes exactly through the centre of the zodiac, longitudinally.

The ancients divided the zodiac into *ten signs*,—Libra being omitted altogether, Virgo and Scorpio being merged into one, thus: Virgo-Scorpio. This accounts for the similarity of their symbols, ♍ ♏.

Ptolemy divides the zodiac into twelve equal parts, of 30 degrees each. He says :—" The beginning of the whole zodiacal circle (which in its nature as a circle can have no other beginning or end, capable of being determined) is, therefore, assumed to be the sign Aries, which commences at the vernal equinox, in March."

One of the many objections urged against Ptolemy's system of astrology is that the signs are continually moving from their positions; but Ptolemy seems to have been aware of this motion of the signs, and has met this objection by what he says in the twenty-fifth chapter of the first book of the "Tetra-biblos," where he makes it clear that the respective influences he ascribes to the twelve signs were considered by him to belong rather to the *places* they occupied in the ambient than to the stars of which they are composed; and he especially speaks of the *ambient* as producing the effects attributed to the respective signs of the zodiac when in the ascendant in a nativity; thus his astrology is just as applicable to modern astronomy as it was to his own.

The signs have been divided into four *triplicities*, thus: *fiery*, ♈, ♌, ♐; *earthy*, ♉, ♍, ♑; *airy*, ♊, ♎, ♒; and *watery*, ♋, ♏, ♓.

The *bicorporal*, or double-bodied, signs are ♊, ♓, and the first half of ♐. The *fruitful* signs are ♋, ♏, ♓; the *barren* signs are ♊, ♌, and ♍.

The tropical signs are Cancer and Capricornus.

The signs of *long-ascension* are ♋, ♌, ♍, ♎, ♏, ♐. The signs of *short-ascension* are ♑, ♒, ♓, ♈, ♉, ♊. The last-named are so-called because they ascend in a shorter period of time (owing to the diurnal motion of the earth being, when they ascend, nearly parallel with its orbit) than the others.

Signs of voice are ♊, ♍, ♒, and the *first* half of ♐, because, it is said, when *any one of* these signs ascends at a birth, and Mercury is strong, the native will be a good orator.

Ptolemy tells us that the signs Aries, Gemini, Leo, Libra, Sagittarius, and Aquarius were denominated *masculine*, and the remainder *feminine*, in alternate order, "as the day is followed by the night, and as the male is coupled with the female." He also says that any two signs configurated with each other at an equal distance from the same, or from either equinoctial point, are termed *commanding* or *obey-*

ing. The signs in the summer semi-circle are commanding, and those in the winter semi-circle, obeying. Any two signs equally distant from either tropical sign are equal to each other in power, and such signs are said to *behold* each other. All signs between which there does not exist any familiarity in any of the modes above specified are inconjunct and separated. For instance, all signs are inconjunct which are neither *commanding* nor *obeying* nor *beholding* each other, as well as all signs which contain between them the space of one sign only, or the space of five signs, and *which do not share* in any of the four prescribed configurations, viz., the Opposition, the Trine, the Quartile, and the Sextile.* All parts which are distant from each other in the space of one sign only are considered inconjunct, because they are averted, as it were, from each other; and because, although the space between them may extend into two signs, the whole only contains an angle equal to that of one sign: all parts distant from each other in the space of five signs are also considered inconjunct, because they divide the whole circle into *unequal* parts; whereas the spaces contained in the configurations above mentioned, viz., the Opposition, Trine, Quartile, and Sextile, produce *aliquot* divisions.

How the modern followers of Ptolemy have been able to reconcile the new aspects,—with the protest contained in the above paragraph,—which is taken from the first book of the "Tetra-biblos,"—is difficult to understand.

As regards the physical influences of the different signs of the zodiac when rising at birth, Ptolemy tells us that it is the general tendency of the quadrant between the vernal equinox and the summer tropic,—that is, of the signs Aries, Taurus, and Gemini,—to produce good complexions, tall stature, and fine eyes, with a temperament abounding in heat and moisture.

---

* It will be remembered that the aspect, or more properly, position of the conjunction is when the planets are in the same sign.

The quadrant from the summer tropic to the autumnal equinox,—Cancer, Leo, and Virgo,—tends to produce an ordinary complexion, proportionate stature, a healthy constitution, large eyes, a stout person, with curled hair, and a temperament abounding in heat and dryness.

The quadrant from the autumnal equinox to the winter tropic,—Libra, Scorpio, and Sagittarius,—causes yellowish complexions, slender, thin, and sickly persons, with a moderate growth of hair, fine eyes, and a temperament abundantly dry and cold.

The other (remaining) quadrant,—Capricorn, Aquarius, and Pisces,—from the winter tropic to the vernal equinox, gives a dark complexion, middle stature, straight hair on the head and some on the body, a goodly figure, and a temperament abounding in cold and moisture.

To speak, however, more particularly, all constellations of human form, both those within and those without the zodiac, act in favour of giving a handsome shape to the body, and due proportion to the figure, while those not of human form vary its due proportions, and incline it towards their own shape, assimilating it, in some measure, to their own peculiarities, either by enlarging or diminishing its size, by giving it additional strength or weakness, or by otherwise improving or disfiguring it. Thus, for example: Leo, Virgo, and Sagittarius enlarge the person; and Pisces, Cancer, and Capricorn tend to make it diminutive; and thus, again, the upper parts of Aries, Taurus, and Leo increase its strength, and their lower parts render it weaker; while, on the other hand, Sagittarius, Scorpio, and Gemini act conversely, for their upper parts produce greater debility, and their lower parts give greater vigour. In the same manner, Virgo, Libra, and Sagittarius contribute to render the person handsome and well proportioned; and Scorpio, Pisces, and Taurus incline it to be misshapen and disfigured.

In the matter of diseases peculiar to the signs, Ptolemy

says :—" Cancer, Capricorn, and Pisces cause diseases of the blood, such as cancer, fistula, scrofula, gout, and leprosy; whilst Sagittarius and Gemini produce disease by falling fits and epilepsy," and if the planets happen to be place l in the latter degrees of the signs, the extremities of the body will be principally affected. Concerning the mental qualities given by the signs, tropical signs, viz., Cancer and Capricorn, dispose those born under them to be fond of distinction, turbulent, ingenious, acute, and studious of astrology and divination.

Bicorporeal or double-bodied signs,—Gemini, Pisces, and Sagittarius,—render the person so born variable, versatile, inclined to duplicity, fond of music, careless, and impressionable. Fixed signs,—Taurus, Leo, Virgo, and Aquarius,—make the native just, constant, prudent, patient, desirous of honour, a little avaricious, and very pertinacious.

These descriptions are useful in showing the modifications brought to bear (by the sign ascending) on the planet's influence. But when no planets are in or near the ascendant at birth, the following descriptions of the temperament and form of body produced by each sign ascending at birth should be used.

Aries (γ) is a hot and fiery sign, and produces a lean body, spare and strong, large bones, grey eyes, with a quick glance, and sandy or red coloured hair. The temper is violent. It governs the head and face ; its colour is white.

Taurus ($\yen$) differs greatly in its effects from the preceding sign; it is cold and dry, gives a broad brow, and thick lips. A person born under it is melancholy and slow to anger, but when roused, furious and difficult to be appeased. It governs the neck and throat ; its colour is red.

Gemini (π) is in nature hot and moist, and produces a person of straight, tall body, sanguine complexion, brilliant eyes, and light brown hair. The temperament of those born under Gemini is lively, and the understanding good. This sign governs the arms and shoulders; its colours are red and white.

Cancer ($\mathfrak{S}$) is by nature cold and moist; it produces a native fair and pale, short in stature, with a round face, sad-coloured brown hair, and grey eyes. Those born under it are phlegmatic, indolent, and gentle tempered. Women born under this sign generally have many children. It governs the breast and stomach; its colour is green and russet brown.

Leo (Ω) is a fiery, hot, and dry sign. When it rises at birth without any planet being near the ascendant, the native will be of tall stature, with yellow hair, ruddy complexion, oval face, and he will have a quick glance and a strong voice. It governs the heart, the back, and the neck; its colours are red and green.

Virgo ($\mathfrak{M}$) is an earthy, cold, barren, feminine sign. When it ascends, it shows a well-formed body, slender, and tall, straight, dark brown hair, and a round face. The mind of the native is ingenious, but rather inconstant. It governs the belly; its colour is black speckled with blue.

Libra ($\triangle$) is an aërial, sanguine, masculine, hot, and moist sign. Rising at birth it produces a well-made body, with long limbs, an oval and beautiful face, sanguine complexion, straight flaxen hair, and grey eyes. Those born under it are courteous, just, and honourable. It governs the loins; and the colours under its rule are black, crimson, and tawny.

Scorpio ($\mathfrak{M}$) is a moist, phlegmatic, feminine sign. It gives a strong, corpulent body, low stature, thick legs, hair growing low on the forehead, and heavy eyebrows. Those born under this sign are reserved, thoughtful, subtle, and malicious. It governs the lower parts of the body; the colour under its rule is brown.

Sagittarius ($\nearrow$) is a fiery, masculine sign. The person born under its rule is handsome, with a rather long face and features, chestnut hair, inclined to baldness, ruddy complexion ; the body strong and active. Those born under this sign are fond of field sports, are good riders, and are lovers of animals. They are kindly, generous, and careless of danger. This sign governs the thighs and hips, and rules yellow and green.

Capricorn (♑) is an earthy, cold, dry, feminine sign. It produces a person of slender stature, with a long neck, narrow chest, and dark hair. The mind is quick, witty, and subtle. It governs the knees and hams, and in colours it rules black or dark brown.

Aquarius (♒) is an airy, moist, masculine sign. In a nativity where no planets are in or near the ascendant, it would produce a person of a well-set, strong body, long face, and delicate complexion, with brown hair. It governs the legs and ankles, and rules the sky-colour or blue.

Pisces (♓) is a watery, cold, and feminine sign. It produces a person of short stature, fleshy body, with a rather stooping gait. Those born under its influence are indolent and phlegmatic. It governs the feet and toes, and presides over the pure white colour. It is needful to remember the colours belonging to the sign, as they are especially useful in horary questions.

CHAPTER IV.

OF THE NATURES OF THE SEVEN PLANETS, AND OF THEIR ESSENTIAL AND ACCIDENTAL DIGNITIES.

OF the seven planets, Jupiter and Venus, because of the heat and moisture predominant in them, are considered by the ancients as benefits or causers of good. The Moon is so considered for the same reasons, though in a less degree.

Saturn and Mars are causes of evil, or malefic ; the

first from his excess of cold, and the other from his excess of heat. The Sun and Mercury are deemed of common influence,—that is, either of good or evil, according to the planets with which they are connected.

The planets have particular familiarity with certain places in the zodiac by means of parts designated as their houses, and also by their *triplicities, exaltations*, and *terms*.

The nature of their familiarity by *houses* is as follows :—

Cancer and Leo are the most northerly of all the twelve signs ; they approach nearer than the other signs to the zenith of this part of the earth, and thereby cause warmth and heat ; they are consequently appropriated as houses for the two principal and greater luminaries ; Leo for the Sun, as being masculine ; and Cancer for the Moon, as being feminine.

Saturn, since he is cold and inimical to heat, moving also in a superior orbit most remote from the luminaries, occupies the signs opposite to Cancer and Leo ; these are Aquarius and Capricorn, and they are assigned to him in consideration of their cold and wintry nature, and because the configuration by opposition does not co-operate towards the production of good.

Jupiter has a favourable temperament, and is situated beneath the sphere of Saturn ; he, therefore, occupies the next two signs, Sagittarius and Pisces.

Mars is dry in nature, and beneath the sphere of Jupiter ; he takes the next two signs, of a nature similar to his own —viz., Aries and Scorpio, whose relative distances from the houses of the luminaries are injurious and discordant.

Venus, possessing a favourable temperament, and placed beneath the sphere of Mars, takes the next two signs, Taurus and Libra. These are of a fruitful nature, and preserve harmony by the sextile distance, and this planet is never more than two signs distant from the Sun.

Mercury never has greater distance from the Sun than the space of one sign, and is beneath all the other planets ;

hence he is nearest to both luminaries, and the remaining two signs, Gemini and Virgo, are allotted to him.

The "houses" of the planets are readily shown by the following table. It is exactly the same as that found in the mummy-case of the Archon of Thebes, in ancient Egypt, as may be seen at the British Museum :—

♌	☉		☽	♋
♍		☿		♊
♎		♀		♉
♏		♂		♈
♐		♃		♓
♑		♄		♒

It will be seen at once from this table that the Sun and Moon have each only one house assigned them. All planets are most powerful in that sign which constitutes one of their houses. Planets receive detriment in the signs opposite to those of their houses. Thus, Saturn would receive detriment in Cancer and Leo, which are the signs opposite to his houses, Capricornus and Aquarius. There are some signs in which the planets are found to be very powerful, though not to the same extent as when in their own houses; these are called the "exaltations" of the planets, and the signs opposite to these are those in which they receive their "fall" when they are considered to be weak in power. Saturn has his exaltation in Libra; his "fall" would therefore be in Aries. He governs the airy triplicity, which is composed of the signs, Gemini, Libra, and Aquarius by day, and in all the twelve signs he has these degrees allotted him by Ptolemy for his Terms :—

In Aries	...	...	27, 28, 29, 30.
In Taurus	...	...	23, 24, 25, 26.
In Gemini	...	...	22, 23, 24, 25.
In Cancer	...	...	28, 29, 30.
In Leo...	...	...	1, 2, 3, 4, 5, 6.
In Virgo	...	...	19, 20, 21, 22, 23, 24.

In Libra ... ... 1, 2, 3, 4, 5, 6.
In Scorpio ... ... 28, 29, 30.
In Sagittarius ... 21, 22, 23, 24, 25.
In Capricornus ... 26, 27, 28, 29, 30.
In Aquarius ... ... 1, 2, 3, 4, 5, 6.
In Pisces ... ... 27, 28, 29, 30.

The meaning of which is that if Saturn should rise in any of these degrees it is a sign that he is not void of essential dignities; or, if he is posited in any of the following degrees (which he is allowed for his Face or Decanate) he is still not devoid of dignities. This is to be understood of all the planets.

Saturn is allotted for his Face these degrees:—
In Taurus ... 21, 22, 23, 24, 25, 26, 27, 28, 29, 30.
In Leo ... 1, 2, 3, 4, 5, 6, 7, 8, 9, 10.
In Libra ... 11, 12, 13, 14, 15, 16, 17, 18, 19, 20.
In Sagittarius 21, 22, 23, 24, 25, 26, 27, 28, 29, 30.
In Pisces ... 1, 2, 3, 4, 5, 6, 7, 8, 9, 10.

Jupiter has his exaltation in Cancer and his fall in Capricornus. He rules the fiery triplicity, Aries, Leo, and Sagittarius, by night.

He has these degrees allotted for his Terms:—

In Aries ... 1, 2, 3, 4, 5, 6.
In Taurus ... 16, 17, 18, 19, 20, 21, 22.
In Gemini ... 8, 9, 10, 11, 12, 13, 14.
In Cancer ... 7, 8, 9, 10, 11, 12, 13.
In Leo ... ... 20, 21, 22, 23, 24, 25.
In Virgo ... 14, 15, 16, 17, 18.
In Libra ... 12, 13, 14, 15, 16, 17, 18, 19.
In Scorpio ... 7, 8, 9, 10, 11, 12, 13, 14.
In Sagittarius 1, 2, 3, 4, 5, 6, 7, 8.
In Capricornus 13, 14, 15, 16, 17, 18, 19.
In Aquarius ... 21, 22, 23, 24, 25.
In Pisces ... 9, 10, 11, 12, 13, 14.

C

He has for his Face, or Decanate,—

Of Gemini ...	1, 2, 3, 4, 5, 6, 7, 8, 9, 10.
Of Leo	11, 12, 13, 14, 15, 16, 17, 18, 19, 20.
Of Libra ...	21, 22, 23, 24, 25, 26, 27, 28, 29, 30.
Of Capricornus	1, 2, 3, 4, 5, 6, 7, 8, 9, 10.
Of Pisces ...	11, 12, 13, 14, 15, 16, 17, 18, 19, 20.

Mars has Aries for his day-house and Scorpio for his night-house. He is exalted in Capricornus, and has his fall in Cancer.

He governs the watery triplicity, viz., Cancer, Scorpio, and Pisces, and he has these degrees in each sign for his Terms :—

In Aries ...	22, 23, 24, 25, 26.
In Taurus ...	27, 28, 29, 30.
In Gemini ...	26, 27, 28, 29, 30.
In Cancer ...	1, 2, 3, 4, 5, 6.
In Leo ...	26, 27, 28, 29, 30.
In Virgo ...	25, 26, 27, 28, 29, 30.
In Scorpio ...	1, 2, 3, 4, 5, 6.
In Aquarius ...	26, 27, 28, 29, 30.
In Pisces ...	21, 22, 23, 24, 25, 26.

He has allotted to him for his Face these degrees :—

In Aries ...	1, 2, 3, 4, 5, 6, 7, 8, 9, 10.
In Gemini ...	11, 12, 13, 14, 15, 16, 17, 18, 19, 20.
In Leo	21, 22, 23, 24, 25, 26, 27, 28, 29, 30.
In Virgo ...	1, 2, 3, 4, 5, 6, 7, 8, 9, 10.
In Pisces ...	21, 22, 23, 24, 25, 26, 27, 28, 29, 30.

The Sun rules the fiery triplicity,—Aries, Leo, and Sagittarius,—by day. He is exalted in the sign of Aries, and receives his fall in Libra.

He has no degrees admitted him for his Terms, but in the twelve signs he has the following degrees for his Face :—

In Aries ...	11, 12, 13, 14, 15, 16, 17, 18, 19, 20.
In Gemini ...	21, 22, 23, 24, 25, 26, 27, 28, 29, 30.

In Virgo   ... 1, 2, 3, 4, 5, 6, 7, 8, 9, 10.
In Scorpio   ... 11, 12, 13, 14, 15, 16, 17, 18, 19, 20.
In Capricornus 21, 22, 23, 24, 25, 26, 27, 28, 29, 30.

Venus governs the earthy triplicity,—Taurus, Virgo, and Capricornus,—by day. She is exalted in Pisces, and has her fall in Virgo. She has the following degrees for her Terms :—

In Aries ...   ... 7, 8, 9, 10, 11, 12, 13, 14.
In Taurus   ... 1, 2, 3, 4, 5, 6, 7, 8.
In Gemini   ... 15, 16, 17, 18, 19, 20.
In Cancer   ... 21, 22, 23, 24, 25, 26, 27.
In Leo ...   ... 14, 15, 16, 17, 18, 19.
In Virgo...   ... 8, 9, 10, 11, 12, 13.
In Libra ...   ... 7, 8, 9, 10, 11.
In Scorpio   ... 15, 16, 17, 18, 19, 20, 21.
In Sagittarius 9, 10, 11, 12, 13, 14.
In Capricornus 1, 2, 3, 4, 5, 6.
In Aquarius   ... 13, 14, 15, 16, 17, 18, 19, 20.
In Pisces   ... 1, 2, 3, 4, 5, 6, 7, 8.

The following degrees are allowed for her Face :—

In Aries ...   ... 21, 22, 23, 24, 25, 26, 27, 28, 29, 30.
In Cancer   ... 1, 2, 3, 4, 5, 6, 7, 8, 9, 10.
In Virgo ...   ... 11, 12, 13, 14, 15, 16, 17, 18, 19, 20.
In Scorpio   ... 21, 22, 23, 24, 25, 26, 27, 28, 29, 30.
In Pisces   ... 1, 2, 3, 4, 5, 6, 7, 8, 9, 10.

Mercury governs the airy triplicity, viz., Gemini, Libra, and Aquarius, by night. He has his exaltation in Virgo, and his fall in Pisces. He has the following degrees for his Terms :—

In Aries ...   ... 15, 16, 17, 18, 19, 20, 21.
In Taurus   ... 9, 10, 11, 12, 13, 14, 15.
In Gemini   ... 1, 2, 3, 4, 5, 6, 7.
In Cancer   ... 14, 15, 16, 17, 18, 19, 20.
In Leo ...   ... 7, 8, 9, 10, 11, 12, 13.
In Virgo...   ... 1, 2, 3, 4, 5, 6, 7.

In Libra ...   ...   20, 21, 22, 23, 24.
In Scorpio   ...   22, 23, 24, 25, 26, 27.
In Sagittarius...   15, 16, 17, 18, 19, 20.
In Capricornus   7, 8, 9, 10, 11, 12.
In Pisces ...   ...   15, 16, 17, 18, 19, 20.

These degrees are assigned him for his Face:—

In Taurus   ...   1, 2, 3, 4, 5, 6, 7, 8, 9, 10.
In Cancer   ...   11, 12, 13, 14, 15, 16, 17, 18, 19, 20.
In Virgo ...   ...   21, 22, 23, 24, 25, 26, 27, 28, 29, 30.
In Sagittarius...   1, 2, 3, 4, 5, 6, 7, 8, 9, 10.
In Aquarius   ...   11, 12, 13, 14, 15, 16, 17, 18, 19, 20.

The Moon governs the earthy triplicity, viz., Taurus,
Virgo, and Capricornus, by night.

She is exalted in Taurus, and has her fall in Scorpio.
The Sun and the Moon have no terms assigned them.

In the Twelve signs she has these degrees assigned
her for her Face:—

In Taurus   ...   11, 12, 13, 14, 15, 16, 17, 18, 19, 20.
In Cancer   ...   21, 22, 23, 24, 25, 26, 27, 28, 29, 30.
In Libra ...   ...   1, 2, 3, 4, 5, 6, 7, 8, 9, 10.
In Sagittarius...   11, 12, 13, 14, 15, 16, 17, 18, 19, 20.
In Aquarius   ...   21, 22, 23, 24, 25, 26, 27, 28, 29, 30.

A planet in his fall is very weak in his influence.   The
Houses count first in dignity, then the Exaltation; afterwards the Triplicities, the Terms, and the Faces.

The meaning of this, is if a planet is in any of the signs
we call his house or houses, he is essentially strong, and
he is allowed five dignities.

If he is in the sign in which he is said to be exalted,
he is allowed four dignities.

If he should be placed in any of the signs allowed him for
his Triplicity, he is allowed three dignities.

If in any of the degrees in the signs which are given as
his Terms, he has two dignities.

If in any of the degrees of the sign given to him as his

Face, he is allowed one essential dignity. Accidental dignities are when a planet is swift in motion, angular or in sextile aspect with Jupiter or Venus.

There was a great difference between the Arabian, Indian, and Greek methods in the disposing of the degrees of the sign to each planet until the time of Ptolemy. Since then almost all astrologers followed the method he left, which is that which has been given in this chapter.

CHAPTER V.

OF THE INFLUENCES OF THE SEVEN PLANETS.

THE planet Saturn is the most remote of the seven planetary orbs recognised by the ancient writers on astrology. He is of a pale ash colour, slow in motion, only finishing his course through the twelve signs of the zodiac in 29 years and about 157 days. His greatest north latitude from the ecliptic is 2 degrees 48 minutes ; his south latitude is 2 degrees 49 minutes.

Those born with this planet well-dignified* are studious, grave, economical, prudent, patient, and in all their actions sober and somewhat austere. They are not much given to the love of women, but they are persons of much depth of feeling, and when they do love they are very constant. They are given to the study of occult matters,† and are of a melancholic, suspicious, and jealous temperament. In person when well-dignified Saturn gives a rather tall stature and long limbs. The hair is dark, the eyebrows much marked and generally meeting between the eyes, which are dark brown, deep set, and close together. The nose is long and generally somewhat bent over the lips, the under jaw slightly protrudes. The complexion is sallow,

---

* The foregoing chapter explains this term.

† The Chaldees averred that when Saturn was powerful in a nativity the person then born was "mystical and confederate in secrecy."

the ears large, and the hands and feet are generally long, but not fleshy.

Those born under the potent aspect of Saturn are generally slow of speech and their voices are harsh; when Saturn rises in a horoscope *devoid of dignities*, the native is envious, covetous, malicious, subtle, untruthful, and of a discontented disposition. In persons frequently deformed, with long and irregular features, the eyes and hair dark, the skin yellow and harsh.

In man's body this planet rules the spleen, the right ear, the lips, and the teeth. In illness he gives ague, palsy, ruptures (especially should he rule in the sign of Scorpio), jaundice, toothache, and all affections of the sight, of the ear, and of the teeth and jaws.

The herbs he governs are the hemlock, hellebore, burdock, sage, henbane, rue, nightshade, and mandrake.

The trees under his rule are the willow, the yew, the cypress, the box-tree, and the pine.

The beasts he governs are the elephant, the wolf, the bear, the dog,* the basilisk, the crocodile, the scorpion, the serpent, the rat, the mouse, and all manner of creeping things; among birds, the crow, the cuckoo, the raven, the owl, and the bat.

Of fish he rules the eel, the tortoise, and all shell fish.

The minerals he governs are lead and the dross of all metals.

His stones are jet, onyx, and all dark stones which are incapable of polish.

He rules Saturday; the first hour after sunrise, and the eighth hour of the same day. In gathering the herbs under his rule the ancients were particular to do so in his hours, as this rendered the medicament more powerful. This is to be observed regarding the herbs ruled by all the planets.

Saturn's orb is nine degrees before and after any aspect; that is, his influence begins to operate when either he applies

---

* This animal has been probably assigned to him by reason of its sagacity and extreme fidelity,—constancy in feeling being one of the attributes given by the planet Saturn when well-dignified.

to any planet or it applies to him within nine degrees of his
perfect aspect, and his influence continues in force until he
is separated nine degrees from the aspect. His angel is
Cassiel. His friends are Jupiter, the Sun, and Mercury ;
his enemies, Venus and Mars.

Jupiter is the next planet below Saturn, and is of a bright,
clear, azure colour. He much exceeds Saturn in motion,
as he finishes his course through the twelve signs in twelve
years. His greatest north latitude is 1 degree 38 minutes,
and his greatest south latitude 1 degree 40 minutes. When
he rises at birth well-dignified he gives an erect, tall stature,
sanguine complexion, oval face, large grey eyes, thick brown
hair, full lips, and good teeth.* In temperament those born
under the good influence of this planet are honourable,
generous, and hospitable, but loving material pleasures, kind
and affectionate to wife and family, charitable, desiring to be
well thought of, and hating all mean and sordid actions. The
voices of those born under Jupiter are clear and sonorous.
When this planet rises *devoid of dignities* the native will
be gluttonous, profligate, vain, boastful, of mean abilities
and shallow understanding, easily seduced to extravagance,
and a tyrant to those of his family and household.

In man's body he rules the lungs and the blood, and of
diseases he gives apoplexy, gout, inflammation of the lungs,
and all illnesses proceeding from corruption of the blood.

The herbs he governs are cloves, mace, nutmeg, gilli-
flower, marjoram, mint, borage, and saffron.

Of trees he rules the mulberry, the olive, the vine, the fig,
the beech, and the pear-tree.

Of beasts, the sheep, the hart, the ox, and all those animals
that are useful to man.

Of birds, the stork, the snipe, the lark, the eagle, the
pheasant, the partridge, and the peacock.

Of fishes, the whale and the dolphin.

* For a more minute description of planetary influences as shown on
the face, see Part the Third, Physiognomy.

His metal is tin.

His stones are the sapphire, the amethyst, and the emerald.

Of colours he rules red mixed with green.

His day is Thursday, and he rules the first hour after sunrise and the eighth hour.

His orb is 9 degrees before and after any aspect.

All the planets except Mars are his friends.

His angel is Zadkiel.

Mars in order succeeds Jupiter. He appears of a red colour, and finishes his course through the zodiac in 1 year 321 days. His greatest north latitude is 4 degrees 31 minutes. His south latitude is 6 degrees 47 minutes. When he is well-dignified in a horoscope, the native is courageous, confident, loving war and all that belongs to it, jealous of honour, hot-tempered, and a great lover of field sports. In person he will be of middle stature, broad shouldered and with big bones; the complexion of a red fairness, the hair is crisp or curly, and also red, but this varies slightly according to the sign rising at birth; in watery signs the hair is not so red, and in earthy signs it is more chestnut; the eyes are grey, and have a bold, fixed glance like that of a hawk.

When he is ill-dignified at birth, the native is turbulent, cruel, boastful, a promoter of sedition, ungracious in manners, and unscrupulous in his actions, with no fear of either God or man. He rules the head and face, the gall, the throat and intestines; and the diseases he gives are fevers, carbuncles, small-pox, all throat affections, all hurts to the head and face, especially by iron, and all diseases which arise from too much heat of blood.

The herbs over which he rules are the nettle, the thistle, onions, scammony, garlic, horehound, cardamons, and all herbs giving heat.

Of trees, all those which are of a prickly nature, such as the holly, the thorn, the chestnut.

Of beasts, all fierce animals,—the tiger, the panther, the wolf, the horse, and the leopard.

Of fish, the pike, the barbel, and the sword-fish.

Of birds, the hawk, the vulture, the kite, the eagle, the magpie.

The metal he rules is iron. The colour he rules is red.

The stones, the carbuncle, the ruby, and the blood-stone.

His orb is 7 degrees before and after any aspect.

He governs Tuesday, the first hour after sunrise, and the eighth.

His friend among the planets is Venus, all the others are his enemies.

His angel is Samael.

The Sun passes through all the twelve signs of the zodiac in one year and a few hours over the 365 days which constitute the year. He has no latitude.

When the Sun rises at a birth well-dignified, the native is of an honourable disposition, but always desiring to rule, loving pomp, yet affable, speaking with gravity and without too many words, and possessing much self-reliance and dignity of manner. In person he will be tall, well made, with golden hair, yellowish skin, large and piercing eyes, and long, straight, and well-formed features.

When ill-aspected the native is arrogant, boastful, a spendthrift, proud, yet in poverty hanging on other men's charity, very loquacious, restless, and without judgment.

He governs the heart, the brain, the right eye and the arms; and the diseases he causes are all illnesses of the heart, such as swoons, palpitations, cramps, also diseases of the mouth, the brain, and the eyes.

Of colours he rules the yellow and orange colour.

The plants subject to the Sun are all those of pungent odours, such as the marigold, heliotrope, rosemary, balsam, spikenard, musk, St. John's-wort, and ginger.

Of trees he rules the palm, the laurel, the cedar, the orange-tree, and the citron-tree.

Of beasts, the lion, the ram, the goat.

Of birds, the eagle, the cock, the buzzard.

Of fish, the star-fish.

Of metals, gold.

Of stones, the topaz, amber, chrisolite, and all yellow stones.

His orb is 15 degrees before any aspect, and as many after separation.

His friends are all the planets except Saturn, who is his enemy.

His angel is Michael.

After the Sun, the planet Venus succeeds in order; she is of a bright shining colour. Her greatest north or south latitude is 2 degrees and 2 minutes. When she rises well-dignified in a nativity, the person born will be of middle stature, rather inclining to shortness, with a beautiful complexion, light brown hair, the eyes large, of a blue or grey colour, and with a slow and rather languishing movement, red lips, and dimples in the cheeks, chin, and about the mouth. In disposition, gracious, very tender, inclined to love-making; easy of belief, and not given to labour about anything; fond of music, plays, and all sorts of merry-makings.

When ill-aspected at birth, Venus causes the native to be over-fat, with thick lips, and much flesh about the chin and cheeks. In disposition, sensual, riotous, and immoral.

Venus governs the lower parts of the body, and the illnesses she gives are cancer and all affections of the womb.

All the herbs she governs have a sweet smell, and generally have smooth leaves and white flowers, such as the lily, both white and yellow, and the lily-of-the-valley, also the water-lily, the myrtle, maidenhair, violets, and roses.

The trees she rules are the walnut, the almond, the apple-tree, the box-tree, the sycamore, and the ash.

Of beasts, the hart, the rabbit, the calf, and all small cattle.

Of birds, the dove, the sparrow, the nightingale, the swan, the pelican, and the swallow.

Her metal is copper.

Her stones, white and red coral, the beryl, turquoise, margasite, and lapis lazuli, because it expels melancholy.

Her colours are white and purple.

Her orb is 7 degrees before and after any aspect.

Her day of the week is Friday, of which she rules the first and eighth hour after sunrise.

Her friends are all the planets.

Her angel is Anael.

Mercury is of a soft silver colour. His greatest north latitude is 3 degrees, 33 minutes. His greatest south latitude is 3 degrees, 33 minutes.

When he rises well-dignified at a birth the native is a person of subtle intellect, an excellent logician, and possessing much eloquence in his speech ; sharp and witty, of admirable memory, curious in occult knowledge, given to divination, and, if he should turn his attention to trade, no man would exceed him in the invention of new ways to gain wealth.

In person, when Mercury rises well-dignified the native is of rather small stature, but elegantly formed, very active and supple in his limbs, and with long arms; he will have a long, narrow face, a high forehead, rather swelling at the temples, grey eyes, with brown spots in them, delicate mouth, straight eyebrows, a skin of a pale yellow or olive colour, the hair of a red-brown, commonly called auburn.

When ill-dignified at birth, Mercury gives a person of very small stature, with small insignificant features, and very small and quickly moving eyes, and in character he is shifty, a boaster, foolishly loquacious, and a great liar.

He rules the liver, the tongue, and the nerves, and the illnesses he gives are epilepsy, giddiness, dry cough, any affection of the tongue, and all nervous affections.

The herbs attributed to him are generally those having a subtle smell, and having effect on the tongue, brain, lungs, or memory ; they are vervain, adder's tongue, aniseseed, dragon-wort, and the reed.

The trees are the elder and the filbert-tree.

The animals are the squirrel, the weasel, the spider, the greyhound, the fox, the ape, and all cunning and quickly-moving creatures.

The birds, the parrot, the magpie, the crane, and the linnet.

Of fish, the jack-fish and the mullet.

His metal is quicksilver.

His stones, all those of divers colours, white and red carnelian, and marcasite, or fire-stone.

In colours he rules azure, and all light-blue colours.

His orb is 7 degrees before and after any aspect.

He governs Wednesday, the first hour and the eighth after sunrise. The Moon, Venus, Jupiter, and the Sun are his friends,—Saturn and Mars his enemies.

His angel is Raphael.

The Moon is the nearest to the earth of all the seven planets. She finishes her course through the whole twelve signs in 27 days 7 hours and 36 seconds. Her greatest north latitude is 5 degrees and about 17 minutes, her greatest south latitude, 5 degrees and 12 minutes.

When she rises well-placed in a horoscope, she signifies a person of soft and gentle manners, timid, imaginative, loving pleasure and ease, yet fond of moving from place to place; rather capricious, but of a poetic and romantic turn of mind. In person, those born under good aspects of the Moon are of middle height, with a round head and face, pale soft skin, large, light eyes, usually one a little larger than the other. The whole body inclined to be fleshy, the lips full, and the hair of a dull, light colour, but not at all inclined to gold.

When the Moon is ill-aspected at birth the native is indolent, sometimes a drunkard and vagabond, generally a liar, and, as Lilly puts it, "a muddling creature."

The Moon governs the left side and the bladder. She gives dropsy, all cold and rheumatic diseases, colds or hurts in the eyes, convulsive fits, hysteria and feminine weaknesses.

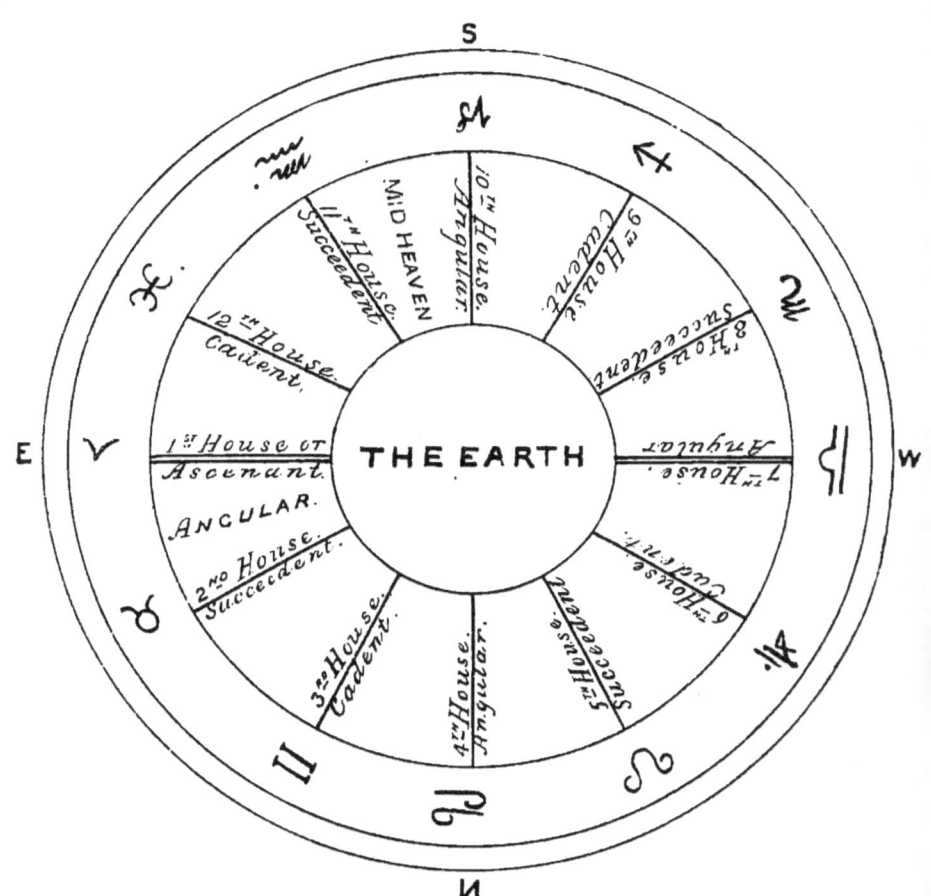

The plants she governs are all those which have soft, juicy leaves, such as the lettuce, the melon, the gourd, the poppy, mushroom, cabbage, and colewort. Of trees, all those which have round spreading leaves, such as the lime-tree and the sycamore.

The beasts she rules are those which love the water, as the otter, the seal.

She rules all sea fowl, and also the goose, the duck, and the night owl.

Of fish, the oyster, the cockle, the crab, and the lobster.

Her colours are light-greenish blue, mixed with white.

Her metal is silver.

Her stones, pearls, diamonds, opals, crystals, and selenite.

Her orb is 12 degrees before and after any aspect.

Her day is Monday; the first hour and the eighth after sunrise are hers.

Her friends are Venus, Jupiter, and the Sun.

Her enemies among the planets are Saturn and Mars.

Her angel is Gabriel.

CHAPTER VI.

CONCERNING THE TWELVE HOUSES OF HEAVEN AND THEIR POWERS.

THE ancient astrologers divided the heavens into twelve houses.

The First House.—This is called the *Ascendant,* and the planet rising therein,—whether well or ill-dignified,—will materially affect the mind, bodily appearance, and fate of the native through his whole existence. This house is masculine and governs the head and face of man, and if the planet Mars be in this house at the time of birth there will always be some blemish or mole in the face of the native;

if a few out of the degrees have ascended, the scar or
blemish is, without fail, on the upper part of the head; if
the middle part of the sign ascends, the mark is in the
middle of the face; if the latter part of the sign is ascending
the mark is near the chin. This house represents the head,
the tongue, and the memory, and it governs in colour
white.

The Second House.—This house has signification of the
native's wealth and worldly goods. The house is feminine,
ruling the neck, and the colour is green.

The Third House.—This governs brothers and sisters,
short journeys, neighbours, letters and writings. It is
masculine, and governs the hands, arms, and shoulders;
its colour is red and yellow mixed.

The Fourth House.—This rules the father, inheritances
or property of the native, and shows his condition at the
close of life. It is feminine, and rules the stomach, breast,
and lungs; its colour is red.

The Fifth House.—This signifies the children of the
native, also his success in speculation, and hazardous
games, the pleasures he enjoys, and the wealth of the
father. It rules the heart, back, and liver, is masculine,
and represents in colour black and white mixed.

The Sixth House.—This concerns the native's servants,
sheep, goats, and small cattle. It also signifies the father's
kindred. This house is feminine. It rules the belly and
intestines, and its colour is black.

The Seventh House gives judgment of marriage, and
describes the man or woman in all love questions. It is
masculine, and it rules the haunches, and its colour is black.

The Eighth House argues of death, of legacies and wills,
also of the kind of death a man shall die; it is a feminine
house. It rules the lower parts of the trunk of the body;
its colours are green and black.

The Ninth House gives judgment on voyages and long
journeys, and also on events happening to the wife's

kindred. It rules the hips and thighs. It is a masculine house; its colours are green and white.

The Tenth House is called the *Mid-heaven*, and is feminine. This concerns the native's mother, and also his calling. It rules the knees and hams, and its colours are red and white.

The Eleventh House represents friends and friendship. It is masculine, and rules the legs.

The Twelfth House.—This house is often called the *Evil Dæmon*, for it is the house of sorrow, self-undoing, enemies, and imprisonment. It governs great cattle. It is feminine, and rules the feet and toes, and in colour it governs green.

The strongest houses are the first (the *Ascendant*) and the tenth (the *Mid-heaven*). The first, fourth, seventh, and tenth are called Angular Houses, and represent the four cardinal points of the compass; thus the first is east, the seventh west, the fourth is north, and the tenth south. The second, fifth, eighth, and eleventh houses are called Succeedent Houses; the third, sixth, ninth, and twelfth houses are termed Cadent Houses (see plate 1). Any planet posited in a Cadent House is regarded as weak in its effects on the native. It is necessary to have thoroughly mastered the influences of the twelve houses, as well as those of the seven planets, and of the signs of the Zodiac, before attempting to cast a nativity or to work a horary question.

CHAPTER VII.

OF THE PART OF FORTUNE, AND OF THE DRAGON'S HEAD AND THE DRAGON'S TAIL.

THE Part of Fortune, thus symbolised (⊕), is very much considered by Ptolemy, yet almost all the modern astrologers are inclined to altogether disregard it, although the ancients found in it considerable effects ; but it is the habit of the modern school to think too much of reason and too little of experience. It is true that we cannot explain the influence of the Part of Fortune; but neither can we do that of any of the planets, and that which,—although inexplicable to what we call reason,—has been made evident to us by experience, should be taken as a principle in so mystical and old-world a study as that of astrology, and therefore, in a book treating it after the manner of the ancients, the Part of Fortune must be considered according to Ptolemy's instructions, and the following is, in brief, what he tells us about it. The Part of Fortune is ascertained by computing the number of degrees between the Sun and the Moon ; it is placed at an equal number of degrees distant from the Ascendant, in the order of the signs. It is in all cases,—both by day and night,—to be so computed, that the Moon may hold with it the same relation as the Sun does with the Ascendant, and it thus becomes, as it were, a lunar horoscope. But it must be seen which luminary follows the other in succession of the signs ; for if the Moon should so follow the Sun, then the Part of Fortune should be numbered from the Ascendant, according to the succession of the signs. But if the Moon should precede the Sun, the Part of Fortune must be numbered from the Ascendant, and contrary to the succession of the signs.

The Part of Fortune is used in the Ptolemaic method to determine the wealth of the native in the following manner:—When the place of the Part of Fortune has been determined (according to the method already given), it must be ascertained to which planets the dominion of it belongs, and their powers and connection, and also the powers of others which may be with them; for, if the planets which assume dominion of the Part of Fortune should be in full force, they will create much wealth, and more especially if the Sun and the Moon give testimony in addition.

Saturn, well placed in the Part of Fortune, will effect the acquirement of riches by means of building, agriculture, mining, or navigation; Jupiter by some office of trust under Government, or some high position in the priesthood; Mars by military command; Venus by means of friends, dowry of wives, or gifts from women; and Mercury by literature, science, or commerce.

The Dragon's Head, thus symbolised (♌), is not a planet, but merely a position in the Zodiac indicating the Moon's north node. If this point happens to ascend in a nativity, it strengthens life with a robust constitution. If it falls in Mid-heaven, it promises great honour and preferment; if in the eleventh house, prosperity and riches. If the benefic planets, Jupiter or Venus, happen to be in these degrees, it makes them much stronger in their benevolent operations; but if the malefics, Saturn or Mars, should be posited there in a nativity, it gives them, on the contrary, a stronger inclination to prove unfortunate.

The Dragon's Tail is the point where the Moon intersects the ecliptic to her southern declination, and it is as barren to all good intents and purposes as the Dragon's Head is fruitful. This point when it ascends at a nativity, blemishes the life, impairs honour and advancement in the Mid-heaven, and wastes riches in the eleventh house. It also weakens the good auspices of Jupiter and Venus, and is altogether of evil significance.

CHAPTER VIII.

AN EXPLANATION OF VARIOUS TERMS USED IN ASTROLOGY.

Ascension, Right.—The distance any body or point in the heavens is from the beginning of the ecliptic, or first point of Aries. It is measured in degrees and minutes of a degree. It is thus abbreviated, A. R.

Ascension, Oblique.—If a star be not on the equator, it will, when it rises, form an angle with that part of the equator which is rising at the same time, and this is called its

Ascensional Difference.—This, added to its right ascension (A. R.) if it have *south* declination, but subtracted from it if it have *north* declination, gives its oblique ascension.

Application signifies the approach of two planets, and is of three kinds: first, when a planet, swift of motion, applies to one of slower progress,—for example, we will suppose Mercury posited in 16 degrees of the sign Gemini, and Mars in 21 degrees of the same sign (*both being in direct motion*), Mercury being swifter would overtake and form a conjunction with Mars, which is termed a *direct application.* The second kind of application is formed by two retrograde planets : thus we will suppose Mercury in 16 degrees of Gemini, and Saturn in 15 degrees of the same sign, both retrograde. Mercury being the swiftest planet, applies to Saturn, a more ponderous planet by retrogradation, and this is called a *retrograde application.* The third kind of application is when one planet, being direct in motion, meets another which is retrograde : for instance, we will suppose Mercury retrograde in 16 degrees of Gemini, and Saturn *direct* in motion in 12 degrees of the same sign ; here Mercury being the higher planet *applies to a conjunction* of Saturn by a retrograde motion. These two last are considered *evil* applications. It should also be remembered that the superior planets, Saturn,

Jupiter, and Mars, never apply to the inferior planets, Venus, Mercury, and the Moon, except by retrograde motion ; but the inferior planets apply in both ways.

Besieging signifies a planet situated between the two malevolent planets, Saturn and Mars : thus, if Saturn were in the 12th degree of Aries, Jupiter in the 14th, and Mars in the 16th, Jupiter would then be *besieged* by the two malefic planets, Saturn and Mars. This is, of course, an evil position.

Combust.—A planet is said to be *combust* when within eight and a half degrees of the Sun, when it loses part of its power. If the planet should be one with much latitude, the Sun has not much power over it, beyond the distance of seven degrees.

Cazimi.—A planet is said to be in *cazimi* when it is in the heart of the Sun ; that is, only 17 minutes before or after the Sun. All astrologers agree that a planet is fortified by this position ; whereas a planet in combustion is of an evil nature.

Direct motion signifies that a planet is moving on its natural course, according to the succession of the signs of the Zodiac : thus a planet is *direct in motion* when it moves from Aries to Taurus, or from Taurus to Gemini.

Frustration means the approach of a swift planet to an aspect with one of slower motion ; but before it can approach near enough to join that aspect, the more weighty planet is joined to some other, by which the first aspect is frustrated. For instance, suppose Saturn placed in 16 degrees of Gemini, Jupiter in 15 degrees of Leo, and Mars in 11 degrees of the same sign ; here Mars applies to a conjunction with Jupiter, but before he can reach it, Jupiter meets a sextile aspect from Saturn, which *frustrates* the conjunction of Mars, and utterly does away with the event promised by the conjunction of Mars and Jupiter.

Hayz is when a masculine diurnal planet is situated above the horizon in the day-time ; or, when a feminine nocturnal planet is placed below the horizon in the night-time ; this is fortunate in its influence.

Increasing in light is when a planet is separating from the Sun, or the Sun from a planet; thus the Moon, at her greatest distance from the Sun, appears with the greatest degree of light, having her whole orb illumined.

Longitude and Latitude.—The longitude of any star or planet is the degree of the Zodiac in which it is found. Numbered from the first point of the sign Aries, the latitude of a star or planet is its distance north or south of the Sun's path, or ecliptic line numbered by the degrees of the meridian.

Lords.—That planet is called the *lord* of a sign whose house the sign represents; thus Saturn is lord of the signs Aquarius and Capricornus. *The lord of a house* is that planet of which the sign is on the cusp of such house. The *lord of the geniture* is the planet which is most exalted at birth.

Lunation.—The ♂, □, or ☍ of ☉ and ☽ ; also the length of time ☽ is going round the ☉, or round the Zodiac.

M. C. or Medium Cœli, or Mid-heaven.—The meridian above the earth.

Meridian.—That point which is always *south* (where ☉ is at noon) is the meridian above the earth; and that point which is always *north* (where ☉ is at midnight) is the meridian below the earth.

Meridian Distance.—The distance any body is by A. R. from the meridian.

Moderator.—The ☉, ☽, Asc., M. C. or ⊕, because each acts in a mode peculiar to itself.

Nocturnal Arc.—The length of time any point in the heavens is below the earth, from its setting till it rises again. It is usually turned into degrees.

Node.—That part of the ecliptic where a planet passes out of north into south latitude is its south node ; that where it goes into north latitude is its north node.

Oriental and Occidental.—A planet when oriental rises before the Sun, when occidental sets after him and is seen bove the horizon when the Sun is down ; consequently, when a planet is oriental it is posited in the east, and when occidental, in the west.

From the fourth house eastward to the tenth is oriental, and from the tenth westward to the fourth is occidental. But ☉ or ☽ are *oriental* between the first and tenth, and its opposite quarter, and are *occidental* between the tenth and seventh, and its opposite quarter.

Parallels, in the *zodiac*, are equal distances from the equator, or having the same declination, whether of the same name or the opposite.

Perigrine is said of a planet when he is posited in a sign where he has no essential dignity by house, triplicity, terms, or face.

Prohibition indicates the state of two planets applying to each other by conjunction, but, before such conjunction can be formed, a third planet, by means of swifter motion, interposes his body and destroys the expected conjunction by forming an aspect himself. For example, suppose Mars posited in 7 degrees of Aries, Saturn in 12 degrees, and the Sun in 6 degrees of the same sign, Mars is the promittor of the event or business in hand, and indicates its completion ·as soon as he comes to a conjunction with Saturn ; but the Sun, being swifter in motion than Mars, passes him and prevents their conjunction by forming that aspect himself. This would indicate that whatever was expected, whether good or evil, from the conjunction of Mars and Saturn is *prohibited*, and will not take place.

Promittor.—The planets ♄, ♃, ♂, ♀, and ☿. If ☉ or ☽ should be directed to each other, the one directed to may be termed a promittor ; so if ⊕ Asc. or M. C. be directed to ☉ or ☽, these become promittors, because they promise the event.

Radical ; radix.—The figure at birth is the *radix* or root

from which everything is judged, and the term radical
refers to it.

Retrograde.—The backward motion which the planets
appear to have sometimes, in consequence of the position
and motion of the earth.

Stationary is understood of a planet when to the eye of
a beholder on earth it appears to stand still. Not that a
planet can ever really be in this state, but is only so
rendered by the inequalities arising from the position and
motion of the earth.

Refranation is when some planet in *direct motion* applies
to another planet, but before they can meet becomes *retrograde*, and thus *refrains* from forming the aspect expected.
For instance, we will suppose Jupiter in the 12th degree of
Gemini, and Mars in the 8th ; here Mars, who is the swifter
planet, promises very soon to overtake Jupiter, and form
the conjunction with him, but just at the instant becomes
retrograde and *refrains* from the conjunction by moving in
an opposite course from Jupiter. The effect of this refranation would be that what was promised by the conjunction
of Mars and Jupiter would not take place.

Separation is when two planets have been in conjunction,
or in any of the other aspects to each other, and have just
departed from that position. Thus, if we suppose Saturn
in 12 degrees of Sagittarius, and Jupiter in 13 degrees of
that sign, Jupiter will then be separated one degree from
a *partile* or *perfect* conjunction with Saturn, but they would
still be in what is called *platic*, or *imperfect* conjunction,
till they were separated nine degrees, when the aspect
would cease.

Translation of Light and Nature.—This happens when
a light planet separates from a heavy one, and joins
with another more ponderous, and it is effected in the
following manner : we must suppose Saturn to be
posited in 20 degrees of Aries, Jupiter in 13 degrees,
and Mars in 14 degrees of the same sign ; here Mars

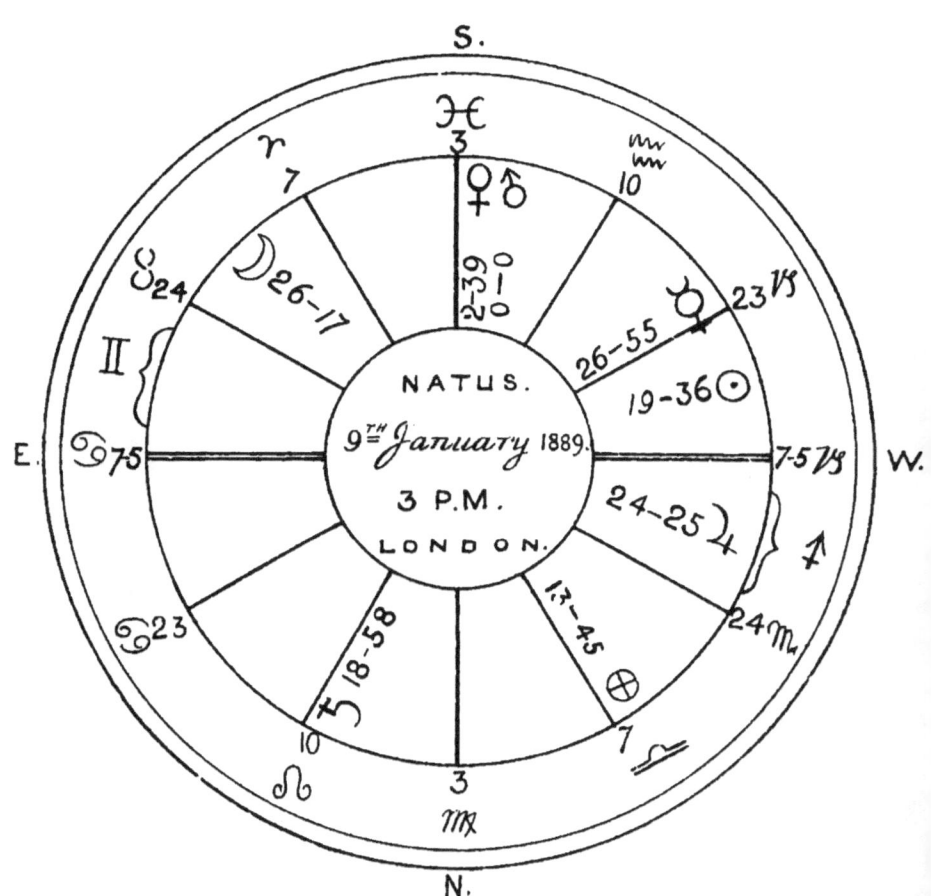

separates from a conjunction with Jupiter and translates the light and nature of that planet to Saturn, to whom he next applies. The effect of this would be that if an event had been promised by Saturn, then, whoever was represented by Mars would obtain all the assistance of *the benevolent* planet Jupiter, and *translate* it to Saturn. This position of the planets would promise success in lawsuits or marriage, or any other questions of the kind.

Swift of course is when a planet moves further than his usual motion in twenty-four hours, and he is *slow* of course when he moves *less* than his ordinary motion in the same course of time.

Void of course is when a planet is separated from another planet, and does not, during its continuance in the same sign, form any aspect with any other planet. This most usually happens with the Moon. The effect of this is that if the planet promising the event be void of course, the matter will not have a good issue.

CHAPTER IX.

OF THE FIGURE OF THE HEAVENS.

THIS was formerly termed a *horoscope*, but is now more generally called a *figure of the heavens*. It is simply a scheme, or plan, representing an accurate picture of the heavens,—that is, of the positions of the Sun, Moon, and planets, and, in some instances, of the fixed stars also, for the moment at which a child is born. In horary questions the figure is drawn for the required time, which may be the moment of the propounding of a question to an astrologer, or of the occurrence of any event of the result of which astrological information is desired.

This map, which contains the twelve divisions already described as the twelve houses of heaven, may be drawn in either a square or circular form. Lilly and other mediæval writers use both forms indiscriminately; modern astrologers seem to prefer the circles, and as this is, perhaps, more easily understood, the following diagram (plate 2) is drawn up in that manner. It will be seen that it is formed of three circles. In the centre space the date, time, and place of the event of a horary question are entered, and in a nativity the name, sex, and moment of birth of the native. The next space (divided into twelve equal parts for the houses) is reserved for the planets, and in the outer space are placed the signs of the Zodiac, with the number of their degrees, on the cusp of heach ouse. The cusps of the Houses are represented by that line between each house. Having obtained an Ephemeris, or astrological almanack* for the year required, we must find the Sidereal Time for the day and month of the birth, or question; then, if the time of the event be *before* noon we must *deduct* the difference between the given time and noon from the Sidereal Time of the day;—for example, on the day of the event (the 9th January, 1889), the Sidereal Time at noon is shown by the Ephemeris to be 19 hours 16 minutes 51 seconds, if the birth had been at 9 a.m. The difference between 9 a.m. and noon is 3 hours. We should, therefore, have to *deduct* 3 hours from 19 hours 16 minutes 51 seconds, which gives 16 hours 16 minutes 51 seconds, the Sidereal Time required.

As the event is supposed to happen at 3 in the *afternoon*, we must *add* the difference between noon and the time given to the Sidereal Time of the day. The difference between noon and 3 p.m. is 3 hours, and, as the Sidereal Time on the 9th January, 1889, is 19 hours 16 minutes 51 seconds, we *add* 3 hours to this amount, which gives 22 hours 16 minutes 51 seconds, the Sidereal Time required.

We must now proceed to place the signs for 3 p.m.

---

* Zadkiel's and Raphael's are both good; the following figure is worked after the Ephemeris of the latter.

on the 9th January, 1889, which is thus done :—we turn
to the " Table of Houses " (which will be found at the end
of the Ephemeris), and having found (under the column
headed " Sidereal Time ") the nearest time to 22 hours
16 minutes 51 seconds, which in this case is 22 hours
16 minutes 48 seconds for the latitude of London, we
see in the next column (headed 10) the sign ♓ (Pisces),
and the number 3° opposite our Sidereal Time, showing
that the third degree of Pisces is on the cusp of the
10th house. In the next column (headed 11) we see
♈ (Aries), and the number 7° ; we, therefore, place
7° ♈ on the cusp of the 11th house, next 24° ♉, on
the 12th ; then 7° 5' ♋ on the Ascendant (or first house),
23' ♋ on the 2nd, and 10° ♌ on the 3rd ; for the remaining
houses we place the signs *in order* opposite to those already
given, keeping the same number of degrees to each corresponding house and sign. The opposite house to the 10th
is the 4th, and the opposite sign to ♓ is ♍; we therefore
place 3° ♍ on the cusp of the 4th house, and so on of the
rest. It will, however, now be seen that the two signs ♊
and ♐ are missing ; these signs are " intercepted," which
means that they lie between two houses without occupying
the cusp of either ; they must, therefore, be placed in their
order *between* the cusps of the houses. This is, of course,
not always the case, and some horoscopes will have no
intercepted signs.

How to Place the Planets.

In the Ephemeris the longitudes of the planets are given
daily for mean noon ; so, to find the *exact* place of a planet
for a given time, we must note the difference of longitude
between the previous noon and noon of the day for drawing
the map for a.m. and for p.m., the difference between
noon of the day and noon of the day after. This *difference*
is the motion of the planet in 24 hours, which we must
work thus:—As 24 hours are to - hours (*i.e.*, the differ-

ence between the given time and noon), so is the daily
motion to the motion required. For example, the ☉ at
noon on the 9th January is (omitting seconds) in 19° 29' ♑,
and on the 10th January at noon he is in 20° 30' ♑, which
gives a daily motion of 59 minutes. We must find his
place for 3 p.m. on the 9th January. As 24 hours are to
3 hours, so are 59 minutes to the time required ; this
equals about 7 minutes, which we add to the ☉'s longitude at noon on the 9th. If the event had been for a.m.
this amount would have been *deducted* from the ☉'s longitude at noon on the day of the event. We must proceed
in the same way for the other planets, and place them in
the map, according to their positions in respect to the
degrees on the cusps of the houses. The ☉ will be in
19° 36' ♑, or about the middle of the 7th house. And
note that the number of degrees of a sign on the cusp
of any house shows that that sign commenced *in* the previous house. Supposing the ☉ had been 1° of ♑, we
should then have placed it in the 6th house, a little below
the cusp of the 7th. When a planet is *Retrograde* (shown
in the Ephemeris thus *R.*), we *add* the amount to the
longitude when the event is before noon or a.m., and *deduct*
it from the longitude when the event is afternoon or p.m.

To Find the " Part of Fortune."

Subtract the place of the Sun in signs, degrees, and
minutes from that of the Moon, and add the result to the
sign, degree, and minute of the cusp of the horoscope, or
ascendant. When the Moon has less signs than the Sun
we have to borrow twelve. For example, we wish to
find the " Part of Fortune " for the 9th January at 3 p.m.

	Signs.	Degrees.	Minutes.
Place of ☽	0	26	17
Subtract place of ☉	9	19	36
Gives	3	6	41
Add place of Cusp of Ascendant	3	7	5
Gives place of ⊕	6	13	45

That is, the Part of Fortune is in 13 degrees 45 minutes of the 7th sign ; Virgo is the 6th sign, but as our amount is 13° 45′ *more* than the 6 signs we place the Part of Fortune (⊕) in 13° 45′ of Libra, just past the cusp of the 5th house, thus completing the map. The mode of giving a general judgment on a horoscope will be shown further on.

CHAPTER X.

OF THE INFLUENCES OF THE FIXED STARS.

THE fixed stars are so called because they appear to keep at the same distance from one another in the heavens. All of these stars have their respective influences analogous to those of the planets. The following table of the principal fixed stars, with their several magnitudes and natures, will be found useful. It is only those of the first and second magnitude which much affect us ; the influence of those stars marked as of fourth magnitude is very slight. The time of the rising and setting of the fixed stars varies according to the latitudes of the places of observation. Their longitudes increase at the annual rate of 50 seconds, but their latitudes vary very little. The right ascension and declinations of the numerous fixed stars are given every year in the Nautical Almanack.

TABLE OF THE PRINCIPAL FIXED STARS, WITH THEIR MAGNITUDES AND NATURES.

Stars.	Magnitudes.	Natures.
South End of the Tail of the Whale	2	Of the nature of Saturn.
The Star in the Wing of Pegasus	2	Mars and Mercury.
The Head of Andromeda	2	Jupiter and Venus.
The Whale's Belly	4	Saturn.
The Girdle of Andromeda	2	Venus.
The Bright Star in the Head of Aries ...	3	Saturn and Mars.
The Left Foot of Andromeda	2	Venus.
The Bright Star in the Jaw of the Whale	2	Saturn.

Stars.	Magnitudes.	Natures.
Caput Algol	2	Saturn and Jupiter.
The Pleiades or Seven Stars	5	Mars and the Moon.
The Middle Star in the Pleiades	3	Mars and the Moon.
Oculus Taurus	3	Venus.
Aldebaran	1	Mars.
Rigel	1	Jupiter and Venus.
The Foremost Shoulder of Orion	2	Mars and Mercury.
The She-Goat	1	Mercury and Mars.
The Middle Star in Orion's Belt	2	Jupiter and Saturn.
The Highest Star in the Head of Orion...	4	Jupiter and Saturn.
The Star in the Horn of the Bull	3	Mars.
Propus	4	Mars.
The Right Shoulder of Auriga	2	Mars and Mercury.
The Foot of Gemini	2	Mercury and Venus.
Castor	2	Mars, Venus, and Saturn.
Pollux	2	Mars.
The Smaller Dog Star	2	Mercury and Mars.
Præsepe*	1	Mars and the Moon.
North Asellus	4	Mars and the Sun.
South Asellus	4	Mars and the Sun.
Cor Leonis or Regulus	1	Mars.
Heart of Hydra	1	Saturn and Venus.
Vindemiatrix	3	Saturn, Venus, and Mercury.
The Back of the Lion	2	Saturn and Venus.
The Tail of the Lion	1	Saturn, Venus, and Mercury.
Crater	4	Venus and Mercury.
Arcturus	1	Jupiter and Mars.
The Virgin's Spike, or Arista	1	Venus and Mars.
The South Balance	2	Saturn and Venus.
The North Balance	2	Jupiter and Mars.
The Left Hand of Ophiucus	3	Mars and Saturn.
The Highest Star in Head of Scorpio ...	2	Saturn and Venus.
The Left Knee of Ophiucus	3	Saturn and Venus.
Cor Scorpio	2	Mars and Jupiter.
Antares	1	Mars.
The Right Knee of Ophiucus	3	Saturn and Venus.
The Bright Star of the Vulture	2	Saturn and Mercury.
The Mouth of Pegasus	3	Venus and Mercury.
The Tail of the Goat	3	Saturn.
Marchab	2	Mars and Mercury.
Fomahaut	1	Venus and Mercury.
Scheat-Pegasi	2	Saturn.

To know when any of these fixed stars will affect the horoscope, we must note the sign and degree on the cusps of the houses, and if (on consulting the Ephemeris) any of these stars should be found to be ascending or descending within five degrees of the signs upon the cusps of the several houses, they must be entered in the same manner

---

* The nebulous mass in the body of the Crab.

as the planets, and their qualities weighed according to the nature of the planet or planets with which they correspond, as shown by the table given.

The influences of the fixed stars are not much considered by the modern astrologers, yet in certain positions their power is undeniable. The conjunction and opposition are the only aspects to be considered in regard to them, as they do not operate on the planets by sextile, square, or trine aspects. When a fixed star happens to be in conjunction with the Sun at birth, certain effects are distinctly traceable. For example, the Sun conjoined with Aldebaran, Hercules, Antares, or any fixed star having the nature of Mars, threatens a violent death, or at best, constant illness to the native. The Sun, with the Pleiades, Castor, Pollux, or Præsepe, show a cruel and headstrong disposition in the native, and the *probability* of violent death. The star Arista, with the Sun, gives great and lasting good fortune. All the stars of the nature of Saturn, conjoined with the Sun, bring calamity and disgrace. When a fixed star, whose latitude does not differ much from that of the Moon, is in conjunction with her, certain effects are produced; for instance, when she is conjoined with Aldebaran or Pollux, violent death is indicated; when with the Pleiades, injury to the eyes or blindness. The Moon with Antares, and in opposition to Saturn with Aldebaran, shows death by strangulation. The moon, with Aldebaran or Antares either in the ascendant or in the mid-heaven, gives brilliant honours, but not without many attendant dangers and hair-breadth escapes. Fixed stars of the *first* magnitude, near the cusp of the seventh house, show a rich wife, but her disposition will sympathise with the planetary qualities of the star. Fomahaut and Rigel, in either the ascendant or mid-heaven, give fame after death. Syrius, the Dog Star, in conjunction with the Sun, either in the ascendant or mid-heaven, gives preferment

and honours from royalty. Caput Algol, in conjunction
with the Sun in the eighth house, and in square to Mars,
shows decapitation.

CHAPTER XI.

OF THE EFFECT OF EACH PLANET IN EACH OF THE TWELVE HOUSES.

SATURN in the first house, or ascendant, shows melancholy
and many sorrows, and if near the ascendant probability
of early death; in the second house pecuniary troubles;
in the third quarrels with brothers and sisters, and dangers
and losses in travelling; in the fourth house death of
father or mother, and loss of friends; in the fifth barren-
ness, death of children; in the sixth illness, worries with
servants, and losses from .cattle; in the seventh an un-
governable wife, and unhappy marriage; in the eighth
violent death and loss of legacies; in the ninth losses
by sea; in the tenth dishonour and imprisonment; in the
eleventh deep depression, and false friends; in the twelfth
sorrow, trouble, and persecution from secret enemies. If
the planet is strong—that is, well dignified—these evils
are much lessened.

Jupiter in the first house gives a good, happy, and long
life; in the second riches; in the third family affection
and fortunate short journeys; in the fourth lands and
inheritance with an honourable life and end; in the fifth
many children who are good and affectionate; in the sixth
faithful servants and fortunate dealings respecting cattle;
in the seventh honourable marriage; in the eighth long life
and natural death; in the ninth profitable sea voyages; in
the tenth preferment and honours; in the eleventh faithful
friends; in the twelfth victory over secret enemies. This,

of course, means when the planet is strong in dignities; if weak the good will be somewhat abated.

Mars in the first house shows shortness of life and scars on the head or face; in the second poverty and troubles; in the third quarrels with kindred and dangers in travelling; in the fourth short life to the fathers; in the fifth disobedient children; in the sixth fevers, bad servants, and loss of cattle; in the seventh sensuality and unhappiness in marriage; in the eighth a violent death; in the ninth irreligion, and losses at sea; in the tenth military preferment, but troubles from great dignitaries; in the eleventh false friends and loss of money; in the twelfth imprisonment. This is when Mars is afflicted, but if well-aspected these evils are somewhat abated.

The Sun in the first house gives honour, glory, and long life; in the second much riches but great extravagance; in the third good brethren and fortunate journeys; in the fourth a noble inheritance and honours in old age; in the fifth few children, yet such as will be a comfort; in the sixth diseases of the mind; in the seventh a good wife, honourable adversaries, and sickness; in the eighth good dowry with the wife, but danger of a violent death; in the ninth gain by the sea, and ecclesiastical dignities; in the tenth gain from princes and noble women; in the eleventh distinguished friendships; in the twelfth powerful adversaries. This is if the Sun is well-dignified; if weak the good fortune is not so pronounced.

Venus in the first house gives good health, but sensuality as regards the opposite sex; in the second riches by means of women; in the third, in a woman's horoscope, by means of lovers above her in rank; in the fourth inheritance; in the fifth many children; in the sixth illness from excesses; in the seventh a good and beautiful wife and very few enemies; in the eighth a good dowry with the wife and a natural death; in the ninth good fortune by sea; in the tenth honour and preferment through the means of some one of the opposite sex; in the eleventh sympathetic friends; in the twelfth freedom from the power of private enemies. This if Venus be strong; if weak, the good fortune is less pronounced.

Mercury in the first house gives noble thoughts, graceful elocution, and love of art and science; in the second profit by intellectual work; in the third mathematical skill, swift and prosperous journeys; in the fourth the gain of an inheritance by craftiness; in the fifth clever children; in the sixth thieving servants, and diseases of the brain; in the seventh a fomenter of quarrels, but a discreet wife; in the eighth death by consumption; in the ninth wonderful ability, especially in occult matters; in the tenth much preferment for ability; in the eleventh inconstant friends; in the twelfth secret enemies, but they will not much affect the destiny. This is when Mercury is well-dignified. If weak, the good fortune is much lessened.

The Moon in the ascendant, or first house, shows the native will travel and will gain the favour of noble persons; in the second she sometimes gives unstable fortune, riches, and poverty alternately; in the third long journeys; in the fourth profit by travelling; in the fifth many children; in the sixth diseases of the brain, but good servants; in the seventh honourable marriage; in the eighth danger by drowning, but otherwise a long and healthy life; in the ninth many long sea voyages, inconstancy in religion, and love of art; in the tenth great honours; in the eleventh the friendship of noble personages; in the twelfth the common people will be the native's enemies and do him much wrong.

The Dragon's Head when posited in the first house shows poverty; in the second a good estate; in the third honest kindred and fortunate journeys; in the fourth gain by travels; in the fifth long life and good children; in the sixth health and good servants; in the seventh a virtuous wife; in the eighth many legacies and a natural death; in the ninth prosperity at sea ; in the tenth honour ; in the eleventh faithful friends ; in the twelfth open enemies.

The Dragon's Tail in the same places signifies the contrary in all things.

The Part of Fortune gives promise of all those things signified by the house in which it is posited, unless afflicted by the presence of one of the malefic planets.

CHAPTER XII.

ON FORMING A GENERAL JUDGMENT ON A NATIVITY.

RESPECTING the distribution of the doctrine of nativities, we are to consider first the *parents,* then the duration of life ; the shape and figure of the body ; after these the quality of the mind ; then as to fortune in regard to honours as well as wealth. In succession to these the character of the employment ; the questions relative to marriage, children, and friendships ; then that concerning travel ; and lastly, that concerning the *kind* of death which awaits the native from the configuration of the heavens at his birth.

The Parents.—In conformity with nature, says Ptolemy, the Sun and Saturn are allotted to the person of the father ; and the Moon and Venus to that of the mother ; and the mode in which these luminaries and planets may be found posited, with reference to each other as well as to other planets and stars, will intimate the situation of affairs affecting the parents.

If Mars should be in bad aspect to the Sun, the father will receive some injury to the face or die suddenly ; but a long life is presaged if Jupiter or Venus be in any mode whatever configurated with either the Sun or Saturn.

If Mars be succedent to the Moon or Venus, or in quartile or opposition to them, or if Saturn be similarly aspected

E

to the Moon only, and both of them be void of course or retrograde, or cadent, adverse accidents and disease will attend the mother ; should they, on the other hand, be swift in motion and placed in angles, they portend that her life will be short, or grievously afflicted.

Should the Sun be configurated, in any mode whatever, with the Moon or Venus, or should Venus herself be harmoniously configurated with the Moon, either by the sextile, the trine, or the conjunction, the mother will live long.

Concerning the duration of the native's own life, the Hylegliacal* places are, according to Ptolemy, the sign on the angle of the Ascendant from the fifth degree above the horizon to the twenty-fifth degree below it ; the thirty degrees in dexter-sextile thereto constituting the eleventh house ; also the thirty degrees in dexter-quartile, forming the Mid-heaven above the earth ; those in dexter-trine making the ninth house ; and lastly, those in opposition belonging to the angle of the west.

Among these places, the degrees which constitute the Mid-heaven are entitled to preference, as being of a more potent influence ; the degrees in the Ascendant are next in virtue ; then the degrees in the eleventh house, succedent to the Mid-heaven ; then those in the angle of the west ; and, lastly, those in the ninth house, which precede the Mid-heaven.

He also holds that " the Sun, the Moon, the Ascendant, and the Part of Fortune are to be considered as the four principally liable to be elected to the office of prorogator " —or HYLEG.

These views are not adopted by the modern astrologers, but, as this is a book setting forth the ancient methods, it is needless to discuss the various objections made by

---

* Hyleg is the word used for that body or point which is the giver of life.

them to this, as to some other of the theories laid down by Ptolemy.

Among the four prorogators already given, the Sun by day is to be preferred, provided he is placed in one of the Hylegliacal places, and if not, the Moon; but if the Moon also should not be so posited, that planet is to be elected as Hyleg which may have most claims to dominion in reference to the Sun, the Moon, and the Ascendant, which means that the planet should have dominion, in any one of the places where these are situated, by at least three dignities. If, however, no planet should be so circumstanced, the Ascendant is then to be taken as Hyleg.

By night the Moon is to be elected as prorogator; provided, in like manner, she should be in some prorogatory place; and if she be not, the Sun; if he also be not in any prorogatory place, then that planet which may have most right of dominion in reference to the Moon, and the antecedent full Moon and the Part of Fortune. But if there be no planet claiming dominion in the mode prescribed, the Ascendant must be taken, in case a new Moon had last preceded the birth; but if a full Moon, the Part of Fortune.

If the two luminaries, and also some ruling planet of appropriate condition, should be each posited in a prorogatory place, then, provided one luminary may be found to occupy some place more important and influential than the others, that luminary must be chosen; but should the ruling planet occupy the stronger place, and have prerogatives of dominion suitable to the conditions of both luminaries, the planet must then be preferred to either of them.

When the Hyleg has been determined by the foregoing rules, then note whether it is supported by benevolent planets in good aspects towards it and free from affliction,—that is, from evil aspects from evil planets,— if so, the life is likely to continue and the constitution to

be strong; but if the Hyleg, whether it be the Sun, the
Moon, the Ascendant, or the Part of Fortune, be afflicted
with evil planets, and there be no assistance from good
planets, the child will die in infancy; if there be some
assistance from good planets, but yet the evil aspects exceed
the good, the constitution will be weak, and the first train
of evil directions will destroy the life.

Concerning the disposition and quality of the mind, we
must look principally to the planets in the ascendant, the
influences of which over mind and body have already been
given in the chapter on the seven planets. We must,
however, always bear in mind that Mercury has chief
dominion over the mental faculties, whilst the sentiment
passions are governed by the Moon and the planet in
the Ascendant. The Moon well aspected, that is in trine,
sextile, or conjunction to Mercury at birth, will give to
the native excellent abilities, ingenuity, versatility, and
wit. Even the evil aspects of the Square and Opposition are
better than no aspects at all, though these sometimes
produce a cynical and obstinate nature.

The abilities of those born when Mercury is in "cazimi"
(that is within seventeen degrees of the Sun's centre) are
of the highest order.

Mercury in conjunction with Saturn at birth gives
clear judgment and a love of occult subjects.

Venus in good aspect with Mercury gives love of music
and an artistic nature.

If Mercury and the Moon throw no aspect to each other,
and are afflicted by Mars and Saturn, the native will be
liable to become insane.

The fortune of wealth is determined, as we have seen, by
the Part of Fortune, the Sun and the Moon; if they are
in good position, that is, angular and well-aspected by the
two luminaries, the native will be rich. If the Sun and
the Moon are well placed, and if there be benefic stars
in the Mid-heaven, the native will rank high in the world.

If the contrary, the native never rises above mediocrity; and if Saturn afflicts the Mid-heaven he meets disgrace. If Mars is strong and in good aspect to the Sun and Moon, he will gain military glory. Jupiter on the Mid-heaven and the Sun and Moon in trine to each other, the Moon having the trine of Jupiter, is one of the best positions for rising in the world. Jupiter in the tenth house will cause the native to do fairly well in the world; but Saturn in that house, if not extremely well-aspected, will bring him to shame and beggary.

Concerning the nature of employment, the dominion of the employment is claimed by the Sun and by the planet on the Mid-heaven. If Mercury should rule alone he produces writers, teachers of science, merchants, and bankers; also, if well aspected to Saturn, astrologers and students of all occult matters; if Jupiter is in conjunction, then the native will be an orator, actor, or painter, and his pursuits will lead him into the society of persons of rank.

Venus ruling makes wine-merchants, dealers in colours, dyes, perfumes, drugs, garments or apparel, &c.; if connected with Saturn, she makes persons have to do with amusement, players, jugglers, &c.; if with Jupiter, persons attending exhibitions, and priests who have much personal decoration—as Catholic priests, bishops, &c., and they will gain by women. Mars ruling alone makes martial men, and, if in Scorpio, Cancer, or Pisces, naval men.* The Sun joined with him, being near the Mid-heaven, or in aspect, makes persons dealing with fire or metals, the latter especially if in Taurus or Leo. If Mars be separated from the Sun, he makes shipwrights, smiths, agriculturists, stonemasons, and carpenters.

If Saturn bear testimony in addition to Mars, persons become mariners, workers in mines, wells, vaults, &c., under ground, keepers of cattle, cooks, butchers. If

---

* At Admiral Nelson's birth Mars was rising in the sign Scorpio.

Jupiter join with Mars, they will be soldiers, innkeepers, tax-gatherers, mechanics. If Mercury and Venus become joint arbiters of employment, they produce musicians, dancers, poets, weavers, and painters, &c. Jupiter in connection with them makes magistrates and senators, and also teachers of youth. Mercury with Mars makes surgeons, statuaries, boxers. If Mercury be more powerful, they will be scientific ; and if Mars be stronger, they will be more violent and cruel in their practices.* If Saturn join these two, they will be thieves (especially if the Moon be in ill aspect to Mercury) ; if ☽ be in ill aspect to ♂, they will be robbers or assassins. If Jupiter join ☿ and ♂, they engage in honourable warfare, and are industrious. If Venus and Mars rule together, persons will be dyers, workers in tin, lead, gold, silver, medical drugs, and also physicians.

The Moon regulating the employment, and, separating from the Sun, and forming an aspect with Mercury, inclines to the pursuit of astrology, spiritualism, and magic.

Concerning Marriage, Ptolemy has laid down some very clear rules. He advises persons about to marry to have a care that the luminaries,—that is, the Sun and Moon in their respective nativities—are in concord. It is of happy augury if the Moon in the bridegroom's nativity is in good aspect—that is in trine or sextile to the Sun in the bride's nativity. The Square or Opposition aspects formed between the luminaries in the two nativities indicate discord and separation, and very evil effects follow if the malefic planets, Saturn and Mars, have a bad aspect to the Sun and Moon in both nativities. If Venus be with them the separation will be caused by adultery. Good planets, such as Jupiter and Venus, placed between the luminaries in both nativities, show much happiness.

In men's nativities the Moon must be chiefly considered

---

* Probably Vivisectionists.

in regard to marriage. Should she be in her first or third quarter at birth, the man will marry under thirty, or if older, his wife will be a very young woman.

If the Moon be configurated with Saturn, she entirely denies marriage. If she should be in a sign of single form, such as Libra or Taurus, the native will marry only once, but if she should be placed in a double-bodied sign, such as Pisces or Sagittarius, the man will marry more than once.

If the Moon make application to the benefics, the wives will be good and true; but if she make application to evil planets, the wives will prove either bad or of a quarrelsome disposition. For example: If Saturn receives the Moon's application the wife will prove troublesome and morose, yet constant and industrious; if Jupiter receive it, the wife will be decorous, good, and economical; if Mars, bold and refractory; if Venus, cheerful, handsome, and agreeable; if Mercury, sensible, prudent, and clever.

Women in whose nativities Venus is configurated with Jupiter or Mercury are virtuous and well-conducted; but when Venus is with Mars alone they are liable to become licentious. Mars in Square to Venus shows adultery.

For women the Sun is to be chiefly regarded in estimating their chances of marriage and happiness. If the Sun be Oriental (i.e., between the Ascendant and Mid-heaven, or between the Descendant and Nadir)—the native will marry in her youth; or, when old, to a young man. If the Sun be occidental, the native will marry late in life; or when young, to an old man. If the Sun be in a sign of single form, she will marry but once; if in a double-bodied sign, or configurated with several oriental planets (in one sign) she will marry more than once. If Saturn be configurated with the Sun, the husband will be steadfast, prosperous, and industrious.

Jupiter configurated with the Sun gives a good, benevolent, and honourable husband. "Mars," says Ptolemy,

" gives a severe husband, void of affection and intractable."
Venus gives an amiable husband of handsome appearance.
Mercury gives one who is provident and expert in business
and of a lively and cheerful temperament.

If Mars be separated from Venus and Saturn, yet have
the assistance of Jupiter, men will lead virtuous lives. If
Mars be configurated with Venus only men are of a licentious temperament.

Saturn, when in the 7th house of a nativity, brings
either unhappiness in marriage or early death of one
or other of the married people. The Sun badly aspected
by Saturn in the nativity of a woman, and the Moon
afflicted by the same planet in the nativity of a man, will
bring trouble in love and marriage.

Description of the Wife or Husband.—The planet, with
the sign in which it is placed, which is posited near the
cusp of the 7th house, must be taken to describe the
person. If no planet should happen to be so placed,
then we must go by the sign alone. Benefic planets in
the 8th house show that the wife or husband will be
rich ; unfortunate planets show the reverse.

Children.—As regards the probability of having children,
the 10th and 11th houses must be consulted, and should
there be no planets in them, then the opposite, the 4th
and 5th houses, must be considered. The Moon, Jupiter,
and Venus are said to be givers of children ; the Sun,
Mars, and Saturn deny children, or give very few, and
those either die early or are a source of trouble to their
parents. Mercury either gives or denies children, according
to the planets with which he may happen to be posited.

If the Sun and malefics be in barren or masculine signs,
and in the before-named houses, there will be no children ;
but if they be in fruitful or feminine, no common signs,
there may be children, but they will be delicate and
short-lived.

If Jupiter, the Moon, and Venus are well-dignified in

the 10th and 11th houses, the children born will attain rank and distinction in the world.

Friends and Enemies.—Persons born under the same sign of the Zodiac are likely to be sympathetic ; so also, if the planet in the ascendant of one person's nativity is one which is friendly to that which rises in the ascendant in the other's. Thus, a person whose ruling planet is Venus would be attracted by one in whose ascendant Mars is dominant, and a person whose ruling planet is the Moon rarely contracts a warm friendship with one who has Mars in the ascendant of his nativity, and *vice versâ.* The friendships and enmities of the planets have already been given in the chapter on the influences of the seven planets.

Mars in bad aspect to the Sun or Moon in the seventh house causes quarrels. Saturn thus placed gives distrust and antipathy. Venus and Mercury well aspected in the eleventh house show intellectual and artistic friendships, and either of the malefics in the twelfth house are indicative of secret foes.

Travelling.—The position of the Moon, Mars, and Part of Fortune are here to be considered. If they, or most of them, should be in a cadent position the native will travel a great deal. The Moon in a watery sign causes much travelling by water. Ptolemy tells us that Mars in Square or Opposition to the Sun or Moon will cause much travelling in foreign countries. If the benefics are conjoined with the Moon, the journeys will be safe and pleasant ; if the malefics they will produce mischances and ill-health in travelling. Mercury ascending at birth in a double-bodied or movable sign gives a great disposition to travel. If a malefic affecting the Moon should be in the watery signs of *Cancer,* Scorpio, or Pisces, shipwreck and even death by drowning may ensue during travelling.

Of the Manner of Death.—If the Hyleg and Ascendant

should be well-aspected, and if either Jupiter, Venus, Mercury, or the Moon well dignified should appear in the eighth house, the native will die a natural death. If either the Sun or Moon should be badly aspected by Mars or Saturn in the eighth house it is significant of a violent or remarkable death. Saturn causes lingering deaths, and Mars those which are sudden. The kind of death depends chiefly on the nature of the planets, the directions of which operate (astrologically speaking) to cause death. The signs in which such planets were posited at birth show in some degree the nature of the fatal illness and the part of the body attacked.

Saturn indicates death by chronic diseases, rheumatism, ague, and paralysis.

Jupiter (when not well aspected at birth) may become a promittor, or cause of death, by apoplexy, inflammation of the lungs, spasms, or gout.

Mars indicates death by acute or eruptive fevers, small-pox, all kinds of hæmorrhage, burns, suicides, and wounds from iron, over which metal he presides.

Venus produces death by cancer, scurvy, dysentery, or wasting away and putrid diseases. If violence attend she causes poison.

Mercury kills by madness, epilepsy, coughs, and obstructions. If violence concur he brings death by accident in sport or by robbers.

The Moon.—When the Ascendant or ☉ be Hyleg, the Moon will assist in causing death by cold phlegmatic diseases, and if she be placed in ♋ ♏, or ♓, by drowning.

The Sun will assist to cause death by his ill aspects to the Ascendant or ☽ if they be Hyleg, and then he acts like Mars, and, if in *Leo*, will produce death by fire, if other testimonies accord. The Moon causes death by dropsy, or other watery diseases. When in the sign Scorpio, Pisces, or Cancer, she causes death by drowning.

Death occurs by violence when Mars and Saturn and

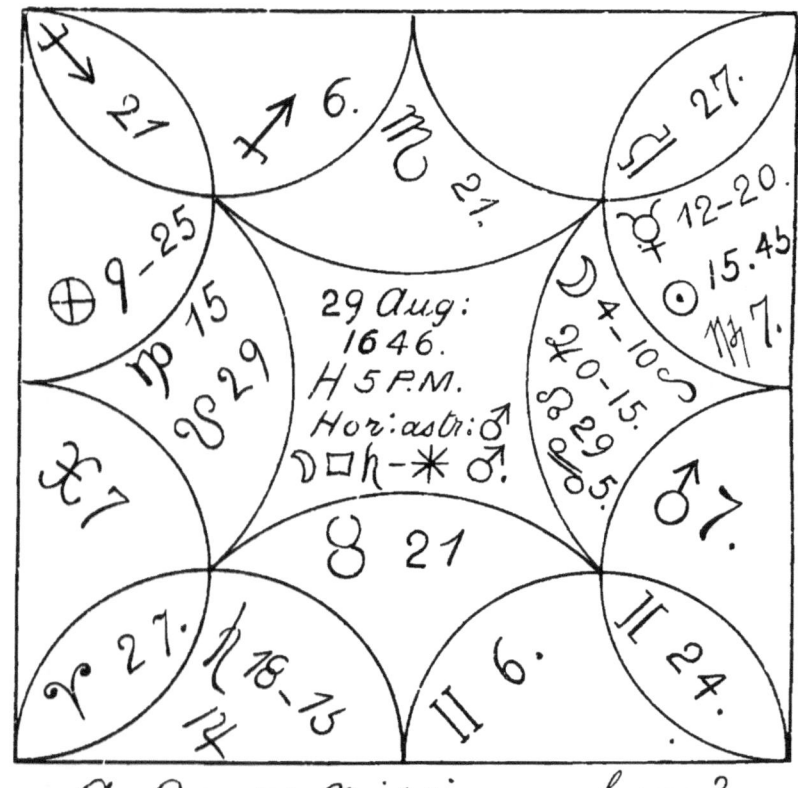

a. Dogge missing—where?

FACSIMILE OF A MAP OF A HORARY QUESTION
FROM LILLYS ASTROLOGY.

evil fixed stars afflict the Hyleg, and are in mutual square or opposition. Saturn, in such case, particularly when in Taurus, indicates death by hanging or suffocation. Saturn in opposition to either the Sun or Moon rising, is said to show death in prison. Venus and Mercury conjoined with Saturn, the last-named afflicting the Hyleg, death is threatened from poison, or through the treachery of a woman. If Saturn be in a tropical or quadrupedal sign, and the Sun be in conjunction or opposition, or Mars be so, death will be caused by the fall of buildings; and if Saturn be in the Mid-heaven, and so configurated with the Sun or Mars, death will result through falls from heights or precipices, especially if Saturn be in an airy sign.

The benefics cannot cause death *of themselves;* and even their □ or ☍ aspects will frequently save life when they fall amidst a train of evil directions. But if the malefic influence is too powerful for them to avert, then they assist to cause death in the various manners above described.

CHAPTER XIII.

CONCERNING DIRECTIONS AND HORARY QUESTIONS.

WE have seen in the chapter on the judgment of a nativity that by the consideration of the position of the planets, and of the Sun and Moon in the twelve houses, what the *general* fortune of the native will be in the whole course of his life; but the art of Direction measures out the time into years, months, weeks, and days, and thus informs us when we may expect in *particular* what is *generally* promised us in nativity.

Directions are of two kinds, *primary* and *secondary*, and are based upon arithmetical calculations of the time of the

events caused by the aspects of the significators (that is, of
the Sun or the Moon), with the places of the planets. They
are founded upon the familiarities of the stars amongst each
other in the Zodiac (*after the nativity*), and show, by calculations, the distance of the place of a significator at the
moment of the nativity from the place it must reach before
it can join the aspect, which distance is called *the Arc of
Direction.* Some astrologers consider what are called
" *Mundane Directions*," which are distances in the world
measured by the semi-arc, and are wholly independent of
the Zodiac. These were invented by Placidus, but as Ptolemy
does not treat of them they will not be considered here.

It must always be remembered that,—in directions,—the
place of a planet, at the time of the nativity, is called the
planet itself, although it may not be there when the significator arrives ; thus, if we wish to direct the Sun to the
conjunction of Jupiter, we must do so to the position which
that planet occupied *at the moment* of the nativity. When
the Arc of Direction is found the Sun's right ascension
must be added to it, and the Sun will be the right ascension
(without latitude) of that place in the Zodiac, at which,
when the Sun arrives, the direction will be completed.
For every day of the Sun's approach to this point a year
must be added, and thus the time when the event is likely
to happen is pointed out ; these primary directions, however, cannot be depended upon to produce an event of
great importance unless the secondary directions agree ;
but where the nativity is weak the primary direction alone
is powerful enough to kill (especially if it should be opposed
to the Hyleg), and misfortune will always happen if the
positions of the planets, at the moment of birth, are unfortunate, *without* the coincidence of any secondary direction.

Secondary Directions are those daily aspects to the
luminaries which happen after birth, every day of which is
reckoned for a year , two hours for a month, thirty minutes
for a week, and four minutes for a day. Thus, whatever

aspects take place in the *first day* of the native's life will develop their effects in the first year, and those of the second day in the second year, so that, should the native live fifty years, his secondary direction for his fiftieth year will arise from the aspects which took place on the fiftieth day after his birth. The ancient astrologers—particularly the Egyptians—used to predict the events of a nativity *wholly* from these secondary directions, in which the Moon should be chiefly considered ; for in those days on which she comes to an evil aspect with the malefics, Saturn or Mars, the years corresponding to those days will be peculiarly unfortunate and dangerous to the native ; and where, on the contrary, the Moon is well aspected to the benefics, the years corresponding to those days will be very fortunate : a good direction gives prosperity in that matter which the significator indicates ; thus we direct the Sun to signify the native's preferment or disgrace, his good or bad health, and the favour or disesteem of great personages.

The direction of the Moon refers to the nature of the native's journeys, whether prosperous or the reverse, his marriage, his wife, his women friends and kinsfolk.

The direction of the Part of Fortune refers to the increase or diminution of riches.

The direction of Saturn signifies the native's inheritance, buildings, possessions, and also his fears, jealousies, and mistrusts.

Jupiter is directed as regards glory, renown, riches, children, and religion.

Mars is directed for the native's law-suits, animosities, and victories ; he also shows the estates of brethren.

Venus is directed for marriage, love, and pleasure, and all matters in connexion with women.

Mercury is directed for a knowledge of the amount of wit, understanding, trade, industry, and journeys of the native ; also for distinction in scholarship and all intellectual pursuits.

The Horoscope or Ascendant is directed to signify the life, affections, and manners of the native.

The Mid-heaven's direction affect the passion and correct the native.

If the directions are to good aspects of benevolent planets, they signify prosperity both of mind and body, cheerfulness, and all manner of earthly happiness ; but if the horoscope should have directions to the ill aspects of the malefics, Mars or Saturn, then evil is to be expected of the nature given by the malevolent star. If directed to the good aspects, such as the trine or sextile of these evil planets, the misfortune is not so great, and even in some instances good may be predicted. As, for example, the horoscope directed to the trine or sextile of Mars gives preferment by arms, the same aspects towards Saturn would indicate success in building or in mines, or some calling connected with metals.

As the working out of these directions requires much precision, and as they are likely to lead to many grave errors when not accurately calculated, the student is advised to thoroughly study the problems given in this matter of directions in " The Text-book of Astrology," by A. J. Pearse ; but those who are devoid of mathematical abilities would do better to leave the matter of directions alone, contenting themselves with working out the dates of the events by the easier method given in the second part of this work—Chiromancy, for the hand bears upon it in the clearest manner the influence of the stars received by the native at the moment of birth, and is, in fact, a horoscope drawn up by the heavens.

Horary questions are questions asked at a certain time when a person feels anxious concerning any undertaking or impending event. A figure or map of the heavens, like that erected for a nativity, is drawn out for the minute in which the question is asked ; and if the astrologer be skilful, and the querist sincere,—that is, not putting the question from frivolous motives,—the answer will, in general, be true, for the whole is the effect of that sympathy which pervades all nature, and which is the key-note of all divination under whatsoever form it is practised.

In horary questions the sign ascending and its lord represent the querent, and to these the Moon is added and must be considered with the lord of the ascendant.

The house to which the thing belongs about which inquiry is made is the significator of that person and thing, and every other house and its lord are to be considered according to their respective significations, so as to indicate the means and persons by which the event, about which the inquiries are made, will be accelerated or retarded.

The dates of events are regulated by the signs and angles. For example, should the significator of the event be in a movable sign and an angle, the event will come to pass in the same number of days as there are degrees between the significator's aspect and the star to which it is directed if the aspect be by *application* ; if by *separation*, the thing will *not* take place at all. In one of the succeedent houses movable signs give months ; common signs years, and fixed signs bring about the event, after much delay, and when all hopes of it are past.

Significators in any of the Cadent houses seldom do anything, and should they bring about an event at all, they do so after much waiting and with much trouble and vexation.

The matter of horary questions is very well treated in Lilly's " Grammar of Astrology," published in 1647, and by way of explaining the manner in which this branch of astrology is worked, we give a *fac-simile* of a map of a horary question to be found in this book with (verbatim) Lilly's method of dealing with that particular question.

Judgment of the Figure given in Plate.—" Living in London, where we have few or no small cattle as in the country, I cannot give example of such creatures, but I once set the figure preceding concerning a dogge (which is in the nature of small beasts), which dogge was missing. The question to me was what part of the city they should search and if he should ever be recovered.

" The querent was signified by the sign ascending and the lord thereof, for, in his person, he was Saturnine and vitiated (according to the Dragon's Tail in the ascendant) in his nature, mind, and understanding : that is, he was deformed in body and of a covetous disposition. The sign of the sixth house and his lord signifies the dogge, for that sign stands for sheep, hogs, and small cattle.

" The sign of Gemini is west, and by south the quarter of the heaven is west ; Mercury (the significator of the dogge) is in Libra, a western sign, but southern quarter of heaven, tending towards the west ; the Moon is in Virgo, a south-west sign, and verging towards the western angle. The strength of the testimonies being thus examined I found the plurality to signify the west, and therefore I judged that the dogge ought to be westward from the place where the owner lived, which was at Temple Bar, wherefore I judged that the dogge was about Long Acre, or the upper part of Drury Lane. In regard that Mercury (the significator of the beast) was in a sign of the same triplicity as Gemini the ascendant, which signifies London, and applied to a trine aspect of the cusp of the sixth house, I judged that the dogge was not out of the lines of communication, but was in the same quarter, of which I was more confirmed by the trine of the Sun and Saturn. The sign in which Mercury appeared was Libra—an airy sign ; therefore I judged that the dogge was in some chamber or upper room, and kept privately, or in great secrecy, because the Moon was under the beams of the Sun ; and Mercury, the Moon, and the Sun were in the eighth house ; and because the Sun on the Monday following would apply by trine to Saturn, the lord of the ascendant ; and the Moon to trine of Mars having exultation in the ascendant, I intimated to the owner of the beast that, in my opinion, he should have his dogge again, or news of his dogge or small beast upon the Monday following, or near that time, which was true; for a gentleman of the querent's acquaintance sent home the dogge the very same day, about ten in the morning, who, by accident, coming to see a friend in Long Acre, found the dogge chained up under a table, and, knowing the dogge to be the querent's, sent him home as above said, to my very great credit," and no doubt also to the great satisfaction of " the dogge " himself.

CHAPTER XIV.

APHORISMS CULLED FROM THE WORKS OF PTOLEMY AND OTHER ANCIENT ASTROLOGERS.

JUDGMENT must be regulated by thyself, as well as by the science; for it is not possible that particular forms of events should be declared by any person, however scientific; since the understanding conceives only a certain general idea of some sensible event, and not its particular form. It is, therefore, necessary for him who practises herein to adopt inference. They only who are inspired by God can predict particulars.

Whosoever may be adapted to any particular event or pursuit will assuredly have the star indicative thereof very potent in his nativity.

Neither put on nor lay aside any garment for the first time, when the Moon may be located in Leo. And it will be still worse to do so, should she be badly affected.

If Virgo or Pisces be on the ascendant the native will create his own dignity; but if Aries or Libra be there he will cause his own death.

Venus gives pleasure to the native in that part of the body which may be ruled by the sign she occupies. It is the same with other stars.

F

Should a disease begin when the Moon may be in a sign occupied at the birth by some malefic, or in quartile or opposition to any such sign, such disease will be most severe; and if the malefic also behold the said sign, it will be dangerous. On the other hand, there will be no danger if the Moon be in a place held at the time of birth by some benefic.

While the Moon is in her first quarter, withdrawing from her conjunction with the Sun, the bodily humours expand until her second quarter; in her other quarters they decrease.

There are, in every day of the week, certain hours of the day and the night which, by the reigning force of the seven planets, are productive of fortunate or unfortunate events. The second hour after sunrise on Monday is evil, and also the hour before midnight, whilst the third hour from sunrise and the hour before noon on that day are extremely fortunate. On Tuesday the first hour after sunrise is of evil influence, whilst the hour immediately after noon and that which precedes midnight would be fortunate. On Wednesday, the third hour from sunrise and the hour before sunset are both evil, but the second hour after sunset and the hour are fortunate, especially as regards matters relating to love and marriage. The hour after mid-day—that is, from twelve to one—is, on Thursday, very unfortunate, but the first hour after sunrise is good. On Friday, nothing should be done in the hour before noontide, or in the hour before midnight; but the second hour before noon and the hour next to sunset are very fortunate. On Saturday, the first hour after sunrise and the second hour after noonday,—that is, from one to two o'clock,—are very unfortunate; in travelling, marriage, or business they should be avoided; the fortunate hours of Saturday are the second hour after sunrise and the last hour before sunset. The unfortunate hours of Sunday are the hour after noon and the hour before the sun sets. The fortunate hours are that before noonday and the hour immediately after sunset.

If the Sun should be in conjunction with the lord of the ascendant in the sign Leo, and there be no benefic in the eighth house, the native will be burnt to death.

A malefic planet, when oriental, signifies an accident; when occidental, a disease.

In a conjunction of Saturn and Jupiter, give judgment according to the nature of that planet which may be most elevated (that is, nearest the Mid-heaven), and follow the same rule with all the other stars.

Those who would evince success in any pursuit or undertaking should observe the course of the Moon, and, above all things, begin nothing of consequence in her decrease, which is from the second day of the full Moon to the next new Moon; for long experience proves that there does not exist half the chance of success to any pursuit if undertaken during that time; whilst affairs and business of any kind which are begun during the increase of the Moon,—that is, from the second day after the new Moon to the time of the full,—are attended with a far greater success.

Those born near noon are generally successful in life, owing to the Sun's influence being then most powerful. Those born near midnight are by no means so fortunate as those born at mid-day, and it is a singular peculiarity in such nativities that the most remarkable events of their lives take place *after* their thirtieth year, and they are also certain of some kind of a name after death, meritorious or otherwise, according to what their horoscope declares. Persons born near midnight are very imaginative, and subject to see visions, dream dreams, and to be for the most part believers in the unseen world.

In all travels consider the Moon, for she is a general significatrix of journeys, whether by sea or land. If, when a ship sets sail, Saturn should ascend in the sign Pisces, and there is no good aspect from the Moon, the ship will founder at sea.

If Mars be in the Ascendant when a man goes to war he will either be killed in battle or at best be dangerously wounded.

The planet Mars has more power to destroy life when he is in the sign Aries, in a diurnal nativity. Saturn is more evil in his influence, as regards the native's life, when he is in the sign Capricornus in a nocturnal geniture.

When the Moon is besieged between Mars and the Sun in a nativity, it argues a short life to the native.

When Saturn is Lord of the Fourth House, and well dignified, it promises to the native good fortune by mines or minerals.

Jupiter in the fourth house, and in the sign Libra, also promises to the native much wealth from metals, especially from tin; and argues a rich inheritance or personal estate from the father.

When the Moon is in the ascendant at birth, and in direct opposition to Mercury and Mars, madness is to be feared.

When Venus is in the fourth house, in opposition or in square to Mars or the Moon, and in the sign Cancer, the native will be of a sensual nature. When in a nativity Saturn appears more elevated than either the Moon or Venus, it is an indication that the native will not marry. The square or opposition of Venus to Saturn gives the same signification.

When Jupiter is well-dignified in a horoscope, and in either trine or sextile to Venus or the Moon, it denotes to the native happy marriage with a person of good birth.

Mercury, if posited in one of the houses of Saturn, and in trine or sextile to that planet, gives excellent understanding; and if the Moon be also well-dignified, the native is much given to the study of occult science, and will have much renown in that particular.

Those born with the Moon powerful in their horoscopes

would do well to be guided by her aspects in their daily avocations. If she should be in trine or sextile to Jupiter, it is a good day to seek favours of the great, or to make arrangements with employers. When she is in trine or sextile to Mercury all intellectual matters taken in hand will be likely to prosper. When she is so aspected to Venus matters undertaken with reference to love, marriage, or friendship will have a happy issue. When she is in square or opposition she would have, of course, the contrary effects.

The Sun and Moon in conjunction with Mercury gives to the native great intellectual abilities.

The Moon in conjunction with Saturn, and posited in one of the earthly signs, causes the native to be of a melancholy temperament, and one likely to see visions, and to be governed by influences from the unseen world.

Mercury and Venus in conjunction in an airy sign in the ascendant will cause the native to be a great scholar and a learned critic.

Mercury in the ascendant, and in the sign Gemini, Libra, or Aquarius, causes the native to be eloquent in discourse.

The Moon in the ascendant at birth in the sign Aries, and in opposition of Mercury, will cause the native to be a lying and treacherous person.

Mercury rising in Pisces, and afflicted of either Mars or the Sun, makes the native a fanatic or a hairbrained, fanciful fellow.

Those who have the benevolent planets Jupiter and Venus well posited in either the Ascendant or the Midheaven at birth will always be much beloved during the whole course of their lives.

He who is born with the Sun in trine to Jupiter is fond of rule, and very famous in his generation.

Venus in square to Saturn at a birth causes the native to be sensual and given to unnatural vices.

All the planets, or most of them above the earth, make

the native eminent and famous, and if all should be well
dignified, he will,—like a comet,—outshine all others in
the world's esteem. If, on the contrary, all the planets
are under the earth at a birth, the native will be of a falling
fame and fortune, or if they promise by their natures
honour, dignity, and fortune (that is, if they appear essentially dignified in nocturnal genitures), these good things
will only come in the latter part of the native's life.

Planets in square or opposition to each other from angles
or cardinal signs declare great misfortune to the native
during his lifetime, and also point to a violent death as
likely to be his end.

Saturn in one man's nativity upon the ascendant of
another's is an absolute token of hatred, but the latter will
be the person injured.

When one of the malefic planets,—Saturn or Mars,—is
posited in the fourth or seventh house, the native will survive
his wife. If the Moon is conjoined with only one planet
which is better fortified than the Moon, the husband dies
first.

Saturn, the Moon, and Mars in conjunction in the
fourth house denote captivity, and Mars in square or
opposition to Saturn in the eighth house indicates perpetual imprisonment.

Mercury in an earthly sign in conjunction with Saturn
shows death by the bite of a mad dog or the sting of some
venomous creature.

Ever note that a planet Peregrine,—that is, having no
essential dignities of term, face, or house where he is placed,
—is malicious beyond expression.

In all horary questions remember that there is no affliction to the Moon so great as when she is in conjunction
with the Sun ; the ill aspects for the malefics must affect
her, but no evil aspect is so powerful as her combustion.

The Sun in conjunction with Venus shows the native to
be much influenced by the opposite sex.

The Sun in conjunction with the Moon in a watery sign gives drunkenness.

Venus in conjunction, trine or sextile, to the Moon, gives happy marriage, but in Square to the Moon prodigality, indolence, and drunkenness.

Mercury in trine or sextile to the Moon gives the capacity for acquiring foreign languages. In bad aspect to the Moon makes the native envious, sarcastic, ill-natured, and given to lying and thieving.

Saturn in trine or sextile to Venus shows much power of attachment to wife and family. In a woman's nativity this is very good, as it indicates constancy and prudence.

Saturn well-aspected to the Sun shows the friendship and support of great personages.

Saturn in Square to Mars means a malicious and murderous temperament, and liability to imprisonment.

It is advantageous to make choice of days and hours at a time well constituted by the nativity. Should the time be adverse, the choice will in no respect avail, however favourable an issue it may chance to promise.

A sagacious mind improves the operation of the heavens, as a skilful farmer, by cultivation, improves nature.

PART II.

CHIROMANCY.

"God has placed signs in the hands of all men, that every man may know his work."—Job xxxvii. 7 (*St. Hierom's translation*).

CHAPTER XV.

CHIROMANCY AND ITS ORIGIN.

CHIROMANCY is a science which teaches us to read not only the character but the whole destiny,—for good or evil, the length of life and often the manner of death, of a man by the lines and marks to be seen in his hand. This study is sometimes called Palmistry, in which case, however, it properly refers *only* to a judgment formed from what appears in the palm of the hand, whilst Chiromancy (taken from the word *Cheir*, a hand, and *Manteia*, divination) signifies the revelations made by the hand, taken as a whole. Chiromancy is nearly as ancient as astrology, with which it is *indissolubly* connected, for the hand represents, as has been before said, a natural horoscope, which is placed upon it at the time both of the conception and the birth by the influence of the stars. The seven planets are all represented in the hand, and also the twelve signs of the Zodiac, so that the casting of a nativity is needless, as by simply examining a hand by the light of Chiromancy we can indicate what planets have been powerful at the time of birth, and what, therefore, will be their effect for good or evil over the existence ; and we can also find the dates of the principal events of the life. We find many allusions to this subject in the Bible, and still more in the ancient Kabbala.

The Holy Kabbala, as it was called by the Magi, must not be confounded with what is called "The Black Art"; it is, on the contrary, the quintessence of reason and morality as they were understood by the ancients, and contains that traditional science of the secrets of nature which, from age to age, is born towards us as the wave is carried by the tide to the shore ; but it has been transmitted obscurely, because the doctrines of the Kabbala were known only, in those early ages, to the adept, and the initiation, later on, of neophytes, was only yielded after a series of severe and terrible ordeals, whilst the revelation of its mysteries to the uninitiated was punished by death.

The necessity of silence was, in fact, one of the principal tenets of the Kabbala, and is represented, in the figure of Adda-Nari,* by the position of the fingers of the hand holding the flowering branch of Abundance; the thumb and the first two fingers, which in Chiromancy represent *will*, *power*, and *fatality*, are held open ; whilst the third and fourth fingers, representing light and science, are closed. This was meant to indicate to the good—the initiated—that they would have, when united, strength and will to direct Fate ; but that they must keep hidden from the wicked and ignorant both light and science. It must, however, in justice to the ancient Kabbalists, be suggested that their inculcation of silence probably arose, not so much from a desire of domination, but rather from the fact that, feeling themselves superior in knowledge, they thought they were obeying a divine law in refusing to the wicked those lights which, when possessed by them, led, as perhaps they had sometimes found, to error. We, seeing things in a wider light, give, or try to give, equal knowledge to all, without submitting the ignorant to the ordeal of initiation to prove their worthiness as recipients ; but, after all, it amounts to much the same thing—give to all men truth and light in abundance, but all will not profit by it. We see this every day in our college system ; the lesson is the same for all, but it is only the few who profit by it ; and although we appear to be obeying a divine law in opening the way of light and life—the life of knowledge—to all, as God makes His sun to shine on good and bad equally, still we can, in some sort, understand the feeling of the ancient Magi, whose motto was : " Know, Dare, Will, but keep Silence."

---

* Adda-Nari, Nature,—that is, the deity known under the name of Isis by the Egyptians.

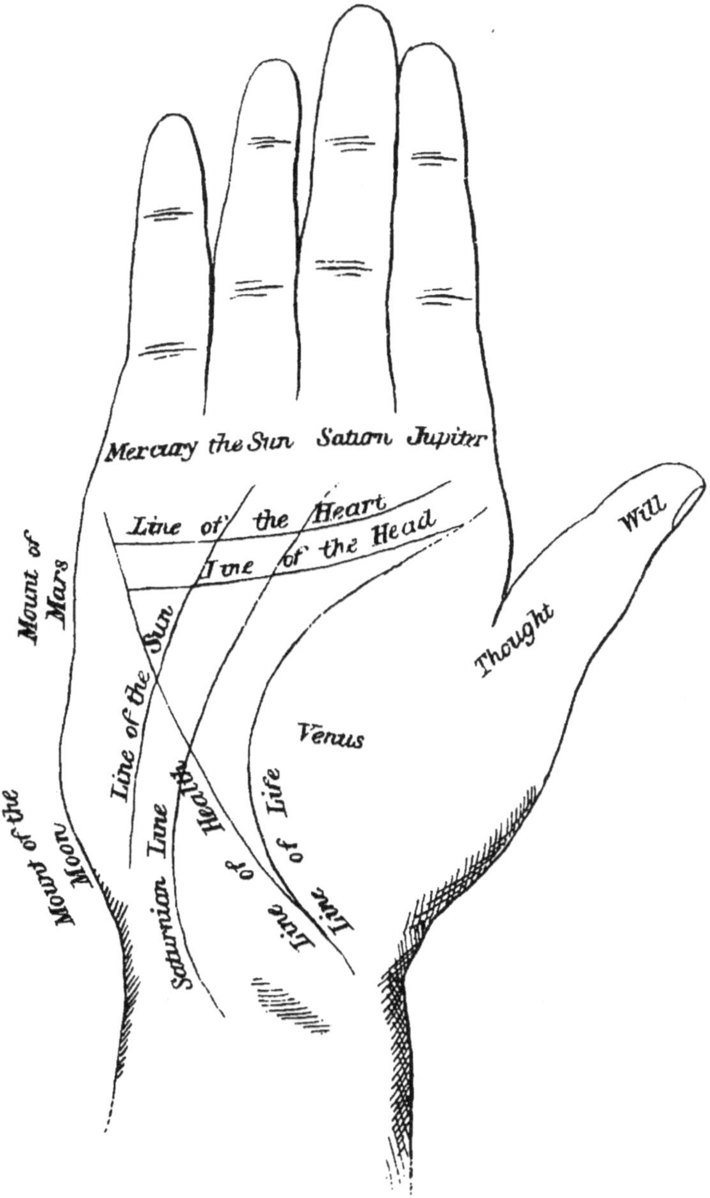

Mercury   the Sun   Saturn   Jupiter

Line of the Heart

Line of the Head

Mount of Mars

Line of the Sun

Thought

Will

Venus

Mount of the Moon

Saturnian Line

Line of Health

Line of Life

CHAPTER XVI.

CONCERNING THE PRINCIPAL LINES IN THE HAND AND THE MOUNTS.

In the plate belonging to this chapter we give a hand on which are marked the principal lines seen on the palm; three of which, viz., the Line of Life, the Line of Head, and the Line of Heart, are found in a clearer or fainter degree on all hands, but which vary, as regards their relative position, in every hand. The first and largest, that which encircles the thumb, is called the Line of Life; by the length, colour, and evenness, or the reverse, of this line the length of life is indicated, and also the illnesses and accidents by which the life is menaced in running its course. The line immediately above it, crossing the palm of the hand, is the Line of Head; by it we are to judge of the intellectual powers. Above it is the Line of Heart, from which we form an opinion of the strength of affection, or the want of it, in the native.

The lines which are not always to be found are the lines going from the wrist to the finger of Saturn, which is called the Saturnian line, and which shows the events of the life; the Line of the Sun, which goes towards the finger of the Sun, and which indicates success in art, literature, or the pursuit of riches; and the Line of Health, which goes from the wrist to the finger of Mercury: this line is often absent in a hand.

All these lines will be more fully discussed further on; at present it is only necessary to name them in order to explain the plate belonging to this chapter.

At the base of each figure there is a mount, more or less developed, on every hand. Now, each of these mounts corresponds with one of the planets from which it has received more or less influence, according to its development, and the signs or marks to be found upon it.

It will be seen also, from the plate, that the ancients gave to each figure the name of one of the planets, thus :—

The first finger represented Jupiter, the mount at its base being called the Mount of Jupiter.

The second, Saturn, the mount at its root being the Mount of Saturn.

The third, the Sun, the mount below being the Mount of the Sun.

The fourth, Mercury, the mount at its base being called the Mount of Mercury.

The thumb is sacred to Venus, and the root of the thumb is called the Mount of Venus.

It will also be seen that the planet Mars (although no finger is dedicated to it) is twice represented in the hand, along the side of the palm by the Mount of Mars, and in the palm, between the Line of Life and the Line of the Head, which is called the Plain of Mars.

The Moon is only represented by the Mount of the Moon, at the lower part of the palm on the opposite side of the hand to the thumb.

When these mounts are well in their places, and clearly but not too strongly defined, they give the qualities of the planet they represent; but when any mount is not well marked, or even, as frequently happens, is quite deficient, there is a want of the qualities shown to exist where the mount is clearly defined. If the mounts are not only ill-defined, but represented by a cavity, that cavity would indicate the existence of qualities which are the reverse of those indicated by the mount; whereas an exceeding development would denote an excess of the qualities given by the mount.

Thus the Mount of Jupiter, which is immediately under the index, when fairly developed, indicates noble ambition, will-power, love of nature, kindliness, generosity, religion, and happy marriage. When in excess—that is, when the mount is so large as to invade that next it, the Mount of Saturn,—it gives superstition, exaggerated pride, and domineering self-assertion. The total absence of this mount (which is sometimes, but rarely, seen) indicates coldness, selfishness, irreligion, and that want of dignity which is produced by the utter absence of self-respect.

The Mount of Saturn is found immediately beneath the second finger, which the ancients assigned to Saturn, the planet of Fatality. Saturn gives extreme misfortune, or extreme good fortune, according to the development of the mount and the signs and lines to be seen upon it, and the course of the Saturnian Line, or Line of Fate (of which we will speak further on), in the palm of the hand. This mount also denotes a tendency to occult science. Those born specially under the influence of Saturn are timid, lovers of solitude, and very seldom marry, but are very persistent in their affections when they do love.

Saturn, when well-developed, gives prudence, wisdom, and, to a certain extent, success; when in excess it gives sadness, taciturnity, asceticism, dread of the after-life, and yet sometimes a predisposition to suicide. The total absence of the mount indicates an insignificant existence.

The Mount of the Sun is placed at the root of the third finger, which was sacred to Apollo, or the Sun; when this mount is well developed it indicates love of art and literature, which shows itself (according to temperament) in poetry, painting, sculpture, or music; it gives also religion of the æsthetic, tolerant sort, grace, riches, and celebrity; in excess it gives love of show, frivolity, and vaingloriousness. The total absence of the mount means a thoroughly material existence; absence of all taste for art—a life without colour, a day without sunlight.

The Mount of Mercury is found at the base of the fourth finger, and, when well-defined, indicates intelligence, success in science, and in occult studies; the love of work, activity,

both of mind and body, and eloquence; in excess it gives
impudence, theft, and falsehood; absence of the mount
indicates no aptitude for science, no intellectuality, a negative existence. Of course, should the Mount of the Sun
be well-defined, the last quality would be overridden by the
success which that indicates.

The Mount of Mars is at the side of the hand, opposite
the thumb, just below the Mount of Mercury and when well-
developed, indicates courage, ardour, and resolution; in excess
it gives cruelty, anger, revenge and tyranny; the absence of
the mount gives cowardice and want of self-command.

The Mount of the Moon is found immediately below that
of Mars and when well-developed, gives imagination of the
dreamy, sentimental order, gentle melancholy, and love of
solitude; in excess it gives morbid melancholy, caprice,
and fantastic imagination; the absence of the mount indicates want of poetry in the nature, positivism.

The Mount of Venus, which is formed by the root of the
thumb, indicates, when fairly developed, love of the beautiful, melody in music, the desire of pleasing and sensuous
tenderness; in excess it gives love of material pleasures,
coquetry, inconstancy and (when other signs, afterwards to
be explained, are also seen in the hand) extreme sensuality.

Each planet has a special influence over certain parts of
the body. Jupiter governs the head and lungs; Saturn, the
spleen and ears; the Sun, heart, eyes, and arms; Mercury,
the liver and legs; Mars, the head and throat; the Moon
and Venus, the lower parts of the body. Any excess in
the length or size of the fingers or mounts argues a tendency to disease in the organs represented by that finger or
mount. When a mount is—instead of being high—broad
and full, it gives the same indications as if it were high;
if much covered with lines it shows an over-abundance of
the quality of the mount, and is equal to an excess of
height. *One* deep perpendicular line upon a mount is a
fortunate sign; *two* show danger of too great force of the

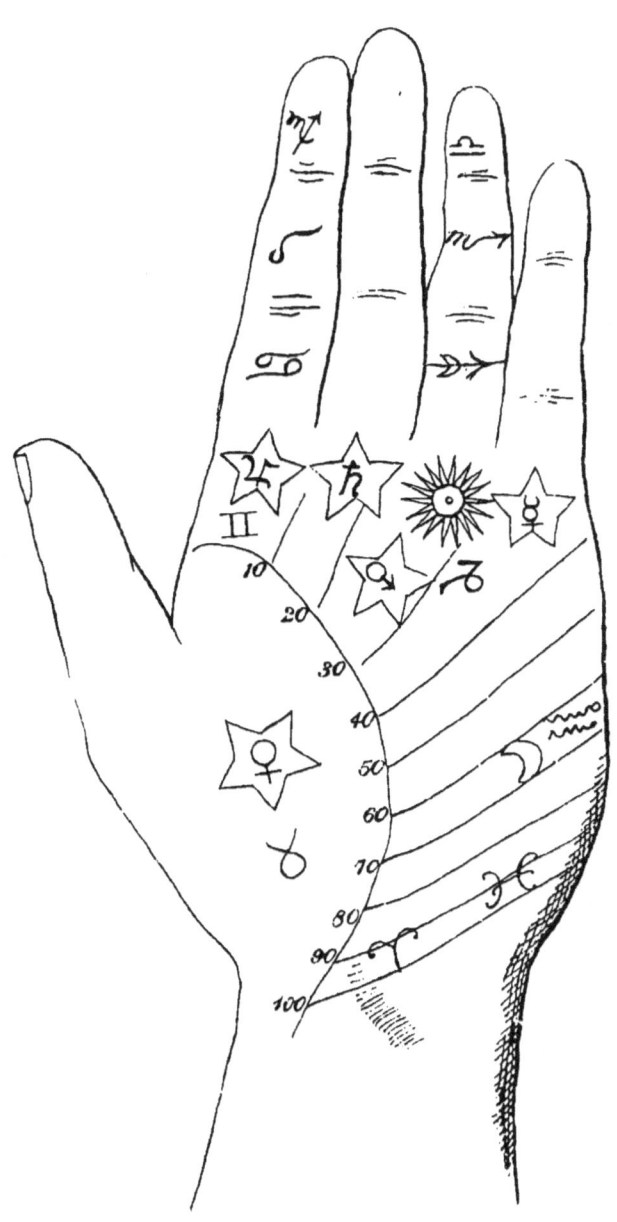

quality; and *three* give misfortune arising from excess of the qualities of the mount. Crossway lines on the mount always denote obstacles. Some old Italian writers affirm that fine cross lines on a mount signify wounds to that part of the body over which the mount on which they are seen has influence.

The mounts are often irregularly placed. If one should lean towards the other, it absorbs some of the qualities of the mount which it invades.

CHAPTER XVII.

THE LINE OF LIFE.

THE ancient Chiromancists divided the Line of Life into ten compartments (see plate), each representing ten years of life, and thus they were enabled to prognosticate at what date in the life the illnesses or dangers indicated by the form or colour of the line would be likely to happen. This plate is copied from one in the Sieur de Peruchio's interesting work, " La Chiromance," published in Paris in 1657.

It will be noticed that the mounts are here indicated by the astrological symbols of the various planets they represent, Mars being placed on the Plain of Mars, gaining the Mount of Mars, which, as we have already seen, lies immediately below the Mount of Mercury. It will also be seen that the signs of the Zodiac are also represented on the hand : Aries (March), which begins the astrological year, is placed at the base of the hand, close to the Mount of Venus ; Taurus (April) is on the Mount of Venus ; Gemini (May) is at the base of the Mount of Jupiter. These represent the spring-tide of the year, and also of life : therefore

G

they are placed on and near Venus, which planets represent happiness and enjoyment. The signs Cancer (June), Leo (July), and Virgo (August), represent the second age, which is given to the accumulation of riches and honours : so these signs appear on the finger of Jupiter. In the third age a person is supposed to enter upon the enjoyment of dignities, therefore Libra (September), Scorpio (October), and Sagittarius (November), are on the third finger, that of the Sun, which is supposed to accord position and reputation. The last months of the astrological year are thus placed : Capricornus (December) is beneath the Mount of the Sun ; Aquarius (January) is on the upper part of the Mount of the Moon ; and Pisces (February) will be seen at the base of the Mount.

When the Line of Life is long, well-formed, slightly coloured and goes all round the thumb, it indicates a long life and free from serious illness ; but when the line is wide and pale in colour, it indicates bad health ; when it is short, it means early death.

If the Line of Life is broken on one hand, but is marked in a continuous line on the other, these signs indicate an illness of a very serious nature ; but if the broken line should appear in *both* hands, it means death at the epoch corresponding with the place on the line where the break occurs. When the Line of Life is not clearly defined, but is formed by a sort of chain of small lines, it indicates continuous small illnesses.

When the Line of Life, instead of starting from the side of the hand, takes its rise in the Mount of Jupiter, which is sometimes, but rarely, the case, it is supposed to indicate a life of successful ambition, honours, and celebrity—qualities given by the influence of Jupiter.

If the Line of Life joins the Line of the Heart, or the Line of the Head, it indicates grave misfortune or violent death, by which the ancients probably meant to infer that when either the heart or the head is dominated by merely vital instincts, the life is menaced by misfortune ; but, when the Line of Life is *very far* from the Line of Head, it indicates a life that accomplishes its course without much intelligence; so also, if the Line of Life is very far from the Line of Heart, it indicates a life without love.

When the Line of Life is bi-forked at its termination, near the wrist, it means a total change in the way of life towards its close, and should one of the branches tend towards the Mount of the Moon, it indicates madness towards the end of existence. A double Line of Life is sometimes, but rarely, seen : this indicates excess of health and long life, and also success in a military career. This line is sometimes called the Line of Mars. To a woman it indicates success in love. Three stars inside the line, but close to it as to be almost on it, show that the subject will be much loved of men or women as the sex will determine, but that these lines will bring distress.

A circle on the Line of Life shows loss of an eye or disease of the eye at the period which it appears on the line. If two circles appear the person will become blind. If the Line of Life terminates with many small lines it means slight illnesses towards the close of life.

A woman having two crosses on the upper part of the Line of Life is sensuous and immodest. A line going from the Line of Life and terminating with an island on the Mount of Jupiter shows lung disease or pleurisy at the time where such line starts. If at the end of the Line of Life, towards the wrist, there is a small triangle, it denotes loquacity and falsehood ; but with a good Line of Head and Heart, tact and eloquence.

When the Line of Life throws branches upwards towards the Plain of Mars it means that, after long struggles, riches and honours will be acquired in old age. A line upwards from the Line of Life to the Mount of Jupiter shows success by the subject's own merits. This often makes its appearance quite suddenly.

A black spot on the Line of Life indicates an illness or a

wound at the period indicated by its position on the line. If the spot is bluish in tint it is a nervous illness attacking heart or head, in which case there is generally a corresponding spot on the Lines of either Heart or Head which determines the nature of the illness. A cross on the Line of Life is always misfortune, which affects the health. Lines going from the base of the thumb across the Mount of Venus and cutting the Line of Life denote illness from money worries if they stop at the Line of Head; and from heart troubles if they go direct to the Line of Heart. A line going from the Line of Life straight to the Mount of Saturn indicates accident from a four-footed beast. A line going from the Mount of Venus to the Line of Heart and terminating with a fork shows separation soon after marriage. When this is seen in conjunction with an island on the Line of Fate, it has a worse indication—that of adultery and divorce. *One* deep line going from the joint of the thumb across the Mount of Venus and just cutting the Line of Life indicates a deep heart sorrow from the death or faithlessness of some one much loved.

CHAPTER XVIII.

THE LINE OF HEART AND LINE OF HEAD.

THE Line of Heart is placed immediately beneath the mounts at the root of each finger. This line, when clear, straight, and well-coloured, rising in the Mount of Jupiter and extending to the outer edge of the hand, signifies that its possessor has a good heart capable of strong affection. If, instead of commencing on the Mount of Jupiter, it does not take its rise till the Mount of Saturn, then the love will, in that nature, be rather of a sensual character.

The Line of Heart sometimes stretches across the whole of the hand; such a line announces a too great amount of tenderness—a passionate and blind devotion in affection.

When the Line of Heart is broken in several places, it means inconstancy, both in love and friendship. Should the breaks be seen immediately beneath the Mount of Saturn it indicates a tragic end to the love; if beneath the Mount of the Sun, by pride*; but if between the Mounts of Saturn and the Sun, the heart-break will be occasioned by folly; if between the Mounts of Apollo and Mercury, by cupidity—the desire to make a better marriage in a worldly point of view; if the break occurs immediately beneath the Mount of Mercury, the evil issue of the love will be from caprice.

When the Line of the Heart appears in the form of the links of a chain instead of in one clear line, it indicates inconstancy and indecision—a tendency towards a series of *amourettes* rather than to a high and serious affection. If it goes round to the percussion of the hand it indicates jealousy.

The Line of Heart of a deep-red colour indicates a power of love ardent even to violence; but when, on the contrary, the Line of Heart is pale and wide, it is an indication of coldness of temperament.

When, at its starting-point, the Line of Heart is seen to turn round the base of the Mount of Jupiter somewhat in the form of a circle, it is what the ancient Chiromancists called " Solomon's Ring," and indicates an aptitude for the occult sciences. If the Line of Heart joins the Line of Life between the thumb and forefinger, it is a sign (if the mark is in *both* hands) of a violent death; if only in one, of a serious, but not fatal, illness connected with the heart.

---

* If the Sun is one of the dominant planets, the Line of Heart broken under the Mount of the Sun shows serious physical affection of the heart; if this sign is on both hands it is fatal.

If the Line of Heart droops towards the Line of Head and touches it, it is a sign of coldness and calculation in the affections; the instincts of the heart are dominated by worldly considerations.

If the Line of Heart is intersected by other lines, it is supposed to indicate as many troubles in the affections as there are crossings to be discerned. *Red* punctures on the Line of Heart mean as many wounds as there are punctures; * but *white* spots on the line indicate as many conquests in love as there are white spots on the line. From the position of these white spots on the Line of Heart, the mental and physical qualities of the lovers can be described. If the spot should appear on the extreme end of the Line of Heart, the character and appearance of the person would be that given by the planet Venus; if immediately under the Mount of Jupiter, he or she would have the mental and physical qualities given by that planet; if under Saturn, those of a Saturnian; if under the Mount of the Sun, those given by the Sun; if under the Mount of Mercury, those of the Mercurians; if nearer the side of the hand, the lover would present the attributes of those born under Mars; and if quite at the percussion of the hand, the qualities given by the Moon would denote the person.

If, on starting, the Line of the Heart is bi-forked, and one branch of the fork rises towards the Mount of Jupiter, it indicates great happiness of a glorious nature; but if the other branch stops between the finger of Jupiter and that of Saturn, it is merely negative happiness—a life passed without great misfortunes. When a hand (but this is rare) is entirely without the Line of Heart, it would indicate an iron will, wickedness, and cruelty.

The Line of the Head rises between the Line of Life and

* If the puncture is beneath the finger of Saturn, the evil will come from a practical person; if under the Sun, from an artist; if under Mercury, from a lawyer or doctor.

the Mount of Jupiter, and when it is long and clear it denotes a sound judgment, good memory, and masterly intellect ; but it must not extend across the hand in a *straight line*, as that signifies a disposition to avarice, or at any rate to extreme economy, because unless corrected by a rich Line of Heart, it would indicate an excess of calculation in the character.

If the Line of Head is long, but droops towards the Mountain of the Moon, it signifies ideality in excess. Life and its numerous duties and cares will be considered from an artistic and unreal point of view, for the Mount of the Moon, it will be remembered, represents imagination in excess, romanticism, and superstition ; and if the Line of the Head droops very low to the Mount of the Moon, it indicates more than superstition—it is then mysticism.

If, instead of drooping towards the Mount of the Moon, the Line of Head rises towards the mounts at its close, the intellect will partake of the qualities of that mount towards which it rises : thus, if it rises beneath the Mount of Mercury, the intellect will be employed successfully in affairs or on the stage ; if towards the Sun, in art and literature.

The Line of the Head pale-coloured and wide indicates a want of intelligence; so also does a very short line, only extending half-way across the hand. This is often seen in persons of medium intellect.

The Line of the Head broken in two immediately under the Mount of Saturn means, where the sign is on both hands, death on the scaffold, or at least, a fatal wound on the head. When this sign appears in only one hand (no matter which), it indicates a probability of madness from an unfortunate passion, or a broken limb, or a blow, but not fatal, on the head.

If the Line of the Head is long, thin, and not deeply marked, it shows infidelity and treachery. If, towards its close, it mounts suddenly to the Line of the Heart, it signifies early death. When this line is cut by a number of small hair lines, it indicates continuous nervous head-aches; a cross in the middle of the line is a sign of approaching death, or of a mortal wound.

When the Line of the Head is not joined to the Line of Life at its starting-point, it indicates self-confidence and impulsiveness, jealousy, and that sort of untruth which springs from exaggeration of facts, from over-impression-ability. With the planets of Mars and Jupiter in excess, the Line of Head separate from the Line of Life gives audacity and enthusiasm, and, therefore, success.

If large, round, red spots are seen on the Line of Head, they indicate so many wounds on the head; whilst white spots on the Line of the Head indicate as many successes in literature as there are spots to be seen.

A star on the Line of Head means a wound on the head, or madness if the line droops much to the Mount of the Moon, and the star appears at its termination.

A sister (or double line) of Head is rarely seen ; but if it appears, it is a sure sign of fortune by inheritance.

CHAPTER XIX.

THE SATURNIAN LINE.

The Saturnian Line, or Line of Fate, overrides the Mount of Saturn, and generally penetrates to the root of the second finger. This line has, in different hands, a different point of departure. Sometimes it rises in the Line of Life, in which case its indications participate in those of the Line of Life in the same hand; sometimes it takes its rise in the Plain of Mars, in which case it announces a troubled life, and still more so when it penetrates beyond the root of the finger of Saturn, and reaches the first joint. When it starts from the Mount of the Moon it signifies happiness, which is the result of a strong affection; if, however, the Saturnian Line, rising in the Mount of the Moon, stops short at the Line of the Heart, it is happiness crushed by an unfortunate attachment or physical disease of the heart. When the Saturnian Line starts from the wrist, exactly below the finger of Saturn, and goes in a direct line to it, cutting through the mount, but stopping at the root of the finger, it is a sign of a life of extreme happiness. If the line goes towards the Mount of Jupiter, this happiness is the result of a marriage bringing both riches and love. If the Saturnian Line stops short at the Line of Head, it is misfortune in affairs through a false calculation; or, taken in conjunction with a troubled Line of Life, it would mean a physical brain affection.

If the Saturnian Line is straight and well-coloured at its termination,—that is, as it nears the finger of Saturn,—it indicates happiness and riches in old age, however troubled the life may have been before. If this line only starts from the Line of Head, it denotes poverty and stupidity.

The Age, on the Saturnian Line, is counted from the wrist upwards; from the wrist to the Line of Head chiromancists count thirty-five years; from the Line of Head to the Line of Heart fifteen years; and from the Line of Heart to the root of the finger are the remaining years of Life.

If the Saturnian Line is broken and irregular, it means trouble and worry in life; and according to whether these breaks occur on the Line of Head or on the Line of Heart, so will the troubles be of the head or heart,—troubles arising from affairs or from the affections. If the Line of Life be irregular, denoting uncertain health, these troubles may be physical evils to the heart or head.

Short Lines crossing the Saturnian show vexations in either the affairs or in love matters. A downward branch from the Saturnian going towards the Moon shows sorrow from the death or treachery of a woman. This is the same whether it be on a man's or a woman's hand.

A triangle between the Saturnian Line and the Line of Life, but touching the Saturnian in the plain of Mars, indicates combats, duels, and success in arms at the time of life where the triangle touches the Saturnian Line. A cross on the Line of Saturn at its termination shows a violent death in old age. A star at the close of the Saturnian Line shows (if there is also a star at the termination of the Line of Life) death by paralysis in old age ; in a bad hand, death on the scaffold.

A line leading upwards from the Saturnian Line almost parallel with it, moving in the direction of the Heart, indicates marriage at the period where it starts from the Line.

Short upward lines going in the same direction indicate loves which do not lead to marriage. An upward branch going towards Mercury or the Sun shows a success in the career; if towards the Sun, in art or literature ; if towards Mercury, in affairs or on the stage.

The Saturnian Line does not always go direct to the finger of Saturn ; it is often seen mounting to the finger of Mercury, when it indicates success in commerce, science, or oratory. If its course goes towards Jupiter, it signifies happiness obtained through satisfied pride and ambition ; if to the Sun, success in art, celebrity, and riches.

If the Saturnian line is twisted in a sort of spiral at the starting-point, but yet the upper part of it goes in a clear, direct line to the Mount of Saturn, and cuts through it to the root of the finger without penetrating beyond, it indicates a troubled and anxious youth, followed by riches and good fortune in middle age. If the twisted line continues, and crosses the Line of the Head and the Line of the Heart, the troubles will continue until old age, and the good fortune be only quite at the close of life. A triangle, or small island at the commencement of the line, shows death of the father or mother in early childhood.

If the Mount of Saturn is much wrinkled, and the Saturnian Line cuts through it, and is of a deep-red colour, and mounts as high as the third joint of the finger of Saturn, it indicates a violent and disgraceful end,— death on the gallows. Upward lines from the Saturnian line mean events of happy omen either in the affections or affairs at the age shown on the line; downward lines have the reverse signification.

There are some hands in which the Saturnian Line is very faintly indicated, and when this is the case it signifies an uneventful, insignificant existence. The Esquimaux, for example, who live in a wretched climate, and live hard, unlovely lives, have absolutely, some of them, *no* Saturnian Line in their hands; and M. Serres, a famous French anthropologist, asserts that this line (which he calls the Caucasian Line) is only to be found in the hands of the white races : whilst M. Desbarrolles, another French writer on this subject, goes farther, and affirms that, among persons condemned to a dry, unintellectual, vegetative life, even among the white races, the Saturnian Line is often found entirely wanting.

The Saturnian Line is one of great importance, for it corrects and modifies the significations both of the lines and of the mounts.

A double Saturnian Line, which is sometimes, but very rarely, seen, indicates great moral corruption and physical infirmities, brought about by the abuse of material pleasures. A cross upon the line shows a change of position or a crisis in the affections at the age indicated by its position on the line.

Downward lines from the Line of Heart towards the Fate Line show heart sorrows at the period when they cross the line. Widowhood is indicated in this way if the Line of Fate breaks, and shows a total change in the way of life immediately afterwards.

CHAPTER XX.

THE LINES OF THE SUN AND LINE OF HEALTH.

THE Line of the Sun takes its rise either in the Line of Life or from the Mount of the Moon, and, ascending, it traces a furrow in the Mount of the Sun, but stops at the root of the finger; it signifies, when straight and well-defined, and taking the course we have described, celebrity in literature or art, whether in poetry, painting, sculpture, or music. The mounts decide in some measure which branch of art is preferred. With Venus large it would probably be music or painting; with the Moon much developed, poetry—or at any rate literature of an elevated kind. Those having the Line of Sun thus traced, even who are not artists by profession, and whom destiny has placed in quite inartistic careers, will always have artistic tastes, eye for colour, ear for music, or a perception of beauty in form or in language. Where the line only begins in the Line of Heart the artistic feeling is only appreciative, not productive, but when it rises as low as the Mount of the Moon, it signifies *creative* power.

If the Line of the Sun sub-divides, in traversing the Mount of the Sun, into several lines, it indicates a tendency to cultivate several branches of art, which prevents the success which generally crowns excess of artistic feeling when confined in its expression to one especial art; it also indicates too great a struggle after effect in art; it is more significative of the dilettante, or patron of art generally, than the artist *pur et simple*. When the Line of the Sun, in its upward course, is barred by several transverse lines, there are obstacles in the career of art; but if the line continues, and marks a single deep furrow in the mount till it reaches the root of the finger, these obstacles will, in the end, be conquered, and success, riches, honours, and celebrity will be attained. In a hand where the Sun Line begins above the Head Line, the hand or deep line at its close only means riches after fifty.

The Line of Health, or, as it is sometimes called, the Line of the Liver, takes its rise at the wrist, near the Line of Life, and mounts in the direction of the Mount of Mercury. If it is well-coloured and the line is not broken, it denotes good health, great power of memory, and success in business pursuits; if the line becomes broken, or is forked at its close, before it reaches the mount, it indicates severe illness in old age. If this line starts from the Line of Life it is a sure sign of weakness of the heart's action. If the line is unequally coloured, and gets redder as it crosses the Line of Head, it indicates a predisposition to apoplexy; if it stops suddenly on the Line of the Heart, a serious physical heart affection is likely.

The Line of Health sometimes takes a curved form on *one* hand—forming a sort of half-circle, from the Mount of the Moon to the Mount of Mercury. In this case it is called the Line of Presentiment, and indicates vivid intuition, especially if Mercury is strong in his influence. When the Line of Health on *both* hands takes this form it indicates mediumistic powers, and powerful second sight. If both the Moon and Mercury are in a long island at the starting point, that is, near the Mount of the Moon of the Line of Presentiment, it indicates somnambulism.

When the Line of Health forms a large and distinct cross with the Line of Head, it shows a disposition for the study of occult science, but this is not the mystical cross which will be described farther on. An island on this line shows some internal illness at the date on which it appears on the line,—that is, if before it reaches the Head Line, it would be *before* 35 ; if after and between the Lines of Head and Heart, it would be between 35 and 50 ; if later, during the remaining years of life. A twisted liver line is a sign of biliousness and indigestion; if it is of a red colour (as it frequently is where Mars is one of the ruling planets) it shows a tendency to feverish complaints.

The Line of Health is sometimes, but rarely, accompanied by another line called the Milky Way; when this line commences side by side with the Line of Health, and mounts with it in an unbroken line towards the finger of Mercury, it signifies a long life of uninterrupted happiness. This line, which is sometimes called the Via Lasciva, gives ardour in love, because a superabundance of health gives force to passion.

CHAPTER XXI.

ON THE RING OF VENUS, THE WRIST LINES, AND THE LETTER M TO BE SEEN IN MOST HANDS.

THE Ring of Venus seems to enclose, as in an island, the Mounts of Saturn and the Sun; this line is not seen in many hands, and, when fully developed, signifies unbridled passion and debauchery of all kinds when, in conjunction with it, the Mount of Venus is strongly developed and marked with crossway lines.

If, with the signs mentioned above, the Ring of Venus is strongly marked, yet *broken* at its centre in *both* hands, it is a sign of eccentric and depraved passion; still, there are always modifications of these bad signs, and a very good Line of Head would, by bringing reason to bear upon passion, considerably mitigate the evil indications of the broken ring.

When the Ring of Venus is seen on a hand where both the planets Venus and the Moon are strongly indicated, and where it is traversed by innumerable fine lines, it is a true sign of an hysterical temperament.

Sometimes the Ring of Venus will be seen to ascend and lose itself on the Mount of Mercury, leaving one end of the semicircle open, which mitigates, in some sort, the terribly strong instincts of voluptuousness indicated by this mark ; but if, on the contrary, the semicircle, after extending itself to the Mount of Mercury, closes itself at the root of the finger, such a mark in the hand would indicate a terrible and absorbing power of passion, which would not hesitate at any means to secure its end.

A line traced on the wrist is a sign of long life ; above all, if there are three of these lines, as is sometimes seen, forms the triple bracelet. These lines indicate, in Chiromancy, thirty years of life each, and the three lines form what is called the magic bracelet, indicating long life, health, and riches. If these lines are formed irregularly, like the links of a chain, and more especially if the first one —that next the hand—is so formed, it indicates a long life of labour, but acquiring ease and competency at its close. If a cross appears in the centre of the wrist, it indicates a rich heritage at the close of life. When lines start upwards from the bracelet, and ascend towards the Mount of the Moon, they denote as many travels by land as there are lines. If a line starts from the wrist, and, after traversing the Plain of Mars, goes to the Mount of the Sun, such a line presages riches and honours coming from royalty.

When these travel lines go as high as the Line of Head and Heart, they denote journeys during which some person is met who influences either the fortunes or the affections, according to whether the line stops at the Line of Head or Heart.

Lines lengthways on the Mount of the Moon mean sea-voyages ; if these lines terminate with a star, it denotes shipwreck ; if on both hands, death by drowning.

The letter M, formed more or less regularly in every

hand by the Line of Life, the Line of Head, and the Line of Heart, represents the three worlds—the material, the natural, and the divine.

The first, the Line of Life, surrounds Love and Generation, as represented by the thumb, which is, as we have seen, sacred to Venus—the material world, or world of sense—but the Mount of Venus may either degenerate love to vice, or perfectionate it to tenderness. With high instincts the Mount of Venus is a good quality, since, *without it*, all the other passions are hard and selfish.

The second line—the Line of the Head—stretches across the natural world ; it traverses the Plain and the Mount of Mars, which represent the struggle of Love and Reason in existence—the natural world, life as it presents itself to most persons. There is in the hand the Plain of Mars and the Mount of Mars ; both mean a struggle ; the mount is the struggle of resistance ; the Plain of Mars (which is between the Lines of Head and Heart) is the struggle of aggression.

The third line, that of the Heart, encloses the divine world, for it surrounds the mounts which represent Religion, Jupiter ; Fate, Saturn ; Art, the Sun ; Science, Mercury ; all of which are especially influenced by the astral light, or fluid, emanating from the planets.

According to the proportions—the relative proportions— which these three lines bear to one another, so the life is influenced by the three different worlds represented. Thus we have a hand in which material (sensual) pleasure dominates : the line of the material world enclosing a space greatly superior to that of the two others. It is needless to give further examples of these differences, for, after all, this matter is but a *résumé* of what has been said before about the power of correction which one line has over the others. Given a wide range to sensual pleasure in the hand, but a good and extensive Line of the Head, the former will be corrected by it, as reason dominates passion ; or given the strong powers of sensuality, with a wide range to the divine world by the space occupied between the Line of Heart and the mounts, and again, religion, love of art and science, will correct and keep under extreme sensuality. In reading the hand, each line must be judged with reference to the others, and the hand must be considered in all its bearings, before an opinion on the tendencies it indicates can be arrived at with any degree of correctness.

CHAPTER XXII.

CONCERNING THE FINGERS AND THUMB AND NAILS.

As the shapes and relative proportions of the fingers to the palm modify the indications given by the lines and mounts, it is necessary to consider them very attentively before giving a judgment in Chiromancy.

Fingers longer than the palm and with pointed tips show idealism ; they are the expression of the Moon's influence when she is well-dignified at a birth. The Mount of the Moon in these hands would always be large. People with these fingers see everything in the golden light of imagination, and find happiness in dreams of intangible beauty ; poetical expression (ethereal, not passionate) is their natural language. They always incline to the marvellous— the sublime, the spiritualistic side of all things! theirs the belief in omens, in occult literature, in the supernatural. Without, perhaps, attaching themselves to any fixed creed, they are, by nature, worshippers ; and the mysterious moan of the sea, the song of the brook, the roar of the torrent, and the sighing of the wind, are to them but as so many revelations of the Deity ! They are loyal to old associations, and are never in advance of their age. They are

H

easily moved to tears, and are graceful in all their gestures. They can, in exalted moments, do without the necessaries of life, and yet, from their intuitive worship of the beautiful, they are lovers of the luxurious superfluities which make up an elegant and refined existence. People with these fingers do not age much ; their hearts are eternally young, for they live a life of perpetual illusion, and though often, alas ! necessarily disappointed in both men and things, they never entirely lose faith in the poetry of existence.

Fingers the same length as the palm, and with slightly pointed tips, show refinement, correct taste, and love of art, —these are the fingers of those born under the dominant influence of the Sun.

Fingers the same length as the palm, but fleshy at their base and square at the tips, show practicality, family affection, love of animals, good judgment, respect for the world's opinion, and much appreciation of material comfort. These fingers show the strong influence of Jupiter.

Long fingers, knotty at the joints and with square tips, show reasoning power and taste for science. Persons with these fingers are always in harmony with progress, and have little or no veneration, and are therefore never stirred by associations ; with the antiquity of Catholicism, its mystical and somewhat sensuous worship, its celibate priesthood, and golden aureole of saints and martyrs, persons having these fingers have no sympathy. If they belong to any fixed creed (and their logical powers are rather against this) they prefer Protestantism—or its offshoot, Dissent— where their real deity, Reason, is permitted full sway. These people love—with all the force of their nature—the study of history, jurisprudence, mathematics, and the exact sciences. They are naturally clever at calculation, and have much sense of order. Such fingers show the influence of Saturn, but not when most dignified ; Saturn when most exalted gives mysticism, but then the fingers are not knotted at the joints and the tips are always spatulated.

Fingers that are shorter than the palm, and with spatulated tips, show sensuality in love and materialism in all things, energy, love of field sports, and indomitable courage. Such fingers indicate the influence of Mars at birth.

Fingers shorter than the palm, but with very pointed tips and thick at the base, show self-indulgence and love of luxury. Persons with such fingers are very sensuous, and are therefore ardent pursuers of material pleasures, but yet with a certain refinement of taste which prevents their becoming grossly sensual. Such fingers are often seen in the hands of singers of both sexes; they indicate the strong influence of Venus in the nativity.

Fingers that are slender and longer than the palm, but with spatulate tips, indicate versatility, wit, and intuitive perception. Such fingers show the dominant influence of Mercury.

In the relative lengths of the three divisions of the fingers Chiromancy also recognises the indications of three separate influences—that of the soul, that of the mind, and that of the body. Fingers that have the first division (that containing the nail) long, show high aspirations and power of veneration—soul; fingers with the second division longer than the other two indicate intellectual force—mind; whilst fingers having the lowest division longest show a love of material pleasure; people having such fingers, unless there are other modifying indications in the hand, are slaves to the body.

The first joint of the thumb (that which is nearest the nail) represents *Will;* therefore, when this is short, such a form indicates want of will—a character very impressionable, and therefore easily led; when this joint is long, it indicates great power of will, and therefore force of character. The second joint represents logic, judgment, and reason; therefore, where this joint is long these qualities exist in excess, and where it is short, they are wanting.

The third joint (that which is outside the Mount of Venus) represents the power which love—more especially the love between the sexes—will have on the character. If

long and thick, it implies the existence of strong passion ;
if short and flat, a cold disposition—no attraction towards
the opposite sex.

Poets have frequently the first joint of the thumb short
(because want of will gives the rein to impulse and impressionability), and whilst the second—the intellectual one—
is fairly long, the third is almost always large, full, and
long. This combination of impressionability, intellectuality,
and warmth of passion gives us the poets full of " the sweet,
sad music of humanity."

These various types of finger-tips are often seen in the
same hand, which shows that several planets have much the
same amount of influence, in which case the following indications should be considered :—the finger of Jupiter
pointed, gives idealistic religion and sense of honour ;
square, it would show reasoning power ; spatulate, energy
and impulse.

The finger of Saturn is rarely pointed, but when it is so
it rather mitigates the melancholy given by the planet, and
shows callousness and (if Mercury is strong in the hand)
frivolity. Square tipped, it indicates prudence, love of
agriculture, and mechanical genius ; spatulate, which is
the ordinary termination of his finger, it betokens sadness
and superstition, and, when the finger is abnormally long, a
tendency to suicide, especially where with it there is a
small weak thumb.

The third finger—that of the Sun—pointed shows
idealism and artistic tastes ; when square-tipped, realism
in art and a love of wealth ; spatulate, it gives spirit of
adventure, especially when it is as long as the first finger ;
when the third finger is *longer* than the first and spatulate,
it indicates love of gambling and of speculation.

The fourth finger—that of Mercury—pointed shows
occultism, intuitive perception, eloquence, and talent for
languages ; square at the tip it denotes logic, facility of
expression, science, and love of research ; spatulate, it gives

movement, vivacity, and, where the rest of the hand is bad, knavery in business and theft; a very short little finger shows unselfishness, and, some old writers say, happiness in marriage.

A pointed thumb gives impressionability; square at its tip, decided but not obstinate will; spatulate, obstinate will. The thumb bending outwards shows generosity and impulse, and when much bent inwards towards the palm of the hand, avarice and reticence. People with short fingers are quicker, more impulsive, and have more intuition than those who possess long fingers. Those with long fingers have much love of detail—often to a worrying extent; they are inquisitive and somewhat distrustful.

As regards the nails, short strong nails show courage, combativeness, and critical faculties. White polished and filbert-shaped nails indicate sensitiveness and refinement, but no force of character. Short, weak, crooked, and black-coloured nails show deceit and slothfulness. Round nails indicate a luxurious, pleasure-loving nature. Very thin nails—especially when the tips are bent inwardly—show delicacy of constitution. Red nails with little white marks on them indicate a choleric and cruel nature.

Many lines on the first joint of a finger denote weakness in the quality given by the finger; a single line shows exaggeration of the quality.

One short line sharply traced on each joint of each finger is a sign of sudden death; cross lines are always obstacles to the proper development of the qualities of the finger. Two crosses on the second phalanx of the first finger are a sign of the friendship of distinguished persons. One star on the third phalanx is said, by many old writers, to be a sign of inchastity. A cross in the third phalanx of the second finger indicates sterility. A single line running the entire length of the third finger shows probability of great renown in literature or art. A cross on the first phalanx of the fourth finger denotes celibacy. Lines on the second phalanx indicate research in occult science. A star on the third phalanx of this finger indicates eloquence; a line going the whole length of the four fingers shows a sense of honour.

Several lines going the entire length of the thumb indicate constancy in love and friendship. Cross lines at the side of the thumb denote riches. If on the first joint, the money comes before fifty; if on the second, late in life. A star on the top phalanx of the thumb, that is, that near the nail, shows licentiousness; two stars on the same place, a fastidious person, who is prone to take offence at trifles. A star or stars on the second phalanx show sweet and amiable manners, and ever inclining to love matters, but without exaggeration of sensuality. Such persons love sweet odours, flowers, beautiful garments, and all things delightful to the senses. Those who have on the root of the Thumb—that is, on the Mount of Venus—many cross bar lines, are sensual and prone to gross indulgence in licentiousness. They who have these marks on their hands will have in their nativity,—Venus in the 6th or 8th house (which houses rule the lower parts of the body), thus showing the entire concordance of Chiromancy with Astrology.

CHAPTER XXIII.

OF THE VARIOUS MARKS TO BE SEEN ON THE HAND.

BESIDES the Lines and Mounts already described there are other signs or marks which, as they modify the qualities given by the lines and mounts, should be carefully considered in giving judgment on the hand as a whole.

A star (fig. 1) indicates something beyond our own power of action—a fatality for good or evil over which we have, personally, no power. A star on the Mount of

FIG. 1

FIG. 2.

FIG 3.

FIG. 4.

FIG. 5.

FIG 6.

FIG. 7.

FIG 8.

FIG 9

FIG 10.

FIG 11.

FIG 12.

Jupiter indicates honours, and distinction in marriage and great and unexpected glory, for Jupiter is always a favourable planet.

A star on the Mount of Saturn means assassination or death on the scaffold; or, in an otherwise good hand, death by paralysis.

A star on the Mount of the Sun, with no Line of the Sun, indicates fatal riches,—fortune which brings with it unhappiness.

A star on the Mount of Mercury indicates dishonour,— a proneness to theft; a star on the Mount of Mars, death in battle; a star on the plain of Mars, honours and military glory.

A star on the Mount of the Moon on a voyage-line means danger of drowning (the Moon has power over the sea); when not on a voyage-line an illness connected with water, such as dropsy, or water on the brain.

A star in the centre of the hand shows that some person of the opposite sex will much influence the life, and generally in an unhappy manner.

A star on Venus means unhappiness caused by love.

Two stars on the top joint of middle finger indicate a shameful death.

A square (fig. 2) announces power and energy of the mount on which it is found, except upon Venus, when it infers imprisonment; it also announces preservation from accident, when seen in the palm of the hand or near any indication of accident.

A circle (fig. 3) on any of the mounts, but above all on the Mount of the Sun, signifies success in the qualities given by the mount on which it appears; but a circle on the lines of the hand has always a bad signification. A circle on the Line of Life means loss of one eye, and two circles would indicate total blindness.

An island (fig. 4) is again always a bad sign; on the Line of Heart it signifies adultery; on the Line of Life, illness, corresponding in time to its position on the Line; on the Line of Head, ruin arising from false speculations or brain illness; on the Line of Health, disorders of the liver and the digestion; on the Saturnian Line, an island indicates happiness from an adulterous liaison; but if the island is broken in shape, it indicates poignant grief arising from an illicit affection. The duration of these affections is shown by the size of the island. An island at the commencement of the Saturnian Line indicates an event of an unfortunate nature, probably death of father or mother, in childhood or very early youth. The lines which are found going lengthways round the side of the hand between the Line of Heart and the root of the finger of Mercury, denote the number of serious attachments; a horizontal line barring these, or a black spot upon them, indicates widowhood; if the lines take the form of islands, the loves will be for cousins or very near relatives.

A triangle (fig. 5) announces aptitudes, and has almost always a favourable signification; on the Mount of Jupiter it signifies diplomatic distinction; on Saturn a man given to the study of mystic science and distinguished in his acquirements of it; on the Mount of the Sun it indicates success in art or literature; on Mars, military glory; on the Mount of the Moon, mysticism; on the Mount of Venus, prudence in love; on Mercury, great aptitude and distinction in science, or in one of the learned professions. On the Mount of the Moon it indicates danger from the water.

A branch (fig. 6) on any of the mounts or lines, shows excess of the qualities indicated by the mount or line on which it appears; but it is generally seen on the lines: on the Line of Heart it means warmth of affection and excess of devotion, extreme unselfishness; on the Line of Head, great intelligence; on the Line of Life, or on the Line of Health—in either case, exuberance of health and long life; on the Saturnian Line, great happiness.

A cross (fig. 7) is generally an unfavourable sign; but

on the Mount of Jupiter it means marriage, and two crosses two marriages.

A cross in the centre of the hand, under the Mount of Saturn, or between the Line of Head and the Line of Heart, indicates love of occult science and mysticism.

A cross on the Mount of Saturn is fatality, and announces the vehement influence of this melancholy planet.

A cross on the Mount of the Sun indicates a serious check in the career of art.

A cross on the Mount of Mercury means perjury and deceit, and (like the star) a predisposition to theft.

A cross on the Plain of Mars indicates a combative nature ; on the Mount of Mars, homicide.

A cross in the base of the triangle formed by the Plain of Mars and the Mounts of Venus and the Moon indicates an event of great importance, generally fortunate, late in life, which will change the whole tenour of existence.

A cross on the Mount of the Moon indicates a man so untrue, that he will lie even to himself.

A cross on the Mount of Venus indicates a single but fatal attachment, unless, on the same hand, the cross is seen on the Mount of Jupiter, indicating marriage, when it only deepens the force of the happy omen, showing the marriage to be one of strong affection.

Chains (fig. 8) always mean obstacles and worries which prevent the free action of the good effects of the lines on which they appear; they must not, however, be confused with islands, which have much the same form, but are much larger, and always appear singly. Chains are most generally seen on the Saturnian Line, when they mean pecuniary worries, more especially, unless they appear just as the line is crossing the Line of Heart, when they would indicate anxiety and sorrow through the affections.

A spot (fig. 9) is sometimes favourable and sometimes the reverse. Red spots on the Line of Heart mean physical ills of the heart. White spots mean, as we have seen, as many

love conquests as there are spots. On the Line of Head, if
red, they mean physical accidents to the head ; but if white,
they indicate, if under the Mount of Mercury, scientific
discoveries ; if under the Sun, success in literature ; if under
Saturn, success in pecuniary matters through intelligent
speculation.

Curved and broken lines (see fig. 10) mean disasters
wherever they are seen ; on the Line of Head madness,
more especially if the line droops toward the Mount of the
Moon.

Hair-lines (fig. 11) show an excess of the quality of the
line, but their very excess sometimes leads to failure. The
people who have these lines on their hands frequently, in
acts of kindness, overstep the mark. Talleyrand must have
had such people in his mind when he said, " *Surtout point
de zèle.*"

Cross-bars (fig. 12) are always obstacles, but on different
parts of the hand they have different significations. On the
mounts they give excess of the qualities. For instance, on
the Mount of Jupiter religion degenerates into superstition,
and self-respect into dominating self-assertion and tyranny ;
on the Mount of Saturn the cross-bars give excess of misfortune ; on the Mount of the Sun, folly, vanity, and error ;
on the Mount of Mercury, cunning, deceit, and theft ; on
the Mount of Mars, violent death ; on the Mount of the
Moon, inquietude, discontent, and morbid imagination,
which always sees the sad side of everything.

Cross-bars on the Mount of Venus mean lasciviousness
and obscenity, unless the Lines of Head and Heart are both
good.

Besides these marks we sometimes see (but these instances
are rare) the sign of a planet traced on a Mount, in which
case the quality given by the Mount is affected by that
of the planet whose symbol it bears. Thus the sign of
Jupiter on the Mount of Mercury would mean honours and
riches by science ; on the Sun, success in art ; on Venus, in

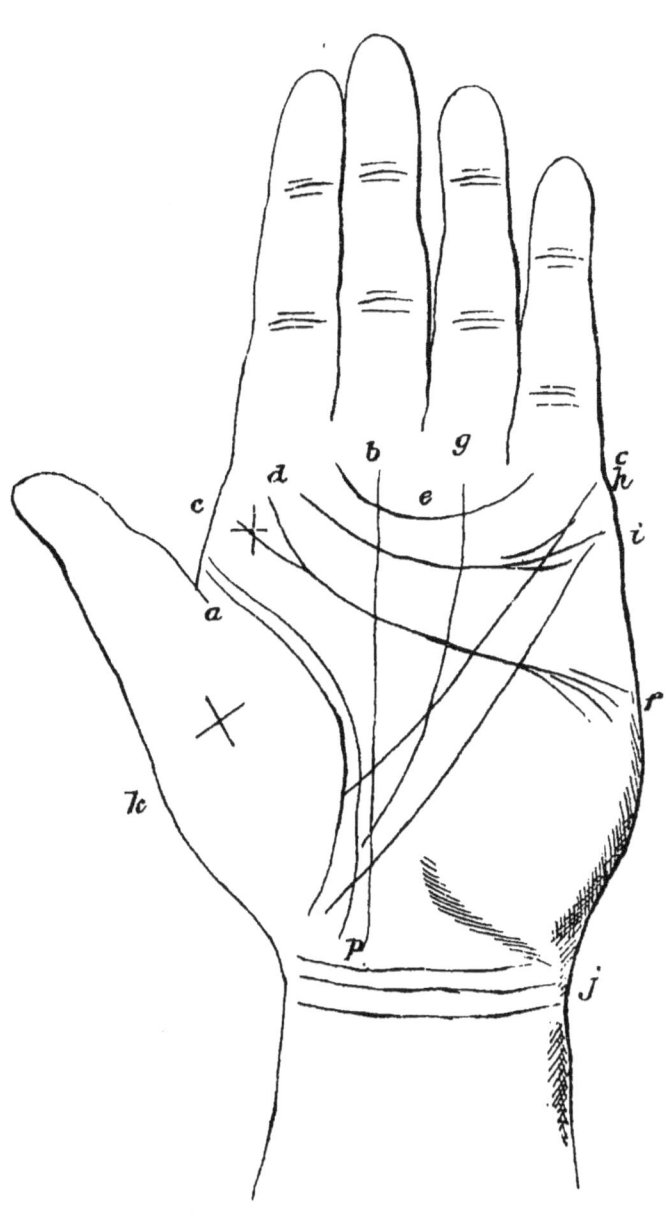

love matters ; on the Moon, celebrity in literature ; on Mars, military renown ; on Saturn, celebrity in occultism. Again, a Mount sometimes (but this is also rare) has its own sign traced upon it as ♃ on Jupiter, ♄ on Saturn, &c. Such marks of course intensify the qualities of the Mounts.

Two lines going from the Mount of Venus to that of Mars denote the pursuit of two love affairs at the same time, and a star joined to these lines shows that the matter has ended or will end in disaster.

A long island, extending from the Mount of Venus to that of Saturn, shows, on a woman's hand, seduction at the age when the sign crosses the Line of Life. Should a square appear on the line, she escapes the temptation.

A Line extending from a star on the Mount of Venus, and terminating with a fork on the Mount of Saturn, shows an unhappy marriage.

A Line going from a star on the Mount of Venus straight to the Mount of the Sun, foretells a great inheritance from the death of a near relation.

CHAPTER XXIV.

THE TRIANGLE, THE QUADRANGLE, AND THE HAPPY HAND.

THE Triangle is the name given to the space enclosed between the Line of Life, the Line of Head, and the Line of Health. If the angle is an equal one and the lines well coloured, it signifies a good disposition both as regards mind and body, and also much health, courage, good reputation, and a long and happy life. When the angles of the Triangle are not well defined, it signifies a dull and mean person, who will not rise above mediocrity. When the Triangle is wide as well as clearly defined, it indicates liberality and nobility of mind. When it is narrow, it signifies avarice, cowardice, and poverty. If the Triangle is altogether wanting in a hand, it portends much evil, a short life, and much illness. A cross in the Triangle shows a quarrelsome disposition, and a crescent in this place indicates inconstancy, whilst a star denotes riches.

The Quadrangle is the square space contained between the Lines of Heart and Head. When it is broad and well-proportioned, it signifies a liberal and courageous person who may attain the highest dignities ; and when the lines which form it are well coloured, that is, not too red or too pale, they represent a person who is just and loyal. Those that have the Quadrangle small and narrow are timid, covetous, cruel, and deceitful. A star in the middle of the Quadrangle shows likelihood of honours and dignities. A cross in the same place shows mysticism.* A line from the Quadrangle to the Mount of Mercury shows the protection of great men.

In the plate at the beginning of this chapter we have a sketch of a hand with all the lines and marks of a happy destiny, which is called in chiromancy " the Happy Hand."

Explanations.

A. Double Line of Life.—Perfect health and a long life.

B. The Saturnian Line, straight and well-defined.—Happiness and good fortune.

C. Branches at the end and beginning of the Line of Heart.—Excess of tenderness.

D. Cross on the Mount of Jupiter.—Love and marriage.

E. Ring of Venus.—Force of passion, but well-directed in consequence of the other good lines in the hand ; in which case the Ring of Venus is not a danger, but makes the organisation richer, because fuller of capacity for pleasure.

---

* This is the " Mystic Cross " which gives great occult powers.

F. Genius.—The Line of Head, long, with branches at each end, and drooping towards the Mount of the Moon, which gives imagination.

G. Direct Line of the Sun.—Success in art and celebrity.

H. Union of Venus with Mercury.—Love and fortune.

I. Line of Health.—Good.

J. Triple Bracelet of the Wrist.—Superabundance of life and health.

K. Cross on the Mount of Venus.—Taken in conjunction with the same on the Mount of Jupiter, one love hallowed by marriage.

Of course, it is seldom that such a combination of good fortune is to be met with on one hand ; many of these lines, however, are sometimes seen together, and in such cases a great deal of happiness may safely be predicted ; but such hands are rare—disappointment, anxieties and griefs being the general rule, and happiness the exception in this world.

PART III.

PHYSIOGNOMY.

"La fisonomia è lo specchio dell' anima."—FINETTA.

THE PLANETS' PLACES ON THE FACE
FACSIMILE FROM AN OLD WOODCUT, DATE 1657.

" THE face is the mirror of the soul," says Finetta, a mediæval Italian writer on the subject of physiognomy, and, to those who take the trouble to study the matter, the intelligence, the sentiments and the instincts of a person are all clearly manifested by the form of the head and features and their relative proportions, by the colouring of the skin, eyes, and hair, by the fugitive expressions which, to an attentive observer, are seen to pass over even the most impassable faces, and " last, but certainly not least," by the lines left by the habitual passage of the expression of strong feeling, which, to the physiognomist, are visible even when the face is in repose.

We are in the habit of applying the term physiognomy to the *face* only ; but the word has really a much wider signification. All things, animate and inanimate, have their physiognomy, and, when judging of the character by the form of the features of the face, it would be impossible to ignore that given by the shape of the head, for, without altogether believing that the brain is mapped out in the manner described by phrenologists, there is no doubt that a good development of the front of the head shows intelligence, whilst a head which is inordinately protuberant at the back indicates the dominance of animal instincts in the organisation. The advantage of this sort of " outline phrenology " is that it may be exercised by the eye without any necessity for feeling for the so-called " bumps " of the cranium. Thus we may be sure, when we see a broad, full, but yet not necessarily high, forehead, that the intellectual faculties are strong ; that if the top of the head is

I

raised from the brow to the centre there is benevolence and the power of veneration,—by veneration we do not mean alone religious belief, but also the quality taken in its wider, though not, perhaps, higher sense; all hero-worship is the result of the faculty of veneration, combined with imagination and ardour, which give enthusiasm. If the head is much raised just before it turns, it gives the same indication as the first joint of the thumb long—a *dominant* will; if the back of the head is fairly but not over-developed, it gives power of affection : this is the same sign as that given by the Mount of Venus, full but without lines on it. If the back of the head projects far beyond the nape of the neck it indicates a sensuous nature ; thus having the same signification as that given by the Mount of Venus inordinately large, with cross bars upon it, and the ring of Venus strongly developed. If the back of the head is quite flat, it indicates coldness—want of passion in the nature. A head which is large just above the ears, shows a tendency to anger, and, if the signs of benevolence on the brow and lips are entirely wanting, it would be mean cruelty; but in physiognomy the signs on both the head and face must be considered as a *whole*, and the qualities shown by *both* weighed one against another, before any right judgment can be arrived at. In this study, as in that of graphology and chiromancy, a deductive power of mind is required. Among twenty persons who may be sufficiently interested in the science to study it, there will be scarcely more than one who will become a good physiognomist. One among the countless objections which have been urged against physiognomy is that many physiognomists make erroneous judgments; but, granted that they do so, it is their want of discernment, or more probably their want of deductivity,—not the science, —which fails. To decry physiognomy, because physiognomists are sometimes wrong in their judgments, is as foolish as to conclude that there is no reason because there is so much *false* reasoning.

There is a certain sort of *instinctive* power of judging character by the face, possessed by children and animals, which is in harmony with the theories of those who have thought and written most upon this interesting subject.

We are all of us,—women, perhaps, more than men,— daily influenced by this sort of *instinctive* physiognomy : for there are few people who do not, when they first see a stranger, form a judgment of him, in which they are, of course, only swayed by his outward appearance, although they may never have even heard the word physiognomy. Although this gift is a natural one, it can be perfected by study ; and there is, in this study, an infinity of ever-varying interest,—faces seen to day are as different to those noticed yesterday as to those one shall come across to-morrow. No two faces are alike, as no two human beings are alike in character ; therefore no society, however seemingly devoid of interest, is altogether so to the physiognomist ; for every human being is a study, and every new discovery a delight. It is interesting to distinguish between people who have created their intelligence and those whose intelligence has created them,—that is, between people whose cleverness is the result of study, and those whose intelligence is intuitive ; between those who hide, or endeavour to hide, their passions, and those who let all their feelings, good or bad, come to the surface. Anyone at all versed in the study of the human face knows that there are, in all physiognomies, the original indications and those given by circumstances. Illness and age both alter the original indications, but experience soon enables one to distinguish these causes, for though they change the face, they do not extinguish the original indications ; thus the intelligent light in the eyes of a seemingly weak and impassive face will show us that the weakness is merely that of circum-stance ; the pleasant smile which suddenly lights up a wearied and down-drooping mouth shows that the depres-sion of age has *tamed*, but not extinguished, the joyous

nature. Illness gives an expression to the face which is
generally so easy to read, that we all at once know a person
to be an invalid from the expression of his face, although
we may never have seen him in health ; and what we say of
illness is, in a measure, true of age. Yet these things act
unequally, and, although they have all the same characteristic signs, they do not show themselves quite in the same
manner on all faces. Some persons are sufferers from a
serious illness without its being apparent to the casual
observer ; but this is merely from the natural vivacity of
temperament, a certain vitality, which brightens the face
whilst speaking ; *in repose*,—a state in which such faces
are seldom to be seen,—the signs of illness would be
apparent ; the same thing applies to the indications of age.
A woman of a bright and happy disposition often looks
younger than her age by ten years whilst she is speaking,
but look at the same face in repose, or more especially in
the deep thought of solitude, and the signs of age will be
more apparent upon it. It is the women,—and the men,
too,—born under Mercury and Venus who retain their
youthful appearance longest, for these planets not only give
beauty, but a happy disposition. People born under them
are always *young* at *heart*, and this, of course, affects the
expression of the face.

The *temperament* has an immense amount of influence
over the character, and this temperament is shown more
especially by the colour and texture of the skin and hair.
It is temperament which precipitates or retards the effects
of illness and age, and temperament is the result of the
astral influence which presided at our birth.

These temperaments have been classified under four
heads,—viz., the sanguine or choleric, the lymphatic, the
bilious, and the melancholic.

The first, the sanguine or choleric, is the result of the
astral influence of Mars and Jupiter ; the lymphatic, of
the Moon and Venus, but more especially of the Moon ; the

bilious (which is especially the intellectual temperament), the Sun and Mercury; and the melancholic temperament is the result of the dominance of the sad planet, Saturn. The sanguine temperament is shown by a skin with a good deal of colour in it, either of a soft pinky white with a rosy peach-like colour on the cheeks, in which case it is Jupiter which dominates in the temperament; or of a deep red colour all over the face, when the sanguine temperament in dominated by Mars, the hair being red or brown, crispy or curling. The lymphatic temperament is shown by a soft, pale skin of a thick dead white, the lips and cheeks being only slightly coloured; the hair is fine and long, but not thick, and is light, not golden, but rather colourless, or what the French call " *un blond cendré* "—that is, of an ash-coloured fairness, sometimes of a soft brown, when Venus is the dominating planet. The bilious temperament is the result of the combination of the astral influences of the Sun and Mercury, the planets which give artistic feeling and intelligence.

Those having this temperament have yellow skins of a soft, fine texture, and when the Sun is the dominant planet they have a vivid colour in the cheeks; the hair of those of the bilious temperament is golden, and is generally curly or wavy; if the melancholic temperament given by Saturn is in combination (and it is frequently so in the bilious temperament) with the yellow-tinted skin of the bilious temperament, we find also the straight, deep black hair peculiar to the Saturnian.

The melancholic temperament is that of those born under the dominant influence of Saturn. People of this temperament are of a pale or livid and, sometimes, of a greenish-tinted or earth-coloured skin, and their hair is always of a dead black. It must be remembered that though one planet may dominate at a birth, there are always present others which have also their influences, though in a secondary degree, so no person is of *one* temperament

without any admixture of the others, although one may,
and often does, dominate the others. Thus no one is
exclusively sanguine, bilious, lymphatic, or melancholic.
One person could be at once bilious, melancholic, and
lymphatic. We sometimes see the apparently contradictory temperaments of the melancholic and sanguine in
the same person, but, generally speaking, one temperament
dominates,—modified by one or more of the others. This
makes one of the sources of the variety of character we see
in those about us, no one person having precisely the same
modification of temperament, to say nothing of the difference of intellectual gifts. Now, as the temperament
produces the character, and the character the passions, it
is very necessary, in order to be a good physiognomist, that
we should be thoroughly expert in being able to assign to
each person under judgment the exact amount of domination of each of these four temperaments ; and this is only
to be done by noting the colour and texture of the
skin and hair. Aristotle has said that though there is a
certain physiognomy of the whole person, the principal
signs to guide us in a knowledge of human beings
are to be found on the face ; and this is perhaps because
the skin of the face is somewhat differently constituted to
that over the other parts of the body. It is more transparent than that of the other parts of the body, and thus
more readily reflects the different colours,—the vivid flush
of joy, the blush of shame, the livid hue of envy, the
pallor of fear,—the different passions by which we are
agitated. The face also is the seat of the eyes and the
lips, both of which features (being continually in movement) make the face, as the old Italian writer has said,
"the mirror of the soul." Even those who habitually
deny the power given by a knowledge of the science of
physiognomy, admit that *in certain moments* they have
been able to judge of what they could ask for, from the
expression they saw on the face of the person with whom

they were dealing. Now, if this were so at one moment, why should it not be so always? When the soul is agitated, that agitation shows itself, at once, upon the face by the variation of its colours and by the contraction of certain muscles about the features. Both this changing of colour and this movement of the features vary according to the passions which produce the agitation, and these different expressions most people can read at a glance. No one confounds the expression of happiness with unhappiness, of love with hatred, of hope with despair, of jealousy with trustfulness, of envy with sympathy. Well, between a face powerfully agitated by any one of these passions and one in which they are (momentarily) at rest,—between the soul agitated and the soul tranquil,—there is not, really, so much difference, for those who are habitually jealous or envious, loving, hopeful, or despairing, will have so often shown this in the forcible manner, in which " he who runs may read," that the expression will have left its trace on the face. Habitual drunkards show their vice on their faces, even when they are perfectly sober ; so also do the other vices show themselves by the lines left on the face by the constant recurrence of the contraction of the features when under the immediate and violent influence of the ruling passion. But these *traces* of past—or, at any rate, slumbering—passion are not always visible to the ordinary observer. As in art, that which is perfectly beautiful in form is easily seen by all, but the refinement of treatment is only appreciated by connoisseurs ; so in physiognomy, whilst the expression of strong feeling is at once seen by all at the moment it is agitating the soul, the traces of it when passed are only discernible to those who have studied the subject. By dint of continually exercising the faculty of observation they come to see expressions and lines on the face which, though perhaps quite lost upon others, give them indications of character which are sometimes startling revelations. Here, again, is another

objection which is often advanced against the study of
physiognomy. Does it not, by laying bare the vices and
weaknesses of human nature, induce a cynical opinion of
human nature ? No ; for, whilst it makes us clear-sighted
as to the vices, it also reveals to us many sweet and noble
qualities in those by whom we are surrounded, which,
perhaps, were never suspected by us. No one better
understood his fellow-men, no one was ever more alive to
" the sweet, sad music of humanity," than Shakespeare.
His large-hearted, sympathetic nature gave him intuitive
perception of character, and this, aided by his wonderful
powers of observation, must have made him a physiognomist. He " looked quite through the thoughts of
men," and yet, with all this wondrous knowledge of human
nature, he says, " What a piece of work is a man ! How
noble in reason ! How infinite in faculties ! In form and
moving, how express and admirable ! In action, how like
an angel ! In apprehension, how like a God ! "

CHAPTER XXVI.

THE FOREHEAD AND EYEBROWS.

" ONE part of the forehead," says a Chinese proverb,
" shows our faculties, the other part the use we make of
them." This is, in a great measure, true ; for the form and
height of the brow show the degree of thought and power
of intellect, whilst the skin of the forehead, its colour, lines,
and tension, denote the passions and the state of mind.
Though the skin of the forehead may be equally wrinkled
in different faces, the forms which these lines take vary very
much. The first line next the hair, which is rarely seen
till past middle age, is referred to the influence of Saturn ;
the second to Jupiter ; the third to Mars ; the fourth, over

the right eyebrow, to the Sun ; the fifth, over the left eyebrow, to the Moon ; the sixth, between the eyebrows, to Venus, and Mercury is assigned his place on the bridge of the nose (see plate).

When the line of Saturn is long and well-defined, it indicates the prudence and sagacity which ought to come with age ; when it is broken or curved in an oblique manner, it shows peevishness and avarice.

The Line of Jupiter, straight and clearly-defined, shows an honourable and just person ; if broken or taking oblique curves it indicates a very voluptuous person.

If the Line of Mars should be long and clear, and stretching across the forehead in one continuous line, it denotes courage and much warlike ambition ; if the line be broken, such a person will be a brawler and quarrelsome, and will experience ill-fortune in war.

The Line of the Sun being perfect, and reaching nearly to the middle of the forehead, shows ambition, good judgment, and success ; being broken or oblique in its form, it shows egotism and love of money.

The Line of the Moon, clear and perfect above the left eyebrow, much imagination and also much travelling into strange places. When this line is broken or much curved, it indicates caprice and want of truth.

The Line of Venus, delicately marked and straight, shows tenderness and success in love matters; if broken and curved, the reverse.

If three lines appear in the place of Mercury across the bridge of the nose, they denote eloquence and wit ; if more than three, loquacity and deceit.

So much for the *lines* on the forehead. As to the *form*, Aristotle tells us that "a very large and prominent forehead shows stupidity," and it is quite true that men of the highest intelligence have foreheads of medium height, but exceptionally broad and full over the eyebrow.

A forehead which is very full over the eyebrows, and

rather low than high, shows intuitive faculty, artistic perception and idealism; we see this form of brow in all the antique statues of Apollo. A very projecting forehead, fuller above than below, and so large as to appear to dominate the whole face, is generally the forehead of a slow if not a dull intellect. A perpendicular forehead, well rounded at the temples, rather high than low, and having straight, well-defined eyebrows, shows solid power of the understanding, love of study, and power of concentrating the attention, but it is not the forehead of the poet, painter, or musician.

Arched foreheads, somewhat low, but full at the temples, with long, sweeping, and mobile eyebrows, appear properly to be feminine, since they show sweetness and sensitiveness of nature. A woman with this sort of forehead, unless her lips were thin, could never be a shrew. This sort of brow, combined with great fulness over the eyes, is the sign of an impressionable, idealistic nature, and is seen in poets, musicians, and artists of all kinds. A forehead with sharp projecting eyebones—that is, the bone on which the eyebrows appear—shows an acute intellect and fondness for research. Yet there are many excellent heads (as far as intellect is concerned) which have not this form of the eyebones, but then these foreheads have full and rounded temples, which indication gives the quality of intellectual power, though not of precisely the same sort.

High, narrow, and wholly unwrinkled foreheads, over which the skin seems tightly drawn, are indicative of weakness of the will-power, want of imagination, and very little susceptibility. They are the foreheads of narrow-minded, commonplace persons. Of course other features may soften these indications: intelligent eyes may give intellect, or a sweet and tender mouth feeling enough to, at any rate, diminish the unpleasant indications of this type of forehead.

Foreheads not altogether projecting, but having angular and knotty protuberances upon them, denote vigour of mind and harsh and oppressive activity and perseverance. To be in exact proportion, the forehead should be the same length as the nose. In Greek art, however, it is generally shorter, which gives softness and elegance to the face. It should be oval at the top, or somewhat square; if the latter, it gives more force—if the former, more sensibility of character. It should be smooth in repose, yet have the power of wrinkling when in deep thought, or when in grief or anger; for foreheads over which the skin is so tightly strained as never to change under these circumstances show a dull, unsensitive, and unintellectual nature. A forehead should project more over the eyes than at the top, and there should be a small cavity in the centre, separating the brow into four divisions; but this should be so slightly accentuated as only to be seen when the forehead is in a strong light coming from above it.

Square foreheads with broad, angular temples, with fine, well-defined eyebrows, show circumspection, resolution, and constancy.

A blue vein, in the form of the letter y, in an open, smooth, and somewhat low forehead, shows a poetic, ardent, and sensitive nature.

Perpendicular wrinkles, those between the eyes, are natural to the forehead where they are sometimes seen in extreme youth. When much accentuated, they show application and thought, habits of concentration; we invariably knit the brows when we wish to grasp a subject. These perpendicular wrinkles on the forehead are, however, often the traces of habitual indulgence in anger; therefore, to be sure of the indication, one should have to consider the temperament. If the skin is of the colour and texture which denotes the choleric or sanguine temperament, one would probably be right in attributing the formation of the perpendicular wrinkles in such a face to the habitual indulgence of anger; but if seen in a person of the lymphatic or melancholic temperament we should be most likely correct

in attributing the lines to the habit of thought. Persons of
the purely lymphatic temperament rarely have these horizontal lines ; they are too indolent to indulge much in study,
and too indifferent to be given to anger. In persons of the
bilious temperament the lines' would probably be produced
from *both* causes—from the deep thought of study, and also
from the indulgence of fits of anger—for the bilious temperament is especially an irritable one, though, at the
same time, highly intellectual, being the result of the
double influence of the Sun and Mercury. Apart from
the deductions to be made from the observations of the
temperament, there is another indication which sometimes
serves to distinguish the perpendicular lines of anger and
thought. Those caused by a habit of concentrated attention, by deep thought, are generally of unequal lengths,
whilst those caused by the perpetually recurrent form of
anger, are shorter, deeper, but both of *equal* lengths. We
sometimes see only *one* of these perpendicular lines between
the eyes—in which case there is no longer any doubt as to
its indication being that of a habit of thought rather than
of anger ; and this *one* line shows also originality.

The eyebrows have so much to do with the indications
given by the brow that it will be well to speak of them in
this chapter.

When the eyebrows are far from each other at their
starting point between the eyes, they denote warmth, frank-
ness, and impulse—a generous and unsuspicious nature.
A woman or man having such eyebrows would never be
causelessly jealous. Eyebrows, on the contrary, which meet
between the eyes in the manner so much admired by the
Persians denote a temperament ardent in love, but jealous
and suspicious : all Saturnians have these eyebrows.

Eyebrows somewhat higher at their starting point, and
which pass in a long sweeping line over the eyes, drooping slightly downwards at their termination, show artistic
feeling and great sense of beauty in form. The Empress

Eugénie's eyebrows are of this form, which gives a sweet and wistful expression to the face, and which some old writers have asserted to be the sign of a violent death.

Eyebrows lying very close to the eyes, forming one direct, clear line on strongly-defined eyebones having the same form, show strength of will and extreme determination of character. This sort of eyebrow appears on the busts of Nero; but then its indications of determination are deepened with cruelty by the massive jaw and the development of the cheekbone by the ear. This form of eyebrow, in conjunction with other good indications, would mean only constancy in affection and power of carrying out a project despite all difficulties, and taste for science.

Eyebrows that are strongly marked at the commencement, and then terminate abruptly without sweeping past the eyes, show an irascible, energetic, and impatient nature.

Thick eyebrows, somewhat arched, show artistic perception of beauty in colour. Delicately marked eyebrows, slightly arched, indicate tenderness and gentle temper. But eyebrows that are so much arched as to give the idea of perpetual astonishment are an indication of a weak and silly nature completely without originality or will-power.

Eyebrows that are straight at their commencement, and are gently arched as they reach the temples, show a pleasant combination of firmness of purpose and tenderness of heart.

Straight eyebrows, that lie very close to the eyes at their termination, show mathematical ability and aptitude for figures; whilst eyebrows which are very much raised, so as to leave a great deal of space between the line of eyebrow and the eyes, show absence of this quality.

When the hair of the eyebrows is ruffled, and growing in contrary directions, it denotes an energetic, easily irritated nature, unless the hair of such eyebrows is fine and soft (a combination sometimes, but not often, seen), in which case this ruffled growth would only indicate an ardent but tender and over-sensitive disposition.

When the eyebrows are formed of short hairs, all lying closely together and leaning one way, it is a very decisive sign of a firm mind and good, unerring perceptions.

Eyebrows that bend downwards close to the eyes, so as almost to meet the eyelashes when they are raised, denote tenderness and melancholy. The beautiful statue of Antinöus has this form of eyebrow.

Angular, strong, and sharply interrupted eyebrows close to the eyes always show fire and productive activity. No profound thinker has weakly-marked eyebrows, or eyebrows placed very high on the forehead. Want of eyebrow almost always indicates a want of mental and bodily force. The nearer the eyebrows are to the eyes, the more earnest, deep, and firm the character; the more remote from the eyes, the more volatile and less resolute the nature.

Eyebrows lighter than the hair show weakness and indecision. Eyebrows much darker than the hair denote an ardent and passionate, but somewhat inconstant temperament.

Eyebrows the same colour as the hair show firmness, resolution, and constancy; but in judging of the eyebrows it must be remembered that if form and colour give different indications, the *form* (as this also means that of the brow) gives the most important indication, the colour and texture of the eyebrow being secondary to its *position* as regards the eyes and forehead.

CHAPTER XXVII.

THE EYES AND EYELASHES.

THE eye has been called " the window of the soul," and not without reason, for it seems more than any other organ to be capable of expressing all its emotions. The most tumultuous passions, the most delicate feelings, the most acute sensations, the eye expresses in all their force and in all their purity, as they arise, and transmits them by variations so rapid as to give to the lookers-on the very image of that with which it is itself inspired; for the eye receives and reflects the intelligence of the thoughts as well as the warmth of the feelings.

The colours most common to the eyes are brown, grey, blue, hazel, and black, or what we *call* black—for those eyes which appear to be black will generally be found to be of a deep yellowish-brown when looked at very narrowly; it is the distance only which makes them seem to be black, because the deep yellow-brown colour is in such strong contrast to the white of the eye that it appears black. There are also eyes of so bright a hazel as to seem almost yellow; lastly, there are eyes that are positively green. Very beautiful, too, are some of the eyes of this colour when they are shaded—as is very often the case—with long, dark eyelashes; but, though beautiful, they are not indicative of a *good* disposition.

Green eyes, although their praises are often sung in Spanish ballads, show deceit and coquetry. We sometimes see eyes which appear to be a combination of yellow, orange, and blue, the latter colour generally appearing in streaks over the whole surface of the iris, while the orange and yellow are set in flakes of unequal size around and at some little distance from the pupil of the eye. Eyes of this variety of tints show intellect, or at any rate a certain originality of character. No commonplace nature has this sort of eye.

There are eyes which are remarkable for being of, what might be said to be, no colour. The iris has only some shades of blue or pale grey, so feeble as to be almost white in some parts, and the shades of orange which intervene are so small that they can scarcely be distinguished from grey or white, notwithstanding the contrast of colours. The black of the pupil is, in these eyes, too marked, because the colour of the iris around it is not deep enough, so that in looking at them we seem to see only the pupil. These eyes are expressionless, for their glance is fixed and dead ; they invariably belong to persons of the lymphatic temperament, and they indicate a listless and feeble disposition, incapable of enterprise, and a cold and indolently selfish nature.

Blue eyes are more significant of tenderness and of a yieldingness of purpose than either brown, black, or grey eyes. There are occasionally to be met strong characters with this tint of eye, but then they will be found to have other indications in the rest of their physiognomy which correct the delicacy and yieldingness of this coloured eye. Blue-eyed people are not inconstant, like those of the hazel and yellow eyes, but they yield from affection.

Angry, irritable persons have frequently eyes of a brownish tint, inclined to a greenish hue. Although the purely green eye of which I have spoken indicates deceit and coquetry, the propensity to greenish tints in the eyes is a sign of wisdom and courage. Very choleric persons, if they have blue eyes, have also certain tints of green in them, and, when under the influence of anger, a sudden red light appears in them. Such eyes as these are generally found in connection with the sanguine, or, as it is sometimes called, choleric temperament ; that is, in those persons who have been born under the double influence of Jupiter and Mars; but, when we see these red tints in the eyes, it would be a sign that, of the two planets presiding over this temperament, Mars was dominant.

Clear grey-blue eyes, with a calm steadfastness in their glance, are indicative of cheerfulness of disposition, of a serene temper, and a constant nature. These eyes are peculiar to the Northern nations; one meets with them among the Swedes, and also sometimes amongst the Scotch. The blue eyes we see among the rare blondes of the South —that is, in Italy and Spain—always have eyes in which there are some greenish tints; and such eyes, though often called light blue, have none of the qualities of serenity and constancy which belong to the light blue eyes of the North. Neither must the pleasant light blue eye, with the honest glance, be confounded with another sort of eye of a pale blue, almost steel-coloured hue, which has a continually shifting sort of motion both of the eyelids and the pupils of the eyes. People with such eyes as these are to be avoided, as they are indicative of a deceitful and selfish nature. Very dark blue eyes, with something of the tint of the violet, show great power of affection and purity of mind, but not much intellectuality.

Grey eyes, of a somewhat greenish grey, with orange as well as blue in them, and which are of ever-varying tints, like the sea, are those which denote most intellectuality. They are especially indicative of the impulsive, impressionable temperament—a mixture of the sanguine and the bilious—which produces the poetic and artistic natures. The line—

" The poet's eye, in a fine phrenzy rolling,"

does not suggest a blue, or even a black, so much as the changeful, ever-varying tinted, grey eye; and it is a fact that in England (where there are more varieties of tints in eyes than in any other country) the poets have almost

K

always grey eyes. A biographer of Byron speaks of his " beautiful, changeful grey eyes, which deepened in colour when he was under the influence of tenderness and passion, and which glowed with a red light when he was angry." Shakespeare also had, we are told, grey eyes, and so had Sir Walter Scott; whilst Coleridge had eyes of a greenish grey. Among the artists, too, eyes of this colour abound.

Black eyes, or what are considered such, are indicative of passionate ardour in love. Brown eyes, when not of the yellowish tint, but pure russet brown, show an affectionate disposition; the darker the brown—that is, the more they verge on to that deepest tint of brown which is seen in eyes we are in the habit of calling black—the more ardent and passionate is the power of affection. The brown eyes which do not appear black—that is, which are not dark enough to appear so—are the eyes of sweet, gentle, and unselfish natures, without the inconstancy of the light brown or *yellow* eyes—" golden eyes," as they were called by a lady novelist—and which are very little more to be trusted than the green eyes already spoken of. The maiden in Long-fellow's " Hyperion," of whom he says,

> " She has two eyes so soft and brown,
> She looketh up, she looketh down;
> Beware, beware, she is fooling thee,"

must have had these *light* brown eyes.

Eyes which show no lines when in sorrow or laughter denote a passionless and unimpressionable nature. Eyes of a long almond shape, with thick-skinned eyelids which appear to cover half the pupil, are indicative of genius; if in conjunction the forehead is that which shows idealism, and has one deep perpendicular line between the eyebrows, which is indicative of originality of mind, and which is generally to be seen in the forehead of distinguished writers and artists. It is very remarkable in all the portraits of Michael Angelo. The almond-shaped eye, however, even without this peculiar form of forehead, always means a susceptible, impressionable nature. Eyes which are large, open, and very transparent, and which sparkle with a rapid motion under well-defined eyelids, denote elegance in tastes, a somewhat susceptible temper and great interest in the opposite sex.

Eyes with weakly-marked eyebrows above them, and with thinly-growing eyelashes which are completely without any upward curve, denote a feeble constitution and a melancholy disposition. These eyelashes are often seen in people who combine the lymphatic and melancholic temperaments—that is, in persons born under the combined influence of the two melancholy planets, Saturn and the Moon. The eyes of these people are either of a pale, colourless sort of blue, or of a dull black without any sparkle in them.

Want of eyelash, like want of eyebrows, shows a general want of force, both of body and intellect.

Strong, dark, and short eyelashes show force of character, and a strong and obstinate will.

Eyes with sharply-defined angles, sinking at the corners, show subtlety of mind ; the sharper the angle, and the more it sinks, the greater the delicacy of perception it denotes ; but when very much developed it shows also craftiness amounting to deceit. Well-opened eyes with smooth eyelids and a steady and somewhat fixed glance denote sincerity. Lines running along the eyelid from side to side and passing out upon the temples denote habitual laughter —a cheerful temperament, or, at any rate, one in which the sense of humour is strong.

We sometimes see (but it is rare) persons whose eyes are of different colours. For instance, one eye will be of a bluish grey, whilst the other will be so flecked with orange or tawny yellow spots as to appear what might be called a brown eye. This peculiarity of having eyes of different colours is sometimes to be seen in dogs, and very often in

cats of the Persian breed, or white cats, but it is very rare
in human beings. An old Italian writer says that people
having eyes of different colours are likely to become mad.
Having, during the whole course of my life, only known
two persons having this peculiarity, I do not feel qualified
to pass an opinion as regards this indication. One of these
persons certainly was mad on several points ; and, when it
is added that the other is the writer of this book, many
of its readers may be inclined to think that the mediæval
physiognomist's theory might very possibly be correct.

CHAPTER XXVIII.

THE NOSE.

We often see fine eyes in an otherwise ugly face, but rarely
is a thoroughly beautiful nose found in a face which could
be called ugly, for the nose is the keynote of the face, and
in it lies the chief characteristic of the countenance.
Beautiful eyes and beautiful lips have, it is true, more
charm—it is the expression of the eyes and lips of those we
love which we most remember in absence—but it is the
nose which, more than any other feature, most affects the
general character of the face. This will be seen if we try
the experiment of drawing the head and face of any beautiful statue—say the Venus of Milo, for instance—and, while
giving it all its fair proportions of brow and cheek and
chin, we substitute a small turn-up nose, or, worse still, a
flat or snub nose, for the noble yet softly gracious line of
the nose in this most perfect head, and how much we
should lower the noble type of beauty this Venus presents !
Of course no one in real life could be unattractive with
such a brow and beautifully shaped eyes, to say nothing of

the perfect lips and softly rounded lines of the chin ; but the nobility of the face would be entirely lost by this alteration of the lines of the nose ; whilst we might alter the beautiful lines of the eyes, narrow the brow, and even take from the softly voluptuous contour of lips and chin, yet by leaving untouched the perfect form of the nose we should still retain the dignity of expression which is so characteristic of this statue.

A nose to be perfect should equal the length of the forehead ; it may, when the forehead is exceptionally low, be even longer than the forehead (and in most of the beautiful antique statues it is so), but on no account should it be shorter than the brow. Viewed in front, the nose should be somewhat broader at its root—that is, where it starts from the brow—than below. The end of it should be neither hard nor fleshy ; but it should be well defined, though neither very pointed nor very broad, for all extremes of forms in any of the features are bad. Viewed in profile, the distance from the line of the wing of the nose to its tip should only be one-third of the length of the nose. Thus, those noses which stand very much out from the face as they near the end of the nose, whilst they are low on the bridge and between the eyes, are out of proportion. Those having such noses are vivacious, but wanting in dignity and force of character. They are impressionable, inquisitive and inconstant.

The nostrils (from the different forms of which many indications are given) should be pointed above and rounded below. The sides of the nose at its root between the eyes should close well with the line of the eye-bone (as one sees them invariably do in the antique statues), and should be at least half an inch in width. Perhaps a better rule of proportion—as regards the whole face—is that the width of the nose between the eyes should be exactly the length of the eye.

Noses which are arched from their starting point between

the eyes show capability of command, energy, and force of character. It will be remembered that the Duke of Wellington—the Iron Duke—had this sort of nose. Of course, this form in excess (as it certainly was in his case), without the characteristics of self-control and other good points in the face, would not have the same indication. A very prominent nose, like the beak of a parrot, with a narrow brow and retreating chin, would give stupid obstinacy; but, in an otherwise good physiognomy, a prominent nose gives force, command, and productive energy.

It cannot, however, be denied that one *sometimes* comes upon noses which are rather small in proportion to the rest of the face, and which are so devoid of arch as to be almost concave in their line when seen in profile, in persons of fairly good understanding; but such noses belong rather to those who appreciate, than to those who produce, works of literature and art. The people having these noses, provided the brows show some intellectuality, will be found to enjoy the beautiful influences of works of the imagination, but they themselves possess little or no creative power.

Straight noses give indications between these two extremes; they may belong to persons of the creative, or simply appreciate, order of mind. The form of the head and brow, and the line of the eyebrows, would determine to which class they especially belong. Arched noses with broad backs denote force of character. Swift and Napoleon Bonaparte had noses of this type. This sort of nose, with an arch starting from the root, is seen in almost all the busts of the Roman emperors; it is, in fact, frequently called the "Roman nose," and is very typical of the race which was for so many ages dominant in Europe; whilst the beautiful straight nose (which we are accustomed to call Grecian, because it is seen in almost all the antique statues) is quite as indicative of the perception of beauty in art and literature and of the subtlety of mind which distinguished the Greeks. The creative force in the antique straight nose is given by its *proportion* to the rest of the face, for it is always larger in proportion to the brow, cheeks, and jaws than the strongly-arched broad-bridged nose which we call Roman, and thus it is indicative of quite as much productive force as the arched Roman nose, with infinitely more delicacy of perception; a small straight nose shorter than the forehead, and set in a large round face, shows timidity and foolishness, and is the nose of an unintelligent person.

High noses that are not broad-backed are often seen in the faces of men of letters, but a high *thin*-backed nose, which seems to start up in a sharp ridge when seen in profile, is more indicative of penetration and acuteness than force of mind. These noses have generally fine, sharp tips, with a downward curve; this is an indication of wit. Voltaire and Sterne had such noses; they are generally seen in combination with thin and flexible lips and a somewhat pointed chin. A nose which is bent downwards is also indicative of sadness of disposition, for it is one of the signatures of the melancholy planet Saturn; but wit may exist (in fact generally does so) with a somewhat sad temperament. Voltaire's wit is almost always cynical, and cynicism grows out of a want of hope, a want of belief in one's fellow creatures; whilst in Sterne (the writer of the inimitable though now little-read work, " Tristram Shandy ") there is always, even in his brightest sallies, an undercurrent of pathetic sadness. People with this sort of nose are sarcastic, somewhat hypochondriacal, and very often reserved and morose. If, with this form of nose, the nostrils are narrow and almost closed, and the wings of the nose pinched, the indications are still more those given by the melancholy planet Saturn; the more elastic and freely-moving the nostril with this form of nose, the more bright and the less sardonic the wit. A person with a broad Roman nose, having this violent downward curve over the mouth, is one to be avoided, for this combination denotes a secretly voluptuous temperament—a man or woman of strong passions hidden beneath a cold and reserved manner. Broad-backed fleshy noses, round and full at the tips, with intellectually good brows, show a genial temperament and a sense of humour. Without the good indications of the brow they would only show love of good cheer and a certain good-humoured carelessness.

Snub-noses—that is, noses short in proportion to the brow and with round fleshy tips—are indicative of common-place, somewhat coarse natures, especially if the nostrils are round and the bridge of the nose very low between the eyes.

What is called a turned-up nose shows vivacity of temperament, jealousy, talkativeness, impudence (growing out of a certain amount of self-esteem), and petulance.

There is a sort of delicately turned-up nose which we often see in pretty women, and which, though it shows wilful-ness and coquetry—things not uncommon in pretty women, since the song tells us—

> " For oh ! these charming women,
> They all have wills of their own—"

is significant of delicate perceptions and a certain intuitive cleverness which is thoroughly feminine, and therefore very attractive to men. These noses—which are especially the noses of charming women—are well raised at the root; in fact, have all the delicacy of line of a straight nose, except that the extreme tip has an upward curve. It must have been of one of these delicate and thoroughly feminine noses that Tennyson must have been thinking when he describes one of his heroines as having a nose—

> " Tip-tilted like a flower."

Flexible nostrils, which quiver under excitement, show an ardent, poetic, and sensitive temperament.

Very open and flexible nostrils show ardour in love, and if seen in conjunction with large, full, and slowly-moving eyes and a full under-lip, indicate a voluptuous and passionate nature.

Closed nostrils show melancholy, timidity, and absence of hopefulness—a person who habitually sees everybody and everything *en noir*.

Round nostrils show animal instincts and a somewhat low type of individuality ; they are generally seen in snub-noses, which of themselves give the same indication.

Noses which have on both sides many wrinkles, which become visible on the slightest motion, and never entirely disappear, even in a state of complete rest, show cunning and sarcasm.

When the line (which, after extreme youth, is always more or less seen from the nose to the mouth) is very strongly marked, and descends at a great distance from the corners of the mouth to the chin, it evidences an anxious and melancholic nature.

CHAPTER XXIX.

THE MOUTH, TEETH, JAW, AND CHIN.

A MOUTH to be beautiful should be in harmony as regards proportion with the rest of the features of the face; that is, it should be neither remarkably large nor remarkably small. Neither the upper nor the lower lip should project beyond the other when the mouth is closed. The lips should shut easily over the teeth, and in doing so should fall into a flowing line of curves without compression. The more the lips are endowed with motion, and the more richly they are coloured, the finer and more delicate are the human passions they indicate.

An excess of even good form is bad ; thus if the full rich lines of a generous mouth are exaggerated, we have the indication of sensuality, whilst the finer susceptibilities shown by delicately moulded lips may, by a little excess towards thinness, give fastidiousness and even avarice.

The middle-sized mouth, which combines strength with warmth of feeling, whilst it steers clear of coarseness, is what gives the best indications. Such a mouth shows courage, generosity, and affection.

A mild, somewhat overhanging upper lip generally signifies goodness, or rather kindliness of disposition ; but if very much overhung it shows weakness of purpose and an irresolute, vacillating character, and, where the under lip is small as well as retreating, and the chin also small, it is an indication of imbecility.

A mouth in which the lower lip projects shows prudence amounting to distrust and melancholy. We often see this form of mouth with the down-drooping nose ; both are indications of the dominating influence of Saturn at the birth of the person possessing such a combination of features. If the under lip should be very full as well as projecting, and droops in a flaccid manner without closing over the teeth when the lips are in repose, it is a sign of a sensual nature. Of course an intellectual brow and a firm and energetic form of nose would lessen the evil of such an indication, but there is always a tendency towards the grosser pleasures of the senses in a person with such a form of lips.

A mouth with lips habitually apart denotes eloquence, if the rest of the face gives intellectual indications ; but if none of the signs of mental power are there it would only signify a chattering person wanting in decision and promptness of action.

A firmly-closed mouth shows courage, fortitude, and determination ; even an habitually open mouth will be seen to close with a sort of forced compression when endurance is necessary. Every one closes the mouth ofter saying, " I am resolved."

A somewhat long mouth, with an upward curve at the corners, and with thin and very flexible lips, indicates wit. Voltaire had this sort of mouth.

Full, flexible lips, with a hollow in the centre of the lower lip, and with the corners turning upwards, denote humour, good-nature, and good spirits.

A mouth with full lips, but in which one side of the lower lip is larger and fuller than the other, was said by the old writers to denote ardour in love and general sensuousness. It is one of the signatures of Venus.

A wart just above the upper lip shows a coarse and cruel nature ; a mole in the same place, love of the opposite sex.

Of course, the shape and placing of the teeth are not without significance in the character given by the mouth. When the upper gum shows above the teeth directly the lips are open, it is a sign of a selfish and phlegmatic nature.

Short, small teeth are held by the old physiognomists to denote weakness and short life, whilst rather long teeth, if evenly set in the head, denote long life.

The more the teeth, in point of size, shape, and arrangement, approach to those of the carnivorous animals, the more violent are the animal instincts in the person ; whilst the more the human teeth in shape and position approach to those of the graminivorous animals, the more placid is the character.

White, medium-sized and evenly-set teeth, which are seen as soon as the mouth is open, but which are never exposed—that is, which do not at any time show the gums —are a sign of good and honest natures.

Projecting teeth show rapacity ; small, retreating teeth, such as are rarely seen unless in laughter, show weakness and want of physical and moral courage. The lower teeth projecting and closing over the upper range are indicative of a harsh nature.

In most faces the mouth or the nose is the more

prominent. Where the nose is the dominant feature, energy, command, and force of will-power, combined (unless the mouth and eyes show great kindness) with selfishness, show themselves in the character.' Where the mouth, jaw, and chin are more prominent, the appetites and passions are strong.

Broad jaws, with a broad forehead, mean both force of intellect and force of animal passion. Byron had this combination of brow and jaw ; but the lips, which were full and flexible, and with upward-curving corners, redeemed the sensuality given by the jaws, and the intellectual qualities shown by the form of the brow were in excess of the indications of voluptuousness given by the lower part of the face.

A person who has the jaw much broader than the brow and head has strong passions and a weak intellect—the very worst possible combination.

When the jaws are massive and yet the head and brow are more so, we have a powerful character, who can exert all his intellectual powers on one subject—one who has the very valuable faculty of concentration.

Where the jaws are much narrower than the head, we have a character where the sensual instincts are feeble, and where intellect is of a subtle and refined order. Wit is shown by this form of face, especially if the nose is delicately outlined, the tip pointed and somewhat drooping over the mouth.

When the lips retreat on each side of the mouth and open into an oval form with a jawbone which comes to a point at the chin, it denotes a subtle intelligence, tact, and refinement of nature.

A sharp indentation immediately above the chin, between it and the lower lip, shows good understanding.

A pointed chin is a sign of craftiness, wisdom, and discretion and intuitive perception.

A soft, fat, double chin shows epicurism and love of

sensual pleasures of all sorts; it also indicates an indolent temperament. We never see such chins in persons of an energetic, restless nature. Charles James Fox, who was excessively indolent, had this chin even in youth.

A flat chin shows avarice and a cold, hard nature; a small chin indicates weakness, want of will-power, and cowardice.

A retreating chin is a sign of silliness, and, if the brow is shallow, of imbecility.

Where the space between the nose and the red part of the lip is short and very sharply cut, it indicates refinement and delicacy of perception, but not much power—no *force* of intellect; where this space is unusually short, it denotes silliness and weakness of purpose. A rather long but not flat upper lip, especially where the serpentine line of the middle of the mouth is much defined and the middle of the lip droops to the lower lip and is very flexible, denotes an eloquent person. We see this form of upper lip in the bust of Demosthenes, the greatest of Grecian orators; in Cicero, whose eloquence was unsurpassed in his age; in Fox, whose powers of oratory were great; in the demagogue Wilkes, in Edmund Burke, in Lord Palmerston, and numerous other orators.

A very long upper lip, which is flat and which belongs to a straight and formless or too thick-lipped mouth, is a sign of a low and vicious type of character. Almost all the faces of great criminals have this defect, combined with massive jaws and high cheek-bones, which last defect is, both Lavater and Perneti (a great French writer on the subject of physiognomy) tell us, a sign of rapacity and egotism.

A round chin, with a dimple in it, denotes kindliness and benevolence, a tender and unselfish nature. In a very massive double chin the dimple increases the quality of love of sensual pleasures. A square and massive chin shows strong perseverance and determined will.

An old Italian writer says that "women with brown, hairy moles on the chin, especially if these excrescences are on the under part of the chin, are industrious, active, and are good housewives"; they are also, he says, "very sanguine and given to love follies. They talk much, and whilst they are easily excited to return a love which is offered them, they are not so readily prevailed upon to become indifferent. For this reason," he goes on, evidently speaking feelingly, and probably, therefore, with personal experience of the matter, "they should be treated with circumspect, calm friendship, and kept at a distance by a mildly cold dignity of demeanour." He gives no directions as to how this effective "demeanour" is to be arrived at, but at once passes on to another remark on the subject of moles, and tells us that "a mole upon the upper lip, especially if it is bristly, will be found in no person who is not defective in something essential." This is rather a wide way of putting the matter. Are people with this blemish morally, mentally, or physically deficient? Wanting in kissableness such a mouth might be, and this, perhaps, where lips are concerned, *is* "something essential."

CHAPTER XXX.

THE HAIR AND THE EARS.

BLACK hair which is perfectly without any wave or curl, and which lies in lank, lifeless masses, shows a melancholic disposition; a black beard which grows sparsely gives also the same indication. Black hair which is wavy or curling, and very thick, shows force of affection, and a certain ardour in love matters; and so also does a thick and crisp-textured black beard and moustache. The lank, thin, and uncurling black hair is one of the signatures of Saturn alone; the crisp, curling, and thickly-growing black hair is the combination of Venus and Saturn. The united influence of these two planets on a life gives force of character, for the warmth and impulse given by Venus is tempered by the distrust of Saturn into prudence; thus people with the crisp dark hair get the ardour, combined with prudence, which produces success in life.

Chestnut hair of a soft and silky texture, and not very thick, gives romance of character. This is not the sort of hair which is ever seen on very common-place realistic persons. This tint of hair, crisp or curling, and growing thickly on the head, indicates a warm and affectionate nature. Men with this sort of hair, and with a thickly-growing beard, also crisp or wavy of texture, are jovial and hospitable, and both women and men of this colouring are fond of society, have a good deal of " go " in them, and an immense amount of confidence in themselves. It is essentially one of the signatures of Jupiter; it indicates pride and generosity of character. Avaricious people never have hair of this colour and texture. With full lips and a round chin with a dimple in it, this sort of colouring would give sensuousness almost amounting to sensuality.

Golden hair of a soft, pale gold without undulation, shows gentleness and tenderness, but no force of character. Men having this sort of hair are somewhat effeminate in their tastes, and are wanting in energy and decision. Both men and women having it are incapable of strong affection; they are attracted by the opposite sex, but they are more given to having a series of small interests than one strong love. If this hair is found in combination with the golden-coloured eyes it is indicative of coquetry in the nature; if with pale blue-grey eyes we have languor and caprice—a sentimental but inconsistent person.

Bright golden hair of a rich, deep colour and of a crisp and waving texture growing thickly on the head and somewhat low on the brow, shows an ardent, poetic, and artistic temperament. It is the signature of the sun. Such people are generally fond of music, painting, or poetry. Both men and women having this sort of hair are intuitive in their judgments ; they do not reason about things, they feel them ; they are a little quick of temper, that is, easily ruffled, but they are quickly appeased ; they are gay, and interest themselves in art, even if they are not artists themselves.

Persons with red hair are ardent and vivacious, especially if, with it, they have hazel eyes, in which case they have a bright and quick intelligence, for reddish hair and bright brown eyes are the signature of Mercury. They have a great deal of natural facility for study, and good memories. Red hair, with blue eyes, shows the same warmth of character, but not so much intelligence, and if, with blue eyes and red hair, the eyebrows and eyelashes are white— as is often the case—it is an indication of a weak and capricious nature.

People with red-brown hair, which is very thick and redder over the ears and at the temples and on the beard than on the head, are courageous and hot-tempered. This coloured hair is the signature of the fiery planet Mars, and (unless the other indications in the face are widely different) shows activity and energy in all things. It augments the indications of force and power given by other features, and, in art, gives sense of colour in painters,—force of language and eloquence in poets,—and power in musical composition.

Hair of that colourless, fair colour which French writers call *blond cendré*, or ash-coloured, denotes persons of an indolent and dreamy temperament. It is the indication given by the dominant influence of the Moon at birth. Persons with this sort of hair, in combination with large blue-grey eyes, with fair, long, but straight eyelashes, and very slightly-defined eyebrows of the same blonde colour, and white, soft skin, are capricious, languid, imaginative, and somewhat melancholic. The imaginative and excessively indolent Théophile Gautier, the French novelist, was of this type in combination with Venus, giving a sensuousness amounting to sensuality.

Women having this sort of colouring of skin and hair are romantic and devoted in a resigned, but not active spirit—that is, they are more generous in words than deeds, for they are incapable of exertion and still less of perseverance.

Persons with soft, wavy brown hair are affectionate, gentle, and loving. Their first instincts are always good and kind. They like society, and are gracious in manners, and, though they are not quite as indolent as those having the soft ash-coloured hair—indicative of the Moon's influence—they are still lovers of repose and elegant comfort.

People with this soft brown hair (which is one of the signatures of the planet Venus) are very open to the impressions of beauty, and they abhor noise, discords, and quarrels; men with this sort of hair, like those with *pale* golden hair, are somewhat effeminate, and are easily moved to tears.

Large, fleshy ears (especially those which have the lobes of the ears red) show coarseness of nature and sensuality.

If the ears stand forward so as to show their entire form when the face is seen from the front, it denotes rapacity and cruelty.

Long-shaped but small ears indicate refinement ; a very small ear, close to the head, shows delicacy of perception, refinement, but also timidity.

The ears should be so placed as not to be higher than the eyebrow, or lower than the tip of the nose ; if set in too sloping a direction they show timidity ; if too upright, animal instincts, courage, amounting to cruelty, especially if they obtrude from the head.

A thin ear shows delicacy and poetry of feeling ; a thick ear, the reverse.

L

A wide space between the wing of the nose and the ear-hole shows coarseness of nature ; too little space, meanness and coldness of temperament.

Ears of a deep red colour show animal instincts ; perfectly colourless ears denote timidity and want of warmth of temperament.

An ear to be perfect should be rather small than not ; in height it should not be higher than the eyebrow and not lower than the nose ; in colour it should be of a very delicate pink, and a little, but a very little, deeper in shade at the lobes.

Middle-sized ears, rather close to the head, are the signature of Jupiter ; large ears of Saturn ; delicate, long-shaped ears of the Sun, and also of Mercury, only those bearing the signature of Mercury are more coloured, whilst those of the Sun are pale. Very upright ears, standing forward, are the signature of Mars ; small, round ears, delicately tinted pink, and close to the head, show the influence of Venus ; whilst middle-sized round ears, of a very pale colour, are indicative of persons born under the influence of the Moon.

CHAPTER XXXI.

THE COMPLEXION.

THE complexion (that is, the colouring of the skin, hair, eyebrows, eyelashes, and beard) is what shows the temperament. The old Italian writers, as well as Holler, Zimmerman, Obereit, and a multitude of others, from Huart to the old mystic Jacob Boëhme, and from him to Lavater, have written at length on this part of physiognomy, all more or less cleverly, none quite satisfactorily ; some, like Jacob Boëhme, admitting the power of astral influence ; others, like Lavater, completely denying it. The classifications of the temperaments given by these various writers are somewhat different ; but, without entering into these differences, I shall pass on to my own theories on the subject, which are, it is needless to say, based on a belief in astral influence.

The temperaments are four in number—the choleric, the melancholic, the nervous, and the lymphatic.

The choleric is the result of the dominant influence of Jupiter or Mars, or both. People born under this influence, when Jupiter is dominant, have a fresh-coloured skin, hair of a reddish and crisp or curly brown, eyebrows and eyelashes and beard of the same colour ; they early become bald, but the baldness is more at the top of the head than over the brow ; they are gay and affectionate, but quick-tempered. Those of the choleric temperament in which Mars is the dominant planet have red hair and beard crisply waving or curly ; their eyebrows are of the same colour, and grow low—that is, close to the eyes ; their eye-lashes are short, thick, and curly upwards; and their skin is of a red-brown tint. They are hot-tempered, jealous, courageous, petulant, and very domineering. In fact, those born under the fiery planet Mars have the choleric or hot temperament more fiercely accentuated than those born under Jupiter.

The melancholic temperament is the result of the influence of the planet Saturn alone. Those of this complexion or temperament have pale or greenish-tinted, or sometimes earth-coloured skins ; their hair, eyebrows, and beard are black, thick, and absolutely without undulation of any sort. The eyebrows of persons of the melancholic temperament are generally set close together, very often meeting over the eyes, and are somewhat raised at their commencement, but droop closely over the eyes at their termination. Persons of this temperament, unmitigated by other influences, are

L 2

morose, melancholy, inclined to avarice, cautious to excess, and generally jealous. They have neither hope nor enthusiasm but they are constant in their affections, patient and persevering. They have an instinctive love of occult science, and are superstitious, whilst at the same time they are often doubters of revealed religion.

The nervous temperament is that given by the influence of the Sun or Mercury, and is the temperament which is more especially that of writers, artists, and musicians. When the Sun is the dominant planet the hair, beard, and eyebrows are of a bright golden colour, which sometimes shows a little red tinge here and there, especially about the beard. The eyelashes are of the same colour, and are always long and curved, and the skin is bright-coloured, but of a yellowish hue. People of this temperament are imaginative, bright, gay, and affectionate, yet not constant; they are generally fond of poetry and all the arts, and are very open to the influences of beauty. Those of the nervous temperament who are under the dominant influence of Mercury have bright brown or auburn hair inclined to curl; their eyebrows, long and delicately marked and slightly arched, are of the same colour; their skin is soft and fine, not very bright-coloured, and of a pale yellowish tint. Those of the nervous temperament especially influenced by Mercury are eloquent and vivacious, and if not writers they are interested in literature or art, and given to the study of the occult sciences.

The lymphatic temperament is that given by the influence of the Moon, or of the Moon in combination with Venus. Those born under the especial influence of the Moon are of a pale complexion; their skin is soft, and their hair long, thin, and quite devoid of curl; their faces are round, and the nose is small in proportion to the size of the cheeks; their eyes are round and of a pale, colourless bluish green, or very light grey-blue colour; their eyebrows are very fair; their chins fleshy and somewhat retreating. People of this temperament are indolent to excess, rather capricious, imaginative, and very dreamy. They love art of the fantastic order, and literature which treats of out-of-the-way subjects. Those of the lymphatic temperament, where Venus is the dominant planet, have hair of a deeper brown, sometimes almost black, and the skin, though inclined to be white, is tinged with colour in the cheeks; the face is still round, but not so large in proportion to the nose and brow as in persons of the lymphatic temperament given by the sole influence of the Moon ; the eyes are generally brown, but have the same languid movements as those of persons born solely under the Moon's influence ; they, too, are gentle, but gayer, and of course warmer in their loves than those born under the influence of the Moon, but, like them, they are a little inconstant.

Of course, it is rarely, if ever, that a person is of one of these four temperaments without some admixture from one or more of the three others.

Persons whose temperaments are both choleric and melancholic are rare, because these temperaments are somewhat contradictory; but they do exist.

Such persons might have the long features and lank black hair given by the melancholic temperament, with the red complexion which belongs to the choleric temperament, in which case the character would be less gay and more gentle, the quickness of temper would be softened, and, on the other hand, the taciturnity and moroseness of the melancholy temperament would be mitigated by the animation of the more choleric nature.

A union of the melancholic temperament with the nervous or artistic temperament gives nobility to the beauty of the latter. The hair might then be chestnut instead of gold, the eyes of a deep dark grey, and the complexion pale. Persons with such a combination of temperaments are eminently poetic ; in fact, it is this union of temperaments (above all when Mercury is the dominant planet) which produces genius.

The union of the lymphatic temperament with the choleric produces a person of fair, delicately-coloured complexion, with soft brown hair and brownish grey eyes, which move more rapidly than those of the purely lymphatic type. Such persons are fitfully energetic, fond of society, but somewhat capricious in their friendships.

The union of the melancholic with the lymphatic temperament gives a person with a soft olive complexion, black hair, a round but not large face, straight but not aquiline features, and very beautiful dark eyes, so dark as to look almost black, or large clear grey eyes with very dark lashes. This union produces a very dreamy nature, yet possessing much reticence (given by Saturn) and the gentleness peculiar to the influence of Venus and the Moon. The evil influence of Saturn is mitigated by this union, and the prudence and logical power belonging to those born under Saturn give force to the weakness and indolence of the lymphatic temperament.

The union of the nervous with the lymphatic temperament gives a pale creamy skin, pale brown hair of a yellowish tinge, large light hazel eyes, delicate, lightly marked eyebrows, and a round face. Persons having this combination of temperament are eloquent, subject to fits of depression, but of pleasing manners. This combination gives science in musical composition, love of beauty in all things, power of affection, but yet no great constancy, for this is especially the impressionable temperament. The old mystic, Jacob Boëhme, at the close of his curiously interesting and quaint little book, " A Consolatory Treatise on the Four Complexions," gives the following sound advice :—

" The melancholy complexion should not perplex his soul with the reading of many books, but rather adhere solely to the Scriptures, in which he shall find durable and steady comfort. The melancholy complexion should also, with great care, avoid drunkenness, that the soul be not overladen and pressed down by the power of the earth."

He goes on to tell the man that is of the choleric complexion that he " must above all things exercise himself in humility, for this complexion has a native lustre of its own, but is commonly void of mildness unless it have Venus in the ascendant"—that is, unless the choleric temperament is softened by the admixture of the lymphatic.

Of the nervous complexion he says, " Thou must live orderly to this noble complexion, but let not hypocrisy take place in it. By the largeness of thy comprehension thou art capable of great inventions ; take heed thou bring not stubble and straw to thy habitation. A sober, temperate life is good for thee ; keep thyself carefully from drunkenness, else thou castest thyself, wilfully, into thine enemies' arms. Thou art much inclined to love ; place it upon the right object, and love not unchastity and pride." Could there be better advice to any one of this artistic temperament ?

CHAPTER XXXII.

CONGENIAL FACES.

By " congenial faces " physiognomists mean such faces as show some dominating quality with few, if any, contradictory indications. Now, as very few people are born under one entirely dominating astral influence (and it is this influence which gives the temperament), such faces are very rare ; but as a physiognomical description of these " congenial faces " would be useful to the students of the science, this chapter will give the indication of special qualities on every feature of the face.

Gentleness and calm, the special qualities of the lymphatic temperament, are shown by a round, smooth forehead,

in which the two arches are not much marked, and of which
the skin is soft and almost without wrinkles—certainly
without the two *short* perpendicular wrinkles between the
eyes, which denote the quick and choleric temperament.
One may sometimes see the long, upright wrinkles between
the eyes, which show thought; but, generally speaking,
the foreheads of gentle and calm natures are quite
unwrinkled, except, of course, in old age; the eyebrows are delicately marked and somewhat arched,
and never of a darker colour than the hair. The
white of the eyes is clear and liquid, and the eyes are
generally blue or of a bluish grey, with well-defined but
not heavy eyelids; the lines of the eye, both above and
below, cut the pupil of the eye; that is, the *whole* circle of
the pupil is not seen either above or below. The eyelashes of calm and gentle natures are rarely curved
upwards, but are very straight, silky, and never of a darker
colour than the hair, which is also fine, soft, and straight,
or, if at all waved, it has loose, large undulations. The
nose is invariably without a rise upon it, and is generally
small in proportion to the face; the nostrils are long and
narrow, and not very flexible or open; the tip of the nose
is never pointed, but softly rounded, and never either turned
up or down, for the upturned nose shows petulance, and the
downward bent nose melancholy. The mouth of very calm
persons is medium size, with moderately full lips closing
evenly; the jaw is not large; the chin is round, rather
small, and somewhat retreating; and the ears are placed in
a sloping position, and lie close to the head, which is
generally round in shape. The skin is fine, soft, and
generally pale, or tinged only with faint colours. Blue
veins showing at the temples are a sign of refinement and
gentleness of nature.

A congenial face, showing energy and quickness of
temper, is one in which the forehead is somewhat square,
and with the two short horizontal wrinkles between the

brow very much developed; the skin of the brow is never very white or very smooth; the eyebrows are short and thickly marked, or they are sharply defined in a long line close to the eyes and nearly meeting over the nose; they are generally darker than the hair, which is of a reddish brown, crisp or curly, and of a coarse, strong texture. The eyes are brown or of a blue-grey, with greenish tints in them, and move quickly, yet fix themselves with a fierce, steady gaze on the person addressed; the eyelids go far back, and show the whole of the pupil of the eye at all times; the nose is always large in proportion to the face, and has a very decided beak-like rise upon it, and the nostrils are large and open; the mouth is small in proportion to the jaw (which is large), and the lips are never full; the teeth are large, long, and pointed; the cheek bones are generally prominent, but the face thin rather than fat; the ears are long-shaped, placed high in an upright direction, and stand out somewhat from the face: this sort of ear is never seen in a gentle or timid nature; the chin is large, pointed, and advancing; the skin is hard and somewhat high coloured.

The congenial melancholic face is long, thin, and pale-coloured, and, after extreme youth, the skin in these faces becomes very much wrinkled, not only across the brow in straight lines, but a multitude of oblique wrinkles also appear, as well as the two perpendicular wrinkles between the eyes, which indicate thought. The hair is long, straight, dark, and never very thick, except in extreme youth. The brow is high and narrow, the head a long oval; the eyes are either sunken or with heavy lids which half cover the pupils. They are generally black, or what we call black, and the white of the eye has a yellowish tinge; the eyes move slowly, and in repose are always bent to the ground; the eyebrows of the melancholic face are black, higher at their commencement over the nose, and very close to one another, and then drooping in a long line near to the eyes

at their termination; the cheeks are thin, and appear
hollow from the largeness of the jaw, the under part of
which is generally projecting. The mouth is large, but the
lips are thin, and droop very much at the corners; the
lower lip generally appears to project, from the form of
the jaw; the teeth of persons of the purely melancholic
temperament are generally of a yellowish white, and are
long shaped and even; their ears are large, and set in
a sloping position, and rather low in the head; the nose is
straight, and long in proportion to the rest of the features,
thin and very pointed at the tip, which is much bent over
the lips; the nostrils are long, closed, and not at all
flexible; the line from the wing of the nose to the mouth
is very much marked in all melancholic faces; the chin is
long, and somewhat heavy, on account of the large form of
the under-jaw.

A congenial face which shows *cheerfulness* is round, fresh-
coloured, with a smooth brow, a short, straight nose,
slightly turned up at its tip; blue or brown well-opened
eyes, with curly eyelashes and arched eyebrows lying somewhat high above the eyes; the hair is bright-coloured, and
generally crisp and not very fine in texture; the mouth is
somewhat large; the lips red, with flexible curves, and very
much turned up at the corners; the cheeks are fleshy and
dimpled, and the chin round.

Avarice is shown by a head which is very flat at the
back, and a forehead which is perpendicular and narrow
and very much covered with oblique wrinkles; the nose is
very thin and pinched, and leaning slightly to one side; the
mouth is long, but the lips are thin and very compressed;
the eyes are small, generally of a dull grey colour, and the
eyelids are thin and very wrinkled; the jaws are very
large, and the cheeks are thin and wrinkled; the chin is
pointed and has no superfluous flesh upon it, and, above
all, no indentation under the lower lip.

Tenderness in a perfectly congenial face would be shown

by a low round forehead, long sweeping eyebrows, with a downward bend in the middle, and stretching across blue-veined temples. The eyes are large, long-shaped, with rather full lids, and are of a blue or blue-grey or soft brown colour; the lashes are long and rather straight, and of a soft and silky texture. The hair of very tender persons is either auburn or brown, and it is always fine and straight, never crisp or curly ; the nose is straight and delicate, with flexible, oval-shaped nostrils ; the lips full, and of a delicate pink-red, closing softly over small, straight, and white teeth ; the jaw is delicate, and not much accentuated ; the chin round, fleshy, and adorned by a dimple, but there is none of the superabundant fleshiness known as a "double chin" beneath it. The complexion—that given by Venus—is a soft roseate tinge on a *blue*-white skin.

Generosity in a congenial face would be shown by a full, almost square yet low brow ; eyebrows richly marked, and sweeping across the forehead in grand and generous lines, not much raised or much drooping to the eyes ; the eyes are large, with decided lines in the eyelids, and are generally a clear blue or honest brown colour; the eyelashes are brown, and have an upward curve ; the nose is short, fleshy, and with a rise upon it ; the lips very full ; the mouth somewhat large with fine flexible curves ; the cheeks are rounded, the complexion well coloured, the chin round, fleshy, and with a strong indentation under the lower lip.

Ardour in a thoroughly congenial face would be shown by a medium forehead, with the short horizontal wrinkles between the eyes, a straight, thin, long nose, with very flexible nostrils ; large, long, almond-shaped eyes, very liquid in their light, but wide open and quick in their movements ; the eyebrows long, near the eye, though very flexible, and very well defined, but delicate, a little ruffled, but not meeting at the starting point over the eyes. The lips well defined, the upper lip rather short, and, when closed, showing a fine line in three curves; the chin rather angular (from the oval-shaped jaw), and quite devoid of dimple or any superabundant fleshiness.

Sensuality.—A thoroughly sensual face, that is, one in which every feature gives indications of this quality, is one in which the forehead is low and flat, with the hair growing thickly upon the temples and low down upon the forehead, so as to leave but little space between it and the eyebrows. At the same time excessive baldness at an age when it is not to be expected, in conjunction with a face in which all the other indications of sensuality are present, would, to the physiognomist, suggest the same reading as the superabundance of hair.

The eye-bones of the sensual face are not strongly defined, but the eyebrows are thick, arched rather than straight, and not at all close to the eyes. The nose is thick and fleshy, either very much sinking between the eyes, flat, and spreading over the face, and with a round and fleshy tip, or it is prominently arched from the root, though still fleshy, and the tip of it bends very much over the lips. The eyes of such a face are large, black, with heavy lids, and very slow in their movement.

The cheeks are fleshy, and there is a wide space from the wing of the nose to the ear, which is large, and of a deep colour, especially about the lobes, which might almost be called red. The space from the nose to the upper lip, in sensual faces, is always long and flat—that is, the cutting between the nose and lip not sharply defined; the lips are very large and deep coloured, the lower one projecting and hanging. The chin is heavy, and has that superabundance of flesh beneath it called a "double chin." A brown wart or mole on the chin, or on the neck immediately beneath the chin, from which spring some harsh and curling hairs, is a sign of extreme sensuality. The form of the head is somewhat flat, with not much elevation above the ears, and with a very great protuberance at the back, and a broad and fleshy throat. The hair, both of the head and beard, is black or dark red bronze—sometimes of a fiery red.

Purity.—A face suggestive of this quality has a somewhat high brow (that is, the brow, if anything, longer than the nose, certainly not shorter), of which the flesh is soft, and what few lines there are on it are only occasionally discernible. The two arches of the forehead are equally, but not much, developed, the line of the eyebrow is well defined, and the eyebrows—long, sweeping, and delicately though clearly marked—are straight and somewhat close to the eyes. The nose is without any rise upon it, taking the pure, straight line from the forehead which we see in the Greek statues of Pysche. It is delicately cut at the wings, and the nostrils are oval and flexible, but not very open. The eyes are medium size, of a clear blue or bluish-grey colour; the iris flecked with white specks, which give to the eye the pure radiance of a star; the eyelids go well back from the eyes, which have a gentle yet fixed glance. The eyelashes are of a soft light brown, and neither they nor the eyebrows are darker than the hair, which is of the same tint or of a pale gold, in which case the eyelashes and eyebrows are also very light. The space between the nose and the mouth is short and sharply chiselled; the upper lip is well defined, but not thick, and meets the lower lip in a curved and somewhat compressed line; the mouth is well defined at the corners, which are raised. The chin is pointed rather than round, making the face of a severely oval form. The head, too, is oval and the back of it but very slightly projecting; the ears are small, especially the lobes, rather long-shaped, without colour, and close to the head. The skin is clear, firm, though not hard of texture, and delicately pale.

Firmness is shown by a face in which the brow is broad and square, with very low-lying, strongly-marked eyebrows; the eyes, of a light grey, are not large, but have a

clear and unflinching glance ; the eyelashes are short, thick,
and very dark ; the hair dark also, and strong, crisp, or
curling. The nose is thick and broad-backed, with a
decided rise upon it. The lips are somewhat thin, or if
thick are very much compressed, the cheek-bones are prominent, the jaw large and strongly defined, the chin square
and somewhat bony. The head is large rather than small,
and rising at the top; the ears are medium size, slightly
coloured, and set somewhat straight on the head.

Deceit is shown by a flat perpendicular brow, in which
there are a quantity of oblique wrinkles ; the eyebrows are
very flexible, somewhat bushy, and often descend so as to
hide the eyes, which are small and sunken, and have a quick
and shifting movement, never fixing themselves for any
length of time on the person addressed. The lines of the
eyes are not arched in the centre, and the corners are oblique ;
the eyes are set very close together, and are black or of a
greenish-blue. The nose is long, thin, and irregular in
form, and has many lines on both sides of it, which become
visible on the slightest motion, and never entirely disappear
even in a state of complete rest. The mouth is thin and
very flexible ; the upper lip has an uneasy, twitching movement, and when the mouth closes (although it does so in
a straight compressed line) the lower lip projects. The chin
is angular and fleshless, the head narrow and flat at the
back, the complexion pale, the hair of that colourless fair
tint which is one of the indications of the Moon's influence,
for the bad aspects of the Moon give deceit.

Stupidity is shown by a very disproportionately large
brow, in which the upper arch is very much more projecting
than the lower one (that over the eyes), and with a perfectly
flat, unwrinkled space between the eyes, which are large
and very far apart, of a dull light-blue or yellow-grey colour,
with the pupil of the eye very small in proportion to the
white, and in which the lines of the eyes both above and
below do not touch the pupil. The eyebrows are only faintly

drawn, and the eye-bones very little defined. The nose is small in proportion to the face, which is generally large, very flat, and fleshy. There is no rise upon the nose, which is flat to the face, broad, and fleshy at the tip, with round nostrils. A *very high* nose, of an exaggerated form, like that of Punch, set in an otherwise stupid face, is quite as suggestive of dulness as the snub or broad, flat nose, only this combination is not so frequent as the other. The lower part of the face in stupid people is always large in proportion to the upper; the space between the nose and mouth is long and flat, and three curved lines go directly from the wings of the nose to the corners of the lips, and are distinctly visible even when the face is in repose, although they become still more accentuated in laughter.

A *timid and vacillating nature* is shown by a long, narrow forehead, intersected by faint and confused lines in all directions, very faintly marked, almost white eyebrows and eyelashes. The eyes are large, somewhat projecting, and have a glance which is continually shifting, or they are small, with an uncomfortable twitching motion in them; the eyelids are thin; and covered with small lines, the nose is invariably long, and lies close to the cheeks without any rise upon it; the wings of the nose are angular, not rounded, and droop somewhat; the nostrils are small, long, and closed; the mouth, which is small, with the upper lip very much advanced and the corners drooping, is never quite closed for any length of time; for after the compression of the lips for a few seconds they part again, the lower lip hanging loosely down; the chin is small and very retreating; the hair is colourless; the ears, small, close to the head, set in a very sloping position, and low down in the head; the skin is soft, and the colour of it continually varying. It should be observed that in all timid people the nose is whiter than the brow.

A face in which every trait is expressive of *Indolence* is one in which the forehead is low, flat, and fleshy, the head is round and with not much elevation above the ears, whilst at the top it is almost flat, and begins to sink after the centre instead of rising, as a firm and energetic head does, before the turn. The eye-bones are never well defined in the congenially indolent face, and the eyebrows (which are placed very high on the forehead) are arched rather than straight, and both they and the eyelashes are generally lighter than the hair, which is of an undecided colourless brown, fine of texture, but thin in its growth and without any crispness or curl in it. The eyes of an indolent person are never brilliant, and are of a grey, greenish-blue, and have a slow movement beneath heavy lids, which invariably in indolent natures are so drooping as to cover quite one-third of the pupil of the eye ; the nose of an indolent person is very low at the starting-point between the eyes, and is short and small in proportion to the rest of the face ; it is also completely without any indication of a rise upon it ; indeed (when seen in profile), the nose of an indolent person generally appears to sink where the energetic nose rises ; the tip of the nose is always round and fleshy ; persistent indolence is impossible to persons with long, sharply-defined, and very pointed noses. If the chins of such persons are round and very fleshy underneath, they may have their *fits* of indolence (after that over-indulgence in the pleasures of the senses which such a form of chin denotes) ; but, with a high and pointed nose, the rest-lessness of the nature belonging to such noses will soon re-assert itself ; but although physiognomy presents us with many and often very puzzling contradictory indications in the same face, it is rarely that the full and fleshy double chin appears in conjunction with the pointed nose. To return to the "congenial" indolent face. The cheeks are large, very fleshy, and meet beneath the chin in that hanging form called a " double chin." The mouth especially denoting indolence of nature is not very large, but is full-lipped and pale coloured, and is rarely quite closed. The skin is soft, somewhat flabby in texture, and without vivid colours of any sort; the ears are somewhat large, but set in a sloping direction, like those of the gentle natures, and lie very close to the head.

A person of thoroughly *envious* nature has a thin, long face and head; the forehead is high (or appears to be so from its excessive narrowness), and is covered with complicated lines or wrinkles in all directions. The eye-bones are very strongly defined, but, instead of taking the slightly arched form belonging to good and generous natures, they are quite straight and appear to overhang the eyes, which are sunken, small, and of a dull, greenish-yellow colour; the eyebrows are long and narrow, but strongly marked, a little raised, but very close at their starting-point, and often meeting over the nose. Between the eyes of envious persons there are four faint perpendicular wrinkles (the result of the continual knitting of the brows in discontented anger at another's success), but they are not so strongly marked as the two short wrinkles, which have been already described as denoting the habitually choleric nature, nor are they as deep and long as the two perpendicular wrinkles which indicate thought, a capacity for concentration, and therefore good intelligence.

The perpendicular wrinkles of the envious face are quite different to these : they are four in number, and they are as finely traced as the many complex wrinkles which cross the brow in all directions, making it appear to be covered with a network of oblique lines. The nose is long and thin, with very large wings and long thin nostrils, and, as the nose in an envious face has the same downward bend as that of the melancholic face, the nostrils appear to turn up at the outer end; from the wing of the nose to the corners of the mouth there are many fine long lines, intersected again by still finer ones crossing the cheeks in all directions. The cheeks are thin and hollow; no thoroughly envious nature is ever fat. Shakespeare, that wonderful reader of human

M

nature in all its aspects, makes Cæsar, after speaking of the " *spare* Cassius," say,—

" Such men as he be never at hearts' ease
Whiles they behold a greater than themselves."

The mouth in an envious face is long and thin, with very little of the lips showing, and closes in a compressed line, of which one side droops more than the other. The chin is long, pointed, and bony, and there is no line or indentation of any kind between the lower lip and the chin, for this is an indication of selfishness, and all envious people are so. The gums of envious people are pale coloured, and the teeth long and of a yellowish white; their smile is forced, hard, and disagreeable, the many lines about the mouth and cheeks becoming then more apparent. The hair, eyes, and eyebrows of envious people are generally dark, the skin harsh and dry, and of a pale yellow colour, with greenish tints under the eyes.

Imagination (poetic nature) is shown by a head which with the face, makes a perfect oval. The brow is low, but very broad and full ; the lower arch,—that of intuitive perception,—being more fully developed than the upper arch, which gives reflection ; but this, of course, is not wanting, only it is not quite so accentuated as the other qualities given by the fulness over the eyes. The brow is especially full at the temples, just above the line of the eyebrows, giving ideality,—creative power. The eyebrows are long, very flexible, raised at their commencement, well defined, and sweeping over the eyes, until they finish in a delicate drooping line on the temples. The brow is clear from lines, with the exception of three almost straight and equidistant horizontal lines immediately above the one deep perpendicular line between the eyes, already described as indicating marked abilities. This perpendicular line has sometimes the two others indicating power of concentration on each side of it. The eyes are large, almond-shaped, and of a blue-grey tint flecked with orange, very varying in colour, and very liquid; the lashes are long, rather straight than curling, and both they and the eyebrows are darker than the hair, which is of a golden brown, or rich chestnut, slightly waving, and of a fine and silky texture. The nose is long and apparently straight, but (when seen in profile) a slight and very delicately-defined rise is apparent upon it. The wings of the nose are also very delicately articulated; the nostrils are long, pointed towards the tip of the nose, and rounded towards the wings; they are very flexible, and inside of a rosy pink colour. The upper lip is well cut, neither very long nor very short, but, like the eyebrows, very flexible, moving with every passing emotion, for, as Dr. Carus, in his " Symbolik der Menschlichen Gestalt," says: " The upper lip is the organ of sensibility, whilst the under lip, being only for the reception of food, is less suited to reproduce the movements of the soul." In the mouth, especially that of the poet, the under lip is full, giving warmth and sensuousness, but it closes well with the upper lip, and is not at all protuberant or hanging; a small dimple is at times apparent, when the person is speaking, at the corner of the left side of the mouth. This is rare, but as it is given by Venus, it is a sign of a sensitive and poetic nature. The chin is round, medium-sized, but not fleshy, forming a soft oval with the cheeks. The ears are small, long-shaped, set in a gentle slope, rather close to the head, and delicately coloured. The complexion is ordinarily pale, but flushing easily with a deep and vivid yet quickly-fading colour. In imaginative people the blue veins on the temple are very apparent, and there is frequently a blue vein, shaped like the letter v, apparent in the middle of the forehead.

CHAPTER XXXIII.

THE SIGNATURES OF THE PLANETS ON THE FACE.

THOSE born under Jupiter have fresh complexions, large, smiling, blue or grey eyes, with thick, well-formed eyelids ; their eyelashes are long and fine ; their hair—which is chestnut, or, if tending towards black, is a brown, not *blue*-black—is curly and supple, and they generally have well-marked and somewhat arched eyebrows ; their noses are straight and well-formed, but somewhat fleshy ; the mouth large, but with generous, curved and full lips, the upper lip projecting over the lower one ; their teeth are large, and the two front ones are generally longer than the rest; their cheeks are fleshy and firm ; the cheek-bones are well-defined, without being prominent; the chin is large, with a dimple in the centre of it ; their ears are of medium size, and lie somewhat close to the head. The men born under Jupiter have thick curly beards, but get bald early in life.

Those born under Saturn have thick, but straight blue-black hair ; they have long-shaped heads, thin, almost hollow cheeks, large jaws and very high cheek-bones. Their eyebrows are very dark, generally meeting between the eyes, raised at their commencement over the nose, then drooping in a long melancholy line towards the eye at their termination on the temples. Their eyes are sunken, very dark and melancholy, and the white of the eye is of a yellowish tinge ; their ears are large, but lying close to the head ; their noses are long, thin and pointed, bending down over the lips, and the nostrils are closed and inflexible ; their mouths are large, the lips thin, and the lower one somewhat projecting ; their teeth are long and white in youth, but they lose them early; the chin is long and rather large, without being fleshy; the jaw is massive, with the under jaw somewhat projecting. Those born under the dominant influence of Saturn never have any colour in their cheeks, and their skin is dark, of a yellow or leaden tint, and wrinkles easily. Of course it is seldom that anyone is born under the *sole* influence of one planet; the ugliness of the Saturnian type is much mitigated by the influence of Jupiter, and the union of Venus with Saturn often produces positive beauty of a serious and melancholic sort. Many of the very strikingly beautiful Spanish faces show the combined influence of Saturn and Venus.

Those born under the dominant influence of the Sun have regular features, and a soft skin of a pale yellow tint, but with colour in the cheeks and lips. Their hair is long, soft, and fine, of a golden fairness, not flaxen, but of a *red*-gold tint; their eyebrows are long and rather sweeping; their foreheads are rounded and prominent, without being high. Their eyes are of a bright golden-brown or greenish-grey, and they are brilliant and well-shaped, the white of them being pure and limpid. The eyelashes are a little darker than their hair, rather long, and curve slightly upwards; their eyebrows are also a shade darker than their hair, and are traced in a long, delicate, slightly arched and sweeping line over the eyes, extending to the temples. Their cheeks are well covered, without being plump; their jaws are a long oval, and neither the cheek-bones nor the jaws are at all prominent. Their teeth are even, but of rather a yellowish-white; their mouths are neither large nor small, but well-formed, with the lips meeting evenly, that is, neither the upper nor the lower lip projecting. Their ears are medium-sized, rather long in shape, lying close to the head, and the lobes of them are fleshy and slightly coloured of a pinkish hue. The chin is rather prominent, round and well-shaped, like those of the antique statues, but not fleshy. Those born under the influence of the Sun have frequently weak sight, especially if their birth has taken place during an eclipse.

Those born under the influence of Mercury have long

faces, and delicate, mobile features. Their skin is fine, soft and honey-coloured, but changes in tint with every passing emotion, for those born under Mercury are of a nervous, impressionable temperament. Their hair is of a reddish, not golden, brown (what is called auburn), very fine and supple. Their foreheads are high and prominent; and their eyebrows, which are long and delicately traced, lie very low over the eyes and are very mobile, moving up and down with every emotion. The eyes of those born under this planet are somewhat sunken, of a hazel or dark-grey colour; they move quickly and have a restless expression; the white of the eye is (like that of those born under Saturn) of a yellowish tint; and the lids of the eyes are thin, and do not droop at all over the eyes. Their noses are straight and long, with delicate nostrils; the tip of the nose is round rather than pointed, and frequently has a small cleft or dimple, which is, however, only faintly perceptible in certain lights, at the extreme tip. They have delicate mouths which droop a little at the corners, and the lips of which are thin, mobile and often a little apart; the upper lip is thicker and more projecting than the lower lip; the teeth are small and even. The chin is long, pointed, and a little projecting at the tip. The head is oval-shaped, and full at the sides.

Those born under the planet Mars have short, square-shaped, but small heads, with high foreheads on which the hair grows far back, leaving the forehead much exposed. Their faces are round, sometimes square at the lower part; and their skin is hard and dry, and of a red colour, especially about the ears, which are long-shaped, set straight, and rather high on the head, and slightly projecting from it. Their eyebrows are short, sometimes stopping midway over the eyes, very bushy, and lying close to the eyes. Between the eyebrows are several short upright wrinkles. The hair is of a red or sandy colour, coarse, and very curly. The beards of men born under Mars are thick, short, and of the same fiery colour as the hair. Their eyes are grey or red-brown, and are large, round, very wide open, and have a fierce and fixed glance; the white of the eye in those born under this fiery planet is often bloodshot. Their mouths are large, but the upper lip is thin and compressed; the lower lip is somewhat thicker than the upper lip. Their noses are short and aquiline, with dilated nostrils. Their chins are projecting and somewhat massive, for the jaw is strongly developed; the cheeks are somewhat hollow, and the cheek-bones very marked.

Those born under the influence of the Moon have round-shaped heads, broad at the temples (showing ideality—the Moon gives imagination). The forehead is full over the eyebrows, but retreats at the top; it is broad and low. The complexion is pale, almost colourless, and the skin is soft. Their hair is fine, soft, of a colourless fairness, no golden tint in it, and it is never very thick. The faces of those born under the dominant influence of the Moon are large and round; the nose is (in proportion to the face) small and short, its tip is rather round than pointed. Their eyes are large, projecting, of a pale blue or grey colour, and have thick, white, and drooping eyelids, fringed with long, straight, pale-brown eyelashes. The eyebrows are of the same colour as the hair, very lightly marked, but joining over the nose. Their mouths are small; but their lips, which are of a pale colour, are full and pouting, and are rarely quite closed. Their teeth are large, and often irregular. Their chins are round, fleshy, and retreating. Their ears are also round, medium size, pale coloured, set in a very sloping direction, and lying close to the head. If born during an eclipse of the Moon, they are sometimes blind.

People born under the influence of Venus have a great resemblance to those born under Jupiter, only their beauty is more feminine. They have the white and delicately tinted skin of the Jupiterians, but it is still softer, finer, and more transparent. They have round faces, the cheek-bones and the jaw-bones are not at all apparent; their cheeks are softly rounded, and generally ornamented with dimples; their foreheads are a delicate. oval, and rather low, and have delicate azure veins at the temples. The eyebrows of persons born under the influence of this beautiful planet are dark, and beautifully marked in long sweeping but very delicate lines, but not meeting over the nose. Their hair is long, thick, soft, undulating, and of a light brown colour. Their noses, which are broad at the root between the eyes, are straight and delicate, not at all pointed, but rather rounded at the tip; * the nostrils are round, but dilated and very flexible. Their eyes are large, clear, humid, and somewhat projecting ; the pupils are large in proportion to the white of the eye, which is limpid and of a clear transparent bluish white ; their eyelids are well-formed, and blue veined. Their mouths are small and of a beautiful red colour ; the lips are full, and especially the lower one, the right side of which is slightly larger than the left. This is a particular Signature of Venus, as is also a small dimple near the corner of the mouth. The teeth are white, small, and evenly set in coral-tinted gums, and the chin is soft and round, and has, like the chin of Jupiterians, a dimple under in it.

Although the signs just described are those given by each planet, as it rarely happens that anyone is born under the influence of one planet only, but generally of two or more, it is rarely that we see a face which gives the pure type of any one planet without admixture. It is for the physiognomist to examine and ascertain which is the dominant planet.

The union of Saturn and Jupiter gives a pale skin without freshness, chestnut hair, and eyes almost black; if the features show the type of Saturn rather than those of Jupiter, then Saturn will be the dominant planet.

The union of Saturn with the Sun would give soft yellow skin, chestnut-coloured hair with a golden tinge in it, and

---

* The noses of those born under Venus are frequently slightly up-turned at the tip ; they are never bent downwards over the lips.

medium-sized dark eyes ; again, the form of features would decide which planet dominated.

Saturn with Mercury would give a pale dark skin, rather long face, quick-moving black eyes; the form of the head, features, and jaw would decide which planet was dominant ; the under-hung jaw is peculiarly Saturnian, and always shows the potent influence of that melancholy planet. The union of Mercury and Saturn (where the former is dominant) gives genius; for Mercury gives bright intelligence, and Saturn concentrative power.

The union of Saturn with Mars gives dark hair with a reddish tint in it, dark eyes and a brown skin with red in the cheeks ; if the nose is short, and there are the short wrinkles between the eyebrows, Mars would be dominant.

The union of Saturn and Venus gives a pale complexion, dark hair, a round face if Venus dominates, and the most beautiful eyes in the world, of dark blue with dark eyelashes, of a soft melancholy brown; the nose is long, but not pinched and pointed, as when Saturn is dominant; the lips, too, are generally beautiful, following the type of Venus. Of course, if Saturn dominates, then Venus only appears in the eyes and tint of the skin.

Saturn with the Moon gives a very dull, colourless skin, beautiful dark eyebrows, and either large dark eyes or light eyes with very dark eyelashes. This combination gives an imaginative and superstitious person. If the Moon is dominant, the face is round and the nose small.

The union of Jupiter with the Sun takes a little of the whiteness from the skin of the Jupiterian, and gives a clear brown skin with colour in the lips and cheeks ; the hair of a golden brown. This conjunction is supposed to give what is called a cast in the eye ; in which case the Sun is the dominant planet, and the eyes would then be of a golden hazel.

The union of Jupiter and Mercury gives a rather dark skin, the face a round oval, and dark grey eyes.

The union of Jupiter and Mars gives a red-coloured skin and large eyes of a blue or grey colour. If Jupiter dominates, the nose will be straight; if Mars, it will be a short aquiline. The union of Venus and Mars is much the same, but the complexion fairer.

The union of Jupiter with the Moon gives a white skin, with a little colour in the cheeks and lips, beautiful eyes of a blue-grey colour, but of which one will be larger and often of a different colour than the other, long brown eyelashes, and well-cut, delicately-marked brown eyebrows; the face will be round; the nose straight, and, if the Moon dominates, somewhat small,—if Jupiter, of medium size.

The union of Jupiter and Venus gives beautiful light brown hair, fine and silky rather than thick, soft brown eyes, long lashes, a beautiful mouth, and a round and dimpled chin. Should Venus be dominant, there will be dimples also either about the lips or in the cheeks.

The union of the Sun and Mercury gives a honey-coloured skin, middle-sized eyes of a light brown, with a quick and penetrating glance, straight, delicate, mobile features ; and if Mercury should be the dominant planet, the forehead will be prominent, the lips parted, and the chin pointed. This union gives a bright intelligence and eloquence of speech.

The union of the Sun and the Moon is rare: it gives much beauty ; straight, regular features, an oval face, light eyes, and hair of a pale gold colour, delicately-marked eyebrows, and long silken lashes, a shade darker than the hair ; the skin is of a pale ivory-white, and the mouth is beautifully formed.

The union of the Moon with Mercury gives an oval face, light brown hair, and large grey eyes with brown flecks in them. The union of the Moon with Mars gives a round face, aquiline nose, and hair of a red fairness : or, in a man, the hair will be of the colourless fairness of the Moon and the beard and moustaches.

The union of Venus with the Sun gives brilliant beauty, a beautiful complexion, hair of a golden brown or rich chestnut, full, bright brown eyes with long eyelashes, delicately-formed nose, and a beautiful mouth. People born under this junction have much charm of manner, but they are not very constant; for, although they have much tenderness, they are of the ardent artistic nature, which, from its very susceptibility, cannot be expected to be as constant as those who are less impressionable; they are people of quick rather than deep feelings; they love readily, but as readily forget.

"Women born under the double influence of Venus and the Sun," says an old Italian writer on the subject, are " loving, lovely, and beloved."

CHAPTER XXXIV.

PATHOGNOMY.

THAT branch of the science of physiognomy which is called pathognomy is the knowledge of the signs of the passions, that is, of character in motion. Character at rest is more especially shown by the form of the solid parts of the head and face, by the colouring and texture of the skin, hair, eyes, and eyebrows, and by the appearance of the movable parts when at rest. Character impassioned manifests itself by the movable parts when in motion; the former shows what persons are in general, the latter what they become at particular moments; and in this part of the study of physiognomy the observer has to combat the arts of dissimulation. There are few physiognomists but must confess that they have been occasionally deceived in their judgments of truth and untruth, honesty and dishonesty; but on most occasions these errors have their root in the fact that the physiognomist has made his observations at the wrong moment. A liar is never *less* capable of deceiv-

ing than at the first moment, before his powers of deception
are set in motion: thus the detection of dishonesty of
purpose is, at the same time, both difficult and easy;
difficult so long as the deceiver imagines he is observed,
easy when he is unaware that he is being judged. Besides,
by looking at the person under judgment before awaking
his powers (if he have them) of deception by accusing him,
we avoid falling into the error of confusing timidity with
guilt. Nervousness, and not dissimulation, may often
make a person who relates a circumstance to another unable
to look that other in the face, and we are thus often apt to
suspect insincerity where there is only weakness; and
though weakness and timidity are often the root of untruth,
they are not necessarily so. Not only in the study of insincerity, but in all physiognomical observations there are
certain precious moments for judgment, as for instance,
the moment of unforeseen, and therefore unprepared, meeting, the moments of welcome and of farewell, the moment
preceding the impetuous burst of passion, the moment of
its subsiding—especially when the outburst has been interrupted by the sudden entrance of a person whose opinion is
of importance, when the powers of dissimulation will be
displayed,—the moments of compassion, of love, of envy,
and of friendship; the moments especially of the greatest
degree of tranquillity and of passion, when the man is
entirely himself or entirely forgets himself,—should tell
the student of physiognomy what the man is and what he
is not,—what he can and what he cannot become.

The passion of *jealousy* wrinkles the forehead with many
complex lines; the eyebrows sink very much, especially in
the middle (this is the case in a paroxysm of jealousy, even
when the eyebrows are naturally arched), and they are
knitted closely together over the bridge of the nose. The
eyeballs are half hidden by the lowering brows, and the
light of the eye has a fierce, lurid glow. The nostrils are
distended, the lines more sharply defined than when the

face is in repose, and they appear to be drawn backwards towards the cheeks, which are wrinkled in broken lines. The mouth is open in the centre, showing the teeth, but is compressed at the corners, which are much drawn downwards; and, where the paroxysm is very strong, there is a twitching, spasmodic motion of the lips. The muscles of the jaw appear to sink; the colour of the face in paroxysms of jealousy in those of the choleric temperament is inflamed; in those of the bilious or artistic temperament it is yellow; in those of the melancholic it is greenish white; whilst in those of the lymphatic temperament it is deadly pale. The lips in all temperaments under this passion are always livid.

In the passion of *anger* the eyebrows are very much raised, yet knitted together; the eyes (especially in those of the choleric temperament, where Mars is the dominant planet) become almost red in colour, the eyeball staring and sparkling with a sort of scintillating light. The horizontal lines across the forehead are deeply furrowed, and the short perpendicular wrinkles between the eyes very strongly accentuated; the nostrils are fiercely distended, and the wings of the nose have a quivering movement. The lips are pressed against one another, and the under one, rising over the upper lip, leaves the corners of the mouth a little open. The more this last indication is accentuated the more savage and cruel is the anger; the face is generally red (sometimes with Saturnians, livid), and patches of disturbed colour appear on the brow.

Love.—In this passion the eyebrows are drawn a little together, but yet are slightly raised, at least do not at all droop over the eyes, which are fully opened and very liquid, and rest with a soft yet fixed gaze on the person loved. The wings of the nose, and with them the nostrils,—which are palpitating,—rise upwards towards the eyes, the mouth falls into soft curves with the lips somewhat apart, and the cheeks flush and grow pale with a soft and ever-varying colour.

In *Scorn* the forehead is somewhat wrinkled, but not so fiercely so as in anger; the eyebrows are very much knitted together, and brought low next the nose, but at the other end they rise very much. The eyebrows show scorn more than any other feature : hence the word superciliousness (from super-cilium, the eyebrow). The eyelids droop somewhat over the eyes, and the eyeball is very much in the centre of the eye, which has a cold light in it ; the nostrils rise, making wrinkles in the cheeks, sometimes extending from the wings of the nose to the lower eye-bones. The mouth closes in a hard way, with the under lip protruding, which causes the corners of the mouth to take a downward curve. The chin is advanced, and the head tossed back.

In *Astonishment* or *Surprise* the eyebrows are raised, the eyes very much opened, and the eyeball very much raised, so that there is a space of white left between it and the lower line of the eye ; the mouth is half open.

Admiration.—In this passion the eyebrow rises, the eye opens a little more than usual both above and below, so that the pupil of the eye is equidistant from both the lines of the eye. The lips are generally parted with a half-smile.

Attention.—In this state of mind the eyebrows sink and approach the sides of the nose; the lips are slightly apart ; the head a little bent forward, but remaining fixed in that position for some moments.

Veneration, which is the result of admiration and esteem, shows itself by a downward bending face, the eyebrows drooping also ; the eyes are almost shut, and the mouth quite shut, but in softly curved lines.

Hope is indicated by a smooth brow; eyebrows raised ; eyes more than naturally open, the eyeball, almost aflame with brightness, places itself in the middle of the eye ; the nostrils expand, and have an upward movement ; the mouth half opens, and the cheeks flush with sudden and vivid colour.

In *Compassion* the forehead is calm, but the eyebrows sink over the eyes as in sorrow ; compassion is sadness for another's griefs. The wings of the nose are gently raised, the nostrils somewhat expanded, and the mouth slightly open, with the upper lip raised and slightly projecting.

In *Envy* the forehead is intersected with many lines ; the eyebrows are lowering ; the eyes have a restless, uneasy motion ; the cheeks are sunken and lined ; the lips are drawn tightly over the teeth, and have a spasmodic, uneasy motion.

In *Despair* the eyebrows descend so as almost to hide the eyes, which are half-closed, with the eyeballs fixed with a strong expression, and without any light in them. The nose seems sunk down, whilst the muscles of the upper part of the cheeks are swelled and drawn down towards the jaws ; the mouth is drawn backwards, is more open at the sides than the centre ; and the lower lip is loose, flaccid, and drooping.

In *Pain* (whether mental or physical) the forehead is intersected with lines ; the eyebrows are drawn near to each other over the nose, but rise towards the middle ; a deep line is formed from the wings of the nose to the middle of the cheek ; the mouth half opens, and is drawn back towards the ears at the corners ; the colour generally leaves both cheeks and lips, which become almost livid.

In *Sorrow* the eyebrows rise at their starting-point near the nose, but droop again suddenly over the eyes ; the eye-lids are swelled, and half cover the eyes, and the colouring around the eyes and eyelids is livid ; the nostrils are drawn downwards ; the mouth is half open, but the corners droop very much ; the head is bent on one side ; the face is of a leaden colour, and the lips are pale.

In *Joy* the forehead is serene ; the eyebrows are without motion, and take only their natural curves ; the eye is open, and brilliant with light ; the corners of the mouth turn up a little and a bright flush of colour suffuses the whole face.

The manner of carrying the head is very indicative of character. The head, bent forward, shows impulse, but not much will-power—one who would be swayed by the opinions of others—and, if with this manner of carrying the head the eyes are raised, it shows hopefulness and enthusiasm of character. The head very much thrown back indicates self-confidence, pride, and ambition. When the head is held perfectly straight, and is erect without being either thrown back or bent forward, it indicates a person of courage and determination, possessing much self-command and force of character. A head bent to one side shows an impressionable and sensuous person somewhat vain and affected. The head bent down—especially if the eyes are also fixed on the ground—shows a melancholy, thoughtful, and unhopeful nature.

CHAPTER XXXV.

CONCERNING THE MOLES OF THE FACE AND THEIR REFERENCE TO THOSE ON THE BODY.

ALL moles are the result of the influences of the planets, or of the sign of the Zodiac rising at birth. The moles which are given by Saturn are black; those by Jupiter are of a purple-brown colour; those by the Sun, yellow; by Venus, light brown; Mercury, honey-coloured; by the Moon, of a bluish-white.

A mole on the right side of the forehead, just beneath or on the line of Saturn (see plate to chapter 25), indicates another on the right side of the breast. This mole shows to a man, if yellow, that he will have good fortune in sowing, tilling the earth, or building; if red, he will have luck all through his life, by his courage and force of character ; if black, his condition will be changeable ; if the mole is purple, he will be advanced to be the head of his family. In a woman a mole in this position shows fortune by inheritance or legacies ; but if black in colour she will not live long.

A mole on the left side of the forehead on the Line of Saturn indicates another on the left side of the back, and shows to a man imprisonment and disaster ; if honey-coloured, his trouble comes from women ; if red, from quarrels with enemies ; if black, he will be unfortunate all his life. To a woman it foretells that she will live out of her own country, and if black she will be a widow.

A mole in the middle of the forehead on the Line of Saturn shows another in the middle of the stomach : and foretells to a man, if it should be black, that he will suffer much ill-fortune for the sake of women ; if red, he will get some pleasure out of his troubles with them, and if yellow, he will rejoice through women ; if of a pale-bluish colour and raised, he will be much beloved of women. To a woman, of whatever colour it may appear, it indicates that she is of a very luxurious nature, and will suffer from her own folly as regards men.

A mole on the right side of the forehead on the Line of Jupiter shows another on the right side over the liver, and indicates, to a man, good fortune in marriage, long life, and large possessions ; but if black, he will not be quite so lucky as regards marriage. To a woman it shows, whatever its colour, good fortune in all that concerns her.

A mole on the left side of the forehead on the Line of Jupiter shows another on the left side of the stomach, and indicates, to a man, love of material enjoyments, especially if it be of a purple colour; if honey-coloured, he is not so sensual. To a woman such a mole shows her to be impudent, and quite regardless of her own honour.

A mole in the middle of the Line of Jupiter shows another in the middle of the breast, and indicates that a man is of a harsh nature; if red, he is furious in temper; if black, he is singularly unfortunate in all his undertakings; but if raised, and of a bluish colour, he is less unlucky. To a woman it indicates that she is foolish, prattling, and idle.

A mole on the right side of the Line of Mars shows another on the right arm, and indicates, if red, military distinction; if honey-coloured, good fortune with horses and other cattle; if black, danger from four-footed beasts; if much raised and somewhat red, it shows good fortune in all things relating to fire. To a woman this mole shows a rich husband, full of kindness and complacency.

A mole on the left side of the Line of Mars indicates another on the left arm, and shows a man to be of a quarrelsome nature; if black, he is treacherous, and loses much by four-footed beasts and by horse-racing; if purple or yellow, he is involved in quarrels about women. Such a mole, whatever its colour, shows a woman to be very unfortunate in her love affairs and likely to be betrayed by her female friends.

A mole in the middle of the Line of Mars indicates another on the left side of the belly; if red, the man is likely to be guilty of manslaughter, and if any other colour he is sensual. To a woman this mole shows vanity, and, if black, she is likely to be the cause of the death of some friend, but more by mischance than by design.

A mole on the right side of the forehead on the Line of the Sun indicates another on the right breast, and intimates, to a man, of whatever colour but black, riches and honours; if black, his good fortune will not be so great and will come, not from his own merits, but from the exertions of friends. To a woman it shows an affluence of the goods of fortune; but if black she will have to be very subservient to her husband.

A mole on the left side of the forehead on the Line of the Moon denotes another on the left breast and shows, to a man, that he will travel much and have good fortune in merchandise, whatever may be its colour. To a woman it shows many travels after marriage.

A mole in the middle of the forehead between the Lines of the Sun and the Moon shows another in the middle of the belly ; and indicates, to a man, that he will be a great orator, but yet given to lasciviousness of all kinds. To a woman it shows that she will be insatiable in her vanity and luxuriousness, and that she will incur much contempt thereby.

A mole in the middle of the Line of Venus, just above the bridge of the nose, indicates another on the middle of the stomach, just above the navel ; and shows, to a man, of whatever colour it may be, good fortune in marriage, and the friendship of women of high position in the world. To a woman it indicates good fortune in marriage ; but if black she will have but a short life.

A mole on the Line of Mercury on the root of the nose indicates another on the middle of the stomach, just below the navel, and indicates, to a man, whatever may be its colour, that he has a pleasant wit and that he will, by his ingenuity, make his fortune. To a woman its shows brilliant success in the world, long life and success in marriage, except it should appear black in colour, when she will be in much danger, by reason of the malice of pretended friends, who will advance false accusations against her.

A mole on the right side of the temples declares another on the right loin ; and signifies, to a man, of whatever colour it may appear, long life, and a considerable portion of the goods of fortune. To a woman it indicates happy marriage ; but if black, she will bury her first husband, yet will also live happily with the second.

A mole on the left side of the temples shows another on the left loin ; and this signifies, to a man, long and perilous illness, whatever may be its colour ; if black, he dies before middle age. To a woman it shows the probability of a violent death.

N 2

A mole near the right ear shows another on the right side of the belly, not low down; and signifies, to a man, a blow on the head, some accident, to that ear, whereby he may lose his hearing ; if black, these evils are the more to be apprehended. To a woman it shows the loss of those things she most values.

A mole on the left ear shows another on the left side, low down on the belly. This mole indicates to a man persecution from enemies. If it be of a red colour, that he will go near to committing murder by reason of women ; if black, or even honey-coloured, it is still of evil indication, and shows quarrels and violent death. To a woman, let it be of whatsoever colour, it shows that she will be the cause of death to some one ; let her, therefore, shun to meddle with poison. A mole on the tip of the nose shows another on the lowest part of the body, and indicates, whatever its colour, a short life by reason of indulgence in sensual practices. To a woman it has much the same unfortunate indication, and shows the chance of having her throat cut by reason of the jealousy of her lovers.

A mole on the right cheek shows another on the right hip; and indicates to a man that he will have great charm of manner towards women, and be much beloved by them; this, whatever its colour. To a woman also it shows happy marriage and that she will be vehemently beloved.

A mole on the left cheek shows another on the left hip ; and indicates to a man a wandering existence, and short life ; if black, he dies by violence. To a woman it threatens sharp and hard fortune, especially in love matters.

A mole on the right side or corner of the mouth shows another at the right side of the lower part of the spine ; and shows to a man that he shall much increase his wealth by reason of his own sagacity ; but if honey-coloured, his good fortune will come by women. To a woman such a mole shows she will abound in wealth, and be vehemently beloved ; if black in colour, with all these advantages, she will yet suffer from the scandal of envious women friends.

A mole on the left side of the mouth indicates another on the left side of the base of the spine; and shows to a man that he will be entangled with a woman he cannot marry, and have illegitimate children. To a woman it shows a likelihood of the same disgrace.

A mole in the middle of the upper lip shows another on the lowest part of the body; and indicates to a man that he shall be miserable from various perils, but above all, from women. To a woman this mole shows sickness and weakness from internal diseases.

A mole beneath the middle of the under lip shows another on the knee; and indicates to a man that he will undertake long and perilous journeys, by reason of which he shall see many strange countries; if honey-coloured, he will gain wealth from strangers and marry a rich foreign wife. Such a mole shows a woman to be thoughtless and likely to marry a foreigner, and live much out of her own country.

A mole upon the middle of the chin shows another upon the right foot; and indicates to a man that he shall have good fortune through women. To a woman it shows happy marriage, but worry from her children.

A mole on the right side of the chin shows another on the right haunch; and indicates to a man that he will be of great intellectual capacity; if black, he will be a searcher in occult matters. In a woman it shows good fortune, happy marriage, and long life, whatsoever may be its colour.

A mole on the left side of the chin shows another on the left haunch; and indicates to a man inconstant fortune, much worry of mind and bodily discomfort. In a woman it shows ill-health, and if of a pale bluish colour, danger by water.

CHAPTER XXXVI.

CONCERNING THE MOLES WHICH HAVE NO CORRESPONDING MOLES ON THE FACE.

A MOLE on the right side of the throat shows to a man great wit but short life, whatever may be its colour. To a woman it indicates a reasonably happy life, but danger and pain from childbirth.

A mole on the left side of the throat threatens a man with dangerous falls from horses or from high places. To a woman the same, and, should the mole be of a pale colour, danger by water.

A mole at the nape of the neck indicates to either man or woman great danger of untimely death by water.

A mole in the midst of the throat—that is on the gullet— shows to a man much danger of death by strangulation or hanging. To a woman peril in sickness ; and if the mole should be black in colour, she dies.

A mole immediately under the right breast shows to a man that he will be lucky in agriculture. To a woman, that she shall receive inheritance from the dead ; if black, her father is killed by accident.

A mole under the left breast shows a man to be of a malignant nature and furious of temper, but strong in love. To a woman it indicates great constancy, and suffering by reason of that constancy.

A mole on the right foot shows to a man that he will be clever in acquiring foreign languages, and that he will be a great student of occult matters. To a woman it promises a fortunate and happy long life ; if black, this good fortune is somewhat chequered with troubles.

A mole on the left foot denotes a man to be rash, and of an evil and vagabond disposition. To a woman it shows much care and trouble and, if black, danger in travelling.

If the second toe in a foot should stretch out much beyond the great toe, it shows, to either man or woman, riches and a happy and prosperous life.

A mole on the knee, whether left or right, predicts, to either man or woman, long and various journeys. Such persons will marry entirely for their own fancy, probably foreigners, and will be very fortunate in their marriages.

A mole on the calf of the right leg shows to a man that by his own ingenuity and learning he shall attain a high position; if black, he will receive some sorrow from women; but if the mole should appear *raised* he marries a lovely person—has only one wife, and lives happily. To a woman it shows a fortunate, good, and rich husband, and that she will have many children and live long.

A mole on the lowest part of the body shows to a man that he is of a very luxurious nature, and that he shall be enriched by marriage. A woman having this mole is rather sensuous, but—on the whole—faithful to her husband.

A mole on the right shoulder shows a man to be fortunate in his undertakings; if red, he has a large fortune with his wife. To a woman it indicates a marriage above her expectations; but if black, she buries her first husband and marries again.

A mole on the left shoulder predicts to a man much worry in money matters. To a woman it shows a life of continual anxiety, and humiliation by reason of her own vanity. If black in colour, she suffers some serious disgrace from her own conduct.

CHAPTER XXXVII.

CONCERNING THE MARKS GIVEN AT BIRTH BY THE SIGNS OF THE ZODIAC.

By a knowledge of the signature given by the signs of the Zodiac, when rising at birth, we may sometimes ascertain the hour of nativity, or, at any rate, go near enough to it to be able to work out the horoscope after a fashion, supposing the exact date to be impossible of attainment.

A person born when the first part of the sign Aries is rising will have a small raised mole amongst the hairs of the head; if the second part of the sign happened to be rising at the birth, the mark or mole would be raised in the form of a pea or wart, and would be seen on the forehead; if the third part of the sign arose at birth, the mark would appear below the mouth, or towards the chin. Those persons having these marks of Aries on any of the parts described will generally be found to have the mark of Mars in the lowest part of the body, also in the form of a raised mole or wart.

When Taurus is rising at a birth, the native bears a mark in the front of the throat; sometimes in the form of a raspberry or red-coloured mole, which mark is always ill in its effects. Should the second part of the sign Taurus have been rising at the nativity, the person will have the mark at the side of the throat. If the third, the same mark will appear on the nape of the neck, but then it will be more raised than the two former moles.

Those born under Gemini have their marks in the arms. If the first part of the sign arose at birth, they bear its mark on the right arm, near the shoulder; if the second on the same part of the left arm; and if the third part of the sign arises at birth, the native bears the mark on the right arm, but below the elbow, and generally near the wrist.

When the sign Cancer is in the ascendant, the mark is on the upper part of the right breast in the form of a flower or a hare's foot, of a whitish colour, and commonly having a hair or two springing from it. In the older days this mark was supposed to be an evidence of witchcraft in a woman, any many poor creatures have lost their lives for this, Those born under the second part of the sign Cancer have the mark lower down on the breast; and when the third part of Cancer is rising at a birth, the sign is nearly under the breast.

When Leo is in the ascendant at birth, the sign is on the left breast; and, in the same manner, if the sign appears high up on the breast it indicates that the first part of the sign was ascending; if near the middle, the second; and if on one side, towards the left armpit, the third part of the sign must have been ascending at birth.

In nativities under Virgo the mark is on the upper part of the stomach, that is—between the two breasts, when the first part of the sign ascends; those born when the second part is rising have the mark near the navel; and those when the third part is rising quite low down on the stomach. Those that are thus marked are very inconstant. The moles given by Virgo are flat, and of a reddish colour.

When Libra is in the ascendant, the marks are raised like warts, and are small, soft, and hairy; when the first part of the sign is rising the mark is near the loins; when the second, towards the centre of the stomach; and the third part of the sign throws the mark to quite the lower part of the body.

Those born under Sagittarius have the mark of the sign in the thighs; and these moles are raised like bulbs, and are very big. When the first part of the sign is rising, the mark is on the right thigh; when the second part is rising, on the left thigh; and those who have the third part of Sagittarius rising at their birth are so marked on the right haunch.

Those born under Capricornus have the marks on the knees, which marks are quite flat. When the first part is rising, the mark is on the right knee; when the second, on the left; and when the third, the mole is under the knee.

It will be remembered that the sign Aquarius governs the legs; therefore those who are born with this sign ascending have the mark of it (which is a long-shaped mole) on the right leg (this mark shows extreme inconstancy); when the second part of the sign is rising at birth, the mark is on the left leg; when the third part of the sign is rising at birth, persons are marked with this oval-shaped mole in the calf or muscles of the leg.

The sign Pisces, or the Fishes, governs the feet; therefore those who have this sign in their ascendant are marked on the feet. Those born under the first part have the marks (which are ordinary flat moles) on the right foot; those under the second, on the left; and those on the third, on the soles of the feet or on the heels. These last are called the royal marks; they are large moles inclining to red, and those who are marked in those places are assured of honours and dignities.

Alfridary for a Diurnal Nativity.

		Years.	Days.			Years	Days.
☉	—	1	156	♄	—	41	208
☉	♀	2	313	♄	♃	43	52
☉	☿	4	104	♄	♂	44	260
☉	☽	5	260	♄	☉	46	104
☉	♄	7	52	♄	♀	47	113
☉	♃	8	208	♄	☿	49	156
☉	♂	10	—	♄	☽	51	—
♀	—	11	52	♃	—	52	260
♀	☿	12	104	♃	♂	54	156
♀	☽	13	156	♃	☉	56	52
♀	♄	14	208	♃	♀	57	313
♀	♃	15	260	♃	☿	59	208
♀	♂	16	313	♃	☽	61	104
♀	☉	18	—	♃	♄	63	—
☿	—	19	313	♂	♃	64	—
☿	☽	21	260	♂	☉	65	—
☿	♄	23	208	♂	♀	66	—
☿	♃	25	156	♂	☿	67	—
☿	♂	27	104	♂	☽	68	—
☿	☉	29	52	♂	♄	69	—
☿	♀	31	—	♂	♃	70	—
☽	—	32	104	☊	—	73	—
☽	♄	33	208	☋	—	75	—
☽	♃	34	313	☉	—	76	156
☽	♂	36	52	☉	♀	77	313
☽	☉	37	156	☉	☿	79	104
☽	♀	38	26	☉	☽	80	260
☽	☿	40	—	☉	♄	82	52

Alfridary for a Nocturnal Nativity.

		Years.	Days.			Years.	Days
☽	—	1	104	☉	—	40	156
☽	♄	2	208	☉	♀	41	313
☽	♃	3	313	☉	☿	43	104
☽	♂	5	52	☉	☽	44	260
☽	☉	6	156	☉	♄	46	52
☽	♀	7	260	☉	♃	47	208
☽	☿	9	—	☉	♂	49	—
♄	—	10	208	♀	—	50	52
♄	♃	12	52	♀	☿	51	104
♄	♂	13	260	♀	☽	52	156
♄	☉	15	104	♀	♄	53	208
♄	♀	16	313	♀	♃	54	260
♄	☿	18	156	♀	♂	55	313
♄	☽	20	—	♀	☉	57	—
♃	—	21	260	☿	—	58	313
♃	♂	23	156	☿	☽	60	260
♃	☉	25	52	☿	♄	62	208
♃	♀	26	313	☿	♃	64	156
♃	☿	28	208	☿	♂	66	104
♃	☽	30	104	☿	☉	68	52
♃	♄	32	—	☿	♀	70	—
♂	—	33	—	☊	—	73	—
♂	☉	34	—	☋	—	74	—
♂	♀	35	—	☽	—	76	104
♂	☿	36	—	☽	♄	77	208
♂	☽	37	—	☽	♃	78	313
♂	♄	38	—	☽	♂	80	25
♂	♃	39	—	☉	☉	81	260

CHAPTER XXXVIII.

CONCERNING ALFRIDARIES.

THIS word is taken from the Greek, and refers to the certain time or number of years of the several planets which in those years dispense their benevolence or malignity according to their natures.

It will be observed from the plate at the beginning of this chapter, that each of the planets has his Alfridary, one after the other,—and in this table will be seen the number of years in which each planet more particularly governs the life.

In all diurnal nativities the Sun begins the first Alfridary, and has ten years of government; Venus succeeds, having eight years of Alfridary; then Mercury, who has seven years of government. After him the Moon rules the existence for seven years; then Saturn for the same number; Jupiter succeeds him for seven years; afterwards Mars dominates the existence for another seven years.

Those that are born in the night have their first Alfridaric years from the Moon, which are nine, followed by those of Saturn, who has seven years; after him Mars is dominant for seven years; then the Sun for the same number of years; succeeded by Venus and Mercury, each only seven years.

The years of an Alfridary are seventy-five—namely, the Sun, ten; the Moon, nine; Saturn, eleven; Jupiter, twelve; Mars, seven; Venus, eight; Mercury, thirteen; the Dragon's Head, three; the Dragon's Tail, two. These two last have their Alfridaric years separate from the others, and they are those which exceed the seventy years of life, which are weak and feeble. For these signs are not (as we have seen) planets, but only symbols of a place in the Zodiac representing the Moon's north and south nodes.

It will be noticed in these tables that, after the years

of seventy-five, the Sun in a diurnal nativity, and the
Moon in a nocturnal nativity, take up again their government, as at the beginning, of the life. These tables are
interesting as shadowing forth the dates and the nature of
the events *likely* to occur during the life of the native.
Thus, in a diurnal nativity, we see Venus ruling with
Jupiter at fifteen, and with the Sun at eighteen. This signifies love and marriage as likely to come into the life
at somewhere about those years; whilst, in a nocturnal
nativity, the strongest marriage influences (that of Jupiter
and Venus) do not appear till about twenty-six.* It will be
remembered that those born under the Sun marry early,
whilst those in whose nativity the Moon is powerful
generally marry rather late than early. In either nativity,
when Saturn comes up, sorrows by death, sickness, and
loss of money may be expected; whilst, when Mars is
powerful, evils of a strong and sudden nature appear, such
as accidents, sudden deaths, quarrels, and contentions of a
vexatious character.

Those born under the Moon have very often serious
and passionate loves quite late in life; this is accounted for
in some measure by the fact that Venus has seven years of
government in a nocturnal nativity from the age of fifty to
fifty-seven. The age of forty-four, in a diurnal nativity,
would be likely to bring about some misfortune during
that year of the native's life; *both the infortunes*, Saturn
and Mars, being then powerful. The same thing occurs in
a nocturnal nativity at the age of thirteen, from which age
up to twenty there is not much good fortune; it will be
remembered that the latter part of the life of a person born
at night is generally much happier and altogether more
fortunate than the earlier years of existence.

---

* It is true that, in a nocturnal alfridary, we see Venus ruling at 16,
but *only in conjunction with Saturn*, so the love would not be fortunate,
and it is remarkable that the early loves of persons born under the
dominant influence of the Moon are rarely happy.

CHAPTER XXXIX.

CONCERNING THE MYSTICAL WHEEL OF PYTHAGORAS AND THE METHODS OF WORKING IT.

THIS mystical figure is copied from a work in old French on Chiromancy and Geomancy, compiled by the Sieur de Peruchio, and published at Paris in 1657.

Arithmancy, or divination by numbers, on which the working of this figure depends, was much practised in various ways during the middle ages ; and much confidence appears to have been placed in this wheel of Pythagoras, which resolves questions by a species of sortilegy by numbers, in which the result depends upon the unfettered agency of the mind and will, or the serious intent to know any difficult thing. The wheel is said by the old-world writers to be able " to resolve all questions on all matters upon the result of which the querent desires information, whether of the past, present, or future."

Concerning the method of working it, the Sieur de Peruchio gives the following explanations :—

The wheel, it will be perceived, is divided into four equal parts, the upper part of which contains the numbers which are *fortunate*, and the lower half those which are *unfortunate*. Around the wheel are seen the letters of the Alphabet, above which are placed certain correspond-ing numbers, which are required in the calculations. The numbers in the right half of the wheel represent *long time*, that is—that the event about which the question is asked will be some time before it comes to pass; whilst those in the left half of the wheel signify *short* time, that is—that the event about which the querent is anxious will be soon accomplished."

The following table of the mystical numbers repre-senting the planets, and also those belonging to the days of the week which each planet governs, is of much importance in working the wheel :—

PLANETS.			DAYS OF THE WEEK.		
♄	Saturn	55'	Saturday	45
♃	Jupiter	78	Thursday	31
♂	Mars	39	Tuesday	52
☉	Sun	34	Sunday	106
♀	Venus	45	Friday	68
☿	Mercury ...	114	Wednesday	102
☽	Moon	45	Monday	52

These several numbers attributed to the days of the week, as well as those of the planet ruling the day, are of very ancient origin, and are, probably, as well as the wheel itself, a relic of former *traditional* foreknowledge by lots and numbers.

The following table gives the numbers to be chosen by chance (as will be explained further on) in working the questions :—

1	11	22	28	29
6	2	12	23	30
15	7	3	13	24
19	16	8	4	14
25	20	17	9	5
27	26	21	18	10

The inquirer, whilst thinking *earnestly* upon the matter he wishes resolved by the wheel, must choose a number out of the above Table. This is better done with the eyes closed, and the number pricked out with a pin, so that there may be no premeditation in the choice. To this number, thus chosen, the inquirer must add the number answering to the first letter of his first name, which number is seen in the wheel itself where the numbers are above the letters of the alphabet. To this number must be added the number of the day of the week on which the question is asked, and of the planet ruling that day. Then add all these numbers together, and divide the sum by 30 as often as it can be done. Then look for that number which is the remainder in the inner circle of the wheel, observing in what part of the wheel it falls. Should there happen to be no remainder, then the number 30 must be looked for. If the question propounded is whether anything about to be undertaken will succeed or not, if the number falls in the upper part of the wheel the thing will succeed ; if, on the contrary, it appears in the *lower* half, then the matter will have an evil issue. In any question where time is concerned, as how long or how short shall be the matter in hand before being accomplished, observe that one-half of the wheel which represents short and long time, as before explained, and so, whether for good or evil, shall the business quickly or slowly come to pass.

All questions are thus to be asked but *one*, and that is, whether a sick person shall recover or die ; in which case, after proceeding to add the numbers of the Christian name, the day of the week, and the planet, the number representing the Moon's age on the day the question is asked must also be added ; for example, if a person whose name is Salome asks on a Wednesday, 20th day of the Moon, if a sick friend should live or die, and chooses from the Table the number of 23, the matter would be worked thus :—

Number chosen	23
Number answering to the letter S . . .	9
Number answering to Wednesday . . .	102
Number answering to the planet Mercury .	114
Number of the age of the Moon . . .	20
	268

This, divided by 30, leaves 28 remainder, which will be found to fall in the unfortunate half on the wheel, and denotes long sickness and death.

There are certain days, however, which are evil days, on which no question should be asked of the wheel of Pythagoras. These days are as follow : —

Of January, the 3rd, 4th, 5th, 9th, and 11th.

Of February, the 7th, 13th, 17th, and 19th.

Of March, the 13th, 15th, and 16th.

Of April, the 5th and 14th.

Of May, the 8th and 14th.

June has but one ill day, which is the 6th.

July has two, the 16th and the 19th.

August has also only two, the 8th and 16th.

September has three, the 1st, 15th, and 16th.

October has only one ill day, which is the 16th.

November has two, the 15th and 16th.

December has three, the 6th, 7th, and 11th.

The above is a very old tradition, and in mediæval ages these days were universally shunned as "ruled by evil influences." In conclusion, those consulting the wheel of Pythagoras are advised not to ask more than one question on the same day, and to refrain from all gibing, sporting, or jesting, and—above all—from all unbelief whilst making use of this mystical wheel in order to know the truth.

ENVOY.

Go—little book—and teach the present age something of the wisdom bequeathed us by the Past.

PRINTED BY
SPOTTISWOODE AND CO., NEW-STREET SQUARE
LONDON

Ludgate Hill; and Paternoster Square,
London,
December, 1890.

KEGAN PAUL, TRENCH, TRÜBNER, & CO.'S PUBLICATIONS.

NOTE.—*Books are arranged in alphabetical order under the names or pseudonyms of author, translator, or editor. Biographies "by the author of" are placed under the name of the subject. Anonymous works and "selections" will be found under the first word of the title. The letters I.S.S. denote that the work forms a volume of the International Scientific Series.*

ABEL, Carl, LINGUISTIC ESSAYS. Post 8vo (*Trübner's Oriental Series*), 9s.
SLAVIC AND LATIN: lectures on comparative lexicography. Post 8vo, 5s.

ABERCROMBY, Hon. Ralph, WEATHER : a popular exposition of the nature of weather changes from day to day, with 96 illustrations. 2nd edition, crown 8vo, 5s. [I.S.S.]

ABRAHAMS, L. B., MANUAL OF SCRIPTURE HISTORY FOR JEWISH SCHOOLS AND FAMILIES, with map. Crown 8vo, 1s. 6d.

ADAMS, Estelle, SEA SONG AND RIVER RHYME, FROM CHAUCER TO TENNYSON, with 12 etchings. Large crown 8vo, 10s. 6d.

ADAMS, W. H. Davenport, THE WHITE KING, or Charles the First and men and women, life and manners, &c., in the first half of the 17th century. 2 vols. 8vo, 21s.

ÆSCHYLUS. SEVEN PLAYS, translated by Prof. Lewis Campbell. Crown 8vo, 7s. 6d.

AHN, F., GRAMMAR OF THE DUTCH LANGUAGE. 12mo, 3s. 6d.
GRAMMAR OF THE GERMAN LANGUAGE. Crown 8vo, 3s. 6d.
METHOD OF LEARNING GERMAN. 12mo, 3s. Key, 8d.
GERMAN AND ENGLISH CONVERSATIONS, or Vade Mecum for English Travellers. 12mo, 1s. 6d.
METHOD OF LEARNING FRENCH, first and second courses. 12mo, 3s.; separately, 1s. 6d. each.
METHOD OF LEARNING FRENCH, third course. 12mo, 1s. 6d.
METHOD OF LEARNING ITALIAN. 12mo, 3s. 6d.
LATIN GRAMMAR FOR BEGINNERS. 12mo, 3s.

ALABASTER, H., THE WHEEL OF THE LAW : Buddhism illustrated from Siamese sources. 8vo, 14s.

ALBÊRÛNÎ'S INDIA : an account of the religion, philosophy, literature, geography, chronology, astronomy, customs, laws, and astrology of India, about A.D. 1030. Arabic text, edited by Prof. E. SACHAU. 4to, £3. 3s.
ENGLISH TRANSLATION, edited by Prof. E. SACHAU. 2 vols. post 8vo (*Trübner's Oriental Series*), 36s.

A 2

ALEXANDER, Major-Gen. *G. G.*, CONFUCIUS, THE GREAT TEACHER. Crown 8vo, 6*s.*

ALEXANDER, *William, D.D., Bishop of Derry*, ST. AUGUSTINE'S HOLIDAY, and other poems. Crown 8vo, 6*s.*

THE GREAT QUESTION, and other sermons. Crown 8vo, 6*s.*

ALEXANDER, S., MORAL ORDER AND PROGRESS : an analysis of ethical conceptions. Post 8vo, 14*s.* [*Philosophical Library.*]

ALLEN, Grant, COLOUR-SENSE : its origin and development. An essay in comparative psychology. Post 8vo, 10*s.* 6*d.* [*Philosophical Library.*]

ALLIBONE, S. A., DICTIONARY OF ENGLISH LITERATURE AND BRITISH AND AMERICAN AUTHORS, from the earliest accounts to the latter half of the 19th century. 3 vols. royal 8vo, £5. 8*s.*

AMATEUR MECHANIC'S WORKSHOP, The : plain and concise directions for the manipulation of wood and metals, by the author of 'The Lathe and its Uses.' 6th edition, numerous woodcuts, 8vo, 6*s.*

AMBERLEY, Viscount, ANALYSIS OF RELIGIOUS BELIEF. 2 vols, 8vo, 30*s.*

AMERICAN ALMANAC AND TREASURY OF FACTS, statistical, financial, and political, edited by AINSWORTH R. SPOFFORD. Crown 8vo, 7*s.* 6*d.*

AMERICAN GYNECOLOGICAL SOCIETY'S TRANSACTIONS, vols. 1 to 14, 8vo, 25*s* each.

AMOS, Professor Sheldon, HISTORY AND PRINCIPLES OF THE CIVIL LAW OF ROME : an aid to the study of scientific and comparative jurisprudence. 8vo, 16*s.*

SCIENCE OF LAW. 7th edition, crown 8vo, 5*s.* [I.S.S.

SCIENCE OF POLITICS. 3rd edition, crown 8vo, 5*s.* [I.S.S.

ANDERSON, J., ENGLISH INTERCOURSE WITH SIAM IN THE SEVENTEENTH CENTURY. Post 8vo (*Trübner's Oriental Series*), 15*s.*

ANDERSON, J., SELUNGS OF THE MERGUI ARCHIPELAGO, with four plates. 8vo, 2*s.* 6*d.*

ANDERSON, William, PRACTICAL MERCANTILE CORRESPONDENCE : a collection of modern letters of business, with notes. 30th edition, revised, crown 8vo, 3*s.* 6*d.*

ANDERSON, W., and TUGMAN, J. E., MERCANTILE CORRESPONDENCE : a collection of letters in Portuguese and English, treating of the system of business in the principal cities of the world. 12mo, 6*s.*

ANTIQUA MATER : a study of Christian origins. Crown 8vo, 7*s.* 6*d.*

ANTIQUARIAN MAGAZINE AND BIBLIOGRAPHER, The, edited by EDWARD WALFORD and G. W. REDWAY. Complete in 12 vols. 8vo, £3 net.

APPLETON, J. H., and SAYCE, A. H., DR. APPLETON : his life and literary relics. Post 8vo, 10*s.* 6*d.* [*Philosophical Library.*]

ARBUTHNOT, Sir A. J., MAJOR-GEN. SIR THOMAS MUNRO : a memoir. Crown 8vo, 3*s.* 6*d.*

ARCHER, William, WILLIAM CHARLES MACREADY (*Eminent Actors*). Crown 8vo, 2*s.* 6*d.*

ARISTOTLE, THE NICOMACHEAN ETHICS, translated by F. H. PETERS. 3rd edition, crown 8vo, 6*s.*

ARMITAGE, *Edward*, LECTURES ON PAINTING, delivered to the students of the Royal Academy. Crown 8vo, 7s. 6d.

ARNOLD, *Sir Edwin*, DEATH—AND AFTERWARDS, reprinted from the *Fortnightly Review* of August 1885, with a supplement. 9th edition, crown 8vo, 1s. 6d.; paper, 1s.

IN MY LADY'S PRAISE : poems old and new, written to the honour of Fanny, Lady Arnold. Imperial 16mo, parchment, 3s. 6d.

INDIA REVISITED, with 32 full-page illustrations. Crown 8vo, 7s. 6d.

INDIAN IDYLLS, from the Sanskrit of the Mahâbhârata. Crown 8vo, 7s. 6d.

INDIAN POETRY, containing the Indian Song of Songs from the Sanskrit, two books from the Iliad of India, and other Oriental poems (*O. S.*). 5th edition, 7s. 6d.

LOTUS AND JEWEL, containing In an Indian Temple, A Casket of Gems, A Queen's Revenge, with other poems. 2nd edition, crown 8vo, 7s. 6d.

PEARLS OF THE FAITH, or Islam's Rosary : being the ninety-nine beautiful names of Allah. 4th edition, crown 8vo, 7s. 6d.

POEMS, NATIONAL AND NON-ORIENTAL, with some new pieces. Crown 8vo, 7s. 6d.

THE LIGHT OF ASIA, or The Great Renunciation : being the life and teaching of Gautama. *Presentation edition*, with illustrations and portrait, small 4to, 21s. *Library edition*, crown 8vo, 7s. 6d. *Elzevir edition*, 6s. *Cheap edition* (*Lotos Series*), cloth or half-parchment, 3s. 6d.

THE SECRET OF DEATH : being a version of the Katha Upanishad, from the Sanskrit. 3rd edition, crown 8vo, 7s. 6d.

THE SONG CELESTIAL, or Bhagavad-Gîtâ, from the Sanskrit. 2nd edition, crown 8vo, 5s.

WITH SA'DI IN THE GARDEN, or The Book of Love : being the 'Ishk,' or third chapter of the 'Bostân' of the Persian poet, Sa'di, embodied in a dialogue. Crown 8vo, 7s. 6d.

POETICAL WORKS, uniform edition, comprising The Light of Asia, Indian Poetry, Pearls of the Faith, Indian Idylls, The Secret of Death, The Song Celestial, and With Sa'di in the Garden. 8 vols. crown 8vo, 48s.

ARNOLD, *Thomas*, CATHOLIC DICTIONARY : an account of the doctrine, discipline, rites, ceremonies, &c., of the Catholic church. 3rd edition, 8vo, 21s.

ARUNDALE, *Francesca*, THE IDEA OF RE-BIRTH, with preface by A. P. Sinnett. Crown 8vo, 4s. 6d.

ASIATIC SOCIETY : Journal of the Royal Asiatic Society of Great Britain and Ireland from the commencement to 1863. First series, complete in 20 vols. 8vo, £10 ; parts, 4s. to 6s. each.

JOURNAL OF THE ROYAL ASIATIC SOCIETY OF GREAT BRITAIN AND IRELAND. New series, 8vo, 1864-88, vols. from 22s., parts from 10s. 6d.

ASTON, *W. G.*, GRAMMAR OF THE JAPANESE SPOKEN LANGUAGE. 4th edition, crown 8vo, 12s.

GRAMMAR OF THE JAPANESE WRITTEN LANGUAGE. 2nd edition, 8vo, 28s.

AUBERTIN, J. J., FLIGHT TO MEXICO, with 7 full-page illustrations and a railway map. Crown 8vo, 7s. 6d.

SIX MONTHS IN CAPE COLONY AND NATAL, with illustrations and map. Crown 8vo, 6s.

A FIGHT WITH DISTANCES, with illustrations and maps. Crown 8vo, 7s. 6d.

AUSTRALIA IN 1890 : the Year-book of Australia, published under the auspices of the Governments of the Australian Colonies. 8vo, 10s. 6d.

AUSTRALIAN ASSOCIATION FOR THE ADVANCEMENT OF SCIENCE : report of the first meeting. 8vo, 20s.

AXON, W. E. A., THE MECHANIC'S FRIEND : a collection of receipts and practical suggestions relating to aquaria, bronzing, cements, drawing, dyes, electricity, gilding, glass-working, &c. Numerous woodcuts. Crown 8vo. 3s. 6d.

BADGER, G. Percy, ENGLISH-ARABIC LEXICON, in which the equivalents for English words and idiomatic sentences are rendered into literary and colloquial Arabic. Royal 4to, £4.

BAGEHOT, Walter, THE ENGLISH CONSTITUTION. 5th edition, crown 8vo, 7s. 6d.

LOMBARD STREET : a description of the Money Market. 9th edition, crown 8vo, 7s. 6d.

ESSAYS ON PARLIAMENTARY REFORM. Crown 8vo, 5s.

ON THE DEPRECIATION OF SILVER, and topics connected with it. 8vo. 5s.

PHYSICS AND POLITICS, or The application of the principles of 'Natural Selection' and 'Inheritance' to political society. 8th edition, crown 8vo, 5s.   [I.S.S.

BAIN, Alex., EDUCATION AS A SCIENCE. 7th edit., crown 8vo, 5s. [I.S.S.

MIND AND BODY : the theories of their relation, with 4 illustrations, 8th edition, crown 8vo, 5s.   [I.S.S.

BALFOUR, F. H., THE DIVINE CLASSIC OF NAN-HUA : being the works of Chuang Tsze, Taoist philosopher. 8vo, 14s.

TAOIST TEXTS, ethical, political, and speculative. Imperial 8vo, 10s. 6d.

LEAVES FROM MY CHINESE SCRAP-BOOK. Post 8vo, 7s. 6d.

BALL, V., DIAMONDS, COAL, AND GOLD OF INDIA : their mode of occurrence and distribution. Fcap. 8vo, 5s.

MANUAL OF THE GEOLOGY OF INDIA. Part III. Economic geology. Royal 8vo, 10s.

BALLANTYNE, J. R., ELEMENTS OF HINDI AND BRAJ BHAKHA GRAMMAR, compiled for the East India College at Haileybury. 2nd edition, crown 8vo, 5s.

FIRST LESSONS IN SANSKRIT GRAMMAR. 4th edition, 8vo, 3s. 6d.

SANKHYA APHORISMS OF KAPILA, with illustrative extracts from the Commentaries. 3rd edition, post 8vo (*Trübner's Oriental Series*), 16s.

BANKS, Mrs. G. Linnæus, GOD'S PROVIDENCE HOUSE. Crown 8vo, 6s.

BARING-GOULD, S., GERMANY, PRESENT AND PAST. New and cheaper edition, large crown 8vo, 7s. 6d.

BARNES, William, GLOSSARY OF THE DORSET DIALECT, with a grammar of its word-shapening and wording. 8vo, sewed, 6s.

POEMS OF RURAL LIFE IN THE DORSET DIALECT. New edition, crown 8vo, 6s.

BARTH, A., RELIGIONS OF INDIA, translated by J. WOOD. 2nd edition, post 8vo (*Trübner's Oriental Series*), 16s.

BARTLETT, J. R., DICTIONARY OF AMERICANISMS : a glossary of words and phrases colloquially used in the United States. 4th edition, 8vo, 21s.

BARTON, G. B., THE HISTORY OF NEW SOUTH WALES, from the Records. Vol. I. illustrated with maps, portraits, and sketches, 8vo, half-morocco, 20s.; cloth, 15s.

BASTIAN, H. Charlton, THE BRAIN AS AN ORGAN OF MIND, with numerous illustrations. 4th edition, crown 8vo, 5s. [I.S.S.

BAUGHAN, Rosa, THE INFLUENCE OF THE STARS : a treatise on astrology, chiromancy, and physiognomy. 8vo, 5s.

BEAL, S., CATENA OF BUDDHIST SCRIPTURES, from the Chinese. 8vo, 15s.

ROMANTIC LEGEND OF SAKYA BUDDHA, from the Chinese-Sanskrit. Crown 8vo, 12s.

BUDDHIST LITERATURE IN CHINA. 8vo, 10s. 6d.

LIFE OF HIUEN-TSAING, by the Shamans HWUI LI and YEN-TSUNG, with an account of the works of I-Tsing. Post 8vo (*Trübner's Oriental Series*), 10s.

SI-YU-KI : BUDDHIST RECORDS OF THE WESTERN WORLD, translated from the Chinese of HIUEN TSAING (A.D. 629), with map. 2 vols. post 8vo (*Trübner's Oriental Series*), 24s.

TEXTS FROM THE BUDDHIST CANON, COMMONLY KNOWN AS DHAMMAPADA, translated from the Chinese. Post 8vo (*Trübner's Oriental Series*), 7s. 6d.

BEAMES, John, OUTLINES OF INDIAN PHILOLOGY, with a map showing the distribution of Indian languages. Enlarged edition, crown 8vo, 5s.

COMPARATIVE GRAMMAR OF THE MODERN ARYAN LANGUAGES OF INDIA : Hindi, Panjabi, Sindhi, Gujarati, Marathi, Oriya, and Bengali. 3 vols. 8vo, 16s. each.

BEARD, Charles, MARTIN LUTHER AND THE REFORMATION IN GERMANY. 8vo, 16s.

BELLEW, Surgeon-General H. W., HISTORY OF CHOLERA IN INDIA from 1862 to 1881, with maps and diagrams. 8vo, £2. 2s.

KASHMIR AND KASHGHAR : the journey of the Embassy to Kashghar in 1873-74. 8vo, 10s. 6d.

BELLOWS, John, FRENCH AND ENGLISH DICTIONARY FOR THE POCKET, containing the French-English and English-French divisions on the same page; conjugating all the verbs; distinguishing the genders by different types; giving numerous aids to pronunciation, &c. 2nd edition, 32mo, morocco tuck, 12s. 6d.; roan, 10s. 6d.

TOUS LES VERBES. Conjugations of all the verbs in the French and English languages. 32mo, 6d.

ENGLISH OUTLINE VOCABULARY FOR THE USE OF STUDENTS OF THE CHINESE, JAPANESE, AND OTHER LANGUAGES. Crown 8vo, 6s.

BENFEY, Theodor, GRAMMAR OF THE SANSKRIT LANGUAGE, FOR THE USE OF EARLY STUDENTS. 2nd edition, royal 8vo, 10s. 6d.

BENEDEN, P. J. van, ANIMAL PARASITES AND MESSMATES, with 83 illustrations. 4th edition, crown 8vo, 5s. [I.S.S.

BENSON, A. C., WILLIAM LAUD, SOMETIME ARCHBISHOP OF CANTERBURY, with portrait. Crown 8vo, 6s.

BENTHAM, Jeremy, THEORY OF LEGISLATION, translated from the French of Etienne Dumont by R. HILDRETH. 5th edition, post 8vo, 7s. 6d.

BENTLEY, W. H., DICTIONARY AND GRAMMAR OF THE KONGO LANGUAGE, as spoken at San Salvador, West Africa. 8vo, 21s.

"BERNARD," FROM WORLD TO CLOISTER, or My Novitiate. Crown 8vo, 5s.

BERNSTEIN, Prof., THE FIVE SENSES OF MAN, with 91 illustrations. 5th edition, crown 8vo, 5s. [I.S.S.

BERTIN, George, ABRIDGED GRAMMARS OF THE LANGUAGE OF THE CUNEIFORM INSCRIPTIONS. Crown 8vo, 5s.

BEVAN, Theodore F., TOIL, TRAVEL, AND DISCOVERY IN BRITISH NEW GUINEA, with 5 maps. Large crown 8vo, 7s. 6d.

BHIKSHU. Subhadra, BUDDHIST CATECHISM. 12mo, 2s.

BICKNELL, C., FLOWERING PLANTS AND FERNS OF THE RIVIERA AND NEIGHBOURING MOUNTAINS, with 82 full-page plates, containing illustrations of 350 specimens. Imperial 8vo, half-roan, gilt edges, £3. 3s.

BICKNELL, H., HAFIZ OF SHIRAZ : selections from his poems, translated from the Persian, with Oriental bordering in gold and colour, and illustrations. Demy 4to, £2. 2s.

BIDDULPH, C. E., AFGHAN POETRY OF THE 17TH CENTURY, with translations, &c. 4to, 10s. 6d.

BILLER, Emma, ULLI : the story of a neglected girl, translated from the German by A. B. DAISY ROST. Crown 8vo, 6s.

BINET, A., and FÉRÉ, C., ANIMAL MAGNETISM. 2nd edition, crown 8vo, 5s.

BLACKET, W. S., RESEARCHES INTO THE LOST HISTORIES OF AMERICA, with numerous engravings. 8vo, 10s. 6d.

BLADES, W., BIOGRAPHY AND TYPOGRAPHY OF WILLIAM CAXTON, ENGLAND'S FIRST PRINTER. 8vo, hand-made paper, imitation old bevelled binding, £1. 1s. ; cheap edition, crown 8vo, 5s.

BLASERNA, Prof. P., THEORY OF SOUND IN ITS RELATION TO MUSIC, with numerous illustrations. 4th edition, crown 8vo, 5s. [I.S.S.

BLATER, Joseph, TABLE OF QUARTER-SQUARES OF ALL WHOLE NUMBERS FROM 1 to 200,000, for simplifying multiplication, squaring, and extraction of the square root. Royal 4to, half-bound, 21s.

TABLE OF NAPIER, giving the nine multiples of all numbers. Cloth case, 1s. 3d.

BLEEK, W. H. I., REYNARD THE FOX IN SOUTH AFRICA, or Hottentot fables and tales. Post 8vo, 3s. 6d.

BRIEF ACCOUNT OF BUSHMAN FOLK-LORE. Folio, 2s. 6d.

BLUNT, Wilfrid Scawen, THE WIND AND THE WHIRLWIND. 8vo, 1s. 6d.

THE LOVE SONNETS OF PROTEUS. 5th edition, elzevir 8vo, 5s.

IN VINCULIS, with portrait. Elzevir 8vo, 5s.

A NEW PILGRIMAGE, and other poems. Elzevir 8vo, 5s.

BLYTH, E. Kell, Life of William Ellis, founder of the Birkbeck Schools. 8vo, 14*s*.

BOGGETT, W., New Scientific Discoveries. Sewed, 1*s*.

BOJESEN, Maria, Guide to the Danish Language. 12mo, 5*s*.

BOLIA, C., The German Caligraphist. Copies for German hand-writing. Oblong 4to, 1*s*.

BOTTRELL, W., Stories and Folk-lore of West Cornwall, with illustrations. 2nd and 3rd series, 8vo, 6*s*. each.

BOWEN, H. C., Studies in English, for the use of modern schools. 10th thousand. Small crown 8vo, 1*s*. 6*d*.

    English Grammar for Beginners. Fcap. 8vo, 1*s*.

    Simple English Poems. English Literature for Junior Classes,. 3*s*. Parts I. II. and III. 6*d*. each. Part IV., 1*s*.

BOWLES, Emily, Madame de Maintenon, with portrait. Large crown 8vo, 7*s*. 6*d*.

BOYD, P., Nágánanda, or The Joy of the Snake World, from the Sanskrit of Sri-Harsha-Deva. Crown 8vo, 4*s*. 6*d*.

BRACKENBURY, Major-General, Field Works : their technical con-struction and tactical application. 2 vols., small crown 8vo, 12*s*.

BRADLEY, F. H., The Principles of Logic. 8vo, 16*s*.

BRADSHAW'S Dictionary of Mineral Waters Climatic Health Resorts, &c., with maps and plans. New edition, crown 8vo, 2*s*. 6*d*.

    A B C Dictionary of the United States, Canada, and Mexico, showing the most important towns and points of interest, with maps, routes, &c. New edition, revised, fcap. 8vo, 2*s*. 6*d*.

BRAITHWAITE, Robert, True Grounds of Religious Faith. Crown 8vo, 3*s*. 6*d*.

Brave Men's Footsteps : a book of example and anecdote for young people, by the editor of 'Men who have Risen.' Illustrations by C. Doyle. 9th edition, crown 8vo, 2*s*. 6*d*.

Breitmann Ballads, by C. G. Leland. Only complete edition. Crown 8vo, 6*s*. Another edition (*Lotos Series*), 3*s*. 6*d*.

BRENTANO, Lujo, History and Development of Gilds and the Origin of Trade Unions. 8vo, 3*s*. 6*d*.

BRERETON, C. S. H., The Last Days of Olympus : a modern myth. Crown 8vo, 3*s*. 6*d*.

BRETSCHNEIDER, E., Mediæval Researches from Eastern Asiatic Sources : fragments towards the knowledge of the geography and history of Central and Western Asia from the 13th to the 17th century, with 2 maps. 2 vols. post 8vo (*Trübner's Oriental Series*), 21*s*.

BRETTE, P. H., and *THOMAS, F.*, French Examination Papers set at the University of London. Part I. Matriculation, and the General Examination for Women. Crown 8vo, 3*s*. 6*d*. Key, 5*s*.

    French Examination Papers set at the University of London. Part II. First B.A. Examinations for Honours and D. Litt. Examinations. Crown 8vo, 7*s*.

BRIDGETT, T. E., Blunders and Forgeries : historical essays. Crown 8vo, 6*s*.

    History of the Holy Eucharist in Great Britain. 2 vols. 8vo. 18*s*.

BRINTON, D. G., ESSAYS OF AN AMERICANIST. 8vo, 12s.

RIG VEDA AMERICANUS. 8vo, 12s.

BRITISH MUSEUM PUBLICATIONS. List on application.

BROOKE, Major C. K., SYSTEM OF FIELD TRAINING. Small crown 8vo, cloth limp, 2s.

BROOKE, Rev. Stopford A., THE FIGHT OF FAITH : sermons preached on various occasions. 6th edition, crown 8vo, 5s.

THE SPIRIT OF THE CHRISTIAN LIFE. 3rd edition, crown 8vo, 5s.

THEOLOGY IN THE ENGLISH POETS, Cowper, Coleridge, Wordsworth, and Burns. 6th edition, post 8vo, 5s.

CHRIST IN MODERN LIFE. 17th edition, crown 8vo, 5s.

SERMONS. Two series. 13th edition, crown 8vo, 5s. each.

LIFE AND LETTERS OF F. W. ROBERTSON, with portrait. 2 vols. crown 8vo, 12s. Library edition, 8vo, with portrait, 12s. Popular edition, crown 8vo, 6s.

BROWN, Horatio F., LIFE ON THE LAGOONS, with 2 illustrations and map. Crown 8vo, 6s.

VENETIAN STUDIES. Crown 8vo, 7s. 6d.

BROWN, Rev. J. Baldwin, THE HIGHER LIFE : its reality, experience, and destiny. 7th edition, crown 8vo, 5s.

DOCTRINE OF ANNIHILATION IN THE LIGHT OF THE GOSPEL OF LOVE. 4th edition, crown 8vo, 2s. 6d.

THE CHRISTIAN POLICY OF LIFE : a book for young men of business. 3rd edition, crown 8vo, 3s. 6d.

BROWNE, Edgar A., HOW TO USE THE OPHTHALMOSCOPE. 3rd edition, crown 8vo, 3s. 6d.

BROWNING, Oscar, INTRODUCTION TO THE HISTORY OF EDUCATIONAL THEORIES. 2nd edition, 3s. 6d. [*Education Library.*]

BROWNING. BIBLIOGRAPHY OF ROBERT BROWNING from 1833 to 1881. 12s.

ILLUSTRATIONS TO BROWNING'S POEMS, 2 parts. 4to, 10s. each.

BROWNING SOCIETY'S PAPERS. 8vo, 1881–84. Parts I. to XI. 10s. each.

BRUGMANN, Karl, COMPARATIVE GRAMMAR OF THE INDO-GERMANIC LANGUAGES. 2 vols. 8vo, 18s. each.

BRYANT, Sophie, CELTIC IRELAND, with 3 maps. Crown 8vo, 5s.

BRYANT, W. Cullen, POEMS. Cheap edition, small 8vo, 3s. 6d.

BRYCE, J., HANDBOOK OF HOME RULE : being articles on the Irish Question. 2nd edition, crown 8vo, 1s. 6d. ; paper covers, 1s.

BUDDHIST CATECHISM, or Outline of the doctrine of the Buddha Gotama, by SUBHADRA BHIKSHU. 12mo, 2s.

BUDGE, E. A., HISTORY OF ESARHADDON (Son of Sennacherib), King of Assyria, B.C. 681–668. Translated from the Cuneiform inscriptions in the British Museum. Post 8vo (*Trübner's Oriental Series*), 10s. 6d.

ARCHAIC CLASSICS, Assyrian texts : being extracts from the Annals of Shalmaneser II., Sennacherib, and Assur-Bani-Pal, with philological notes. Small 4to, 7s. 6d.

BULKELEY, H. J., ALYPIUS : and other poems. Small crown 8vo, 2s. 6d.

BUNGE, Prof. G., TEXT-BOOK OF PHYSIOLOGICAL AND PATHOLOGICAL CHEMISTRY, for physicians and students, translated from the German by L. C. WOOLDRIDGE. 8vo, 16s.

BUNSEN, Ernest de, ISLAM, or True Christianity. Crown 8vo, 5s.

BURGESS, James, THE BUDDHIST CAVE-TEMPLES AND THEIR IN-SCRIPTIONS, containing views, plans, sections, and elevation of façades of cave-temples ; drawings of architectural and mythological sculptures ; fac-similes of inscriptions, &c. ; with descriptive and explanatory text, and translations of inscriptions. With 86 plates and woodcuts. Royal 4to, half-bound, £3. 3s. [Archæological Survey of Western India.]

ELURA CAVE-TEMPLES, AND THE BRAHMANICAL AND JAINA CAVES IN WESTERN INDIA, with 66 plates and woodcuts. Royal 4to, half-bound, £3. 3s. [Archæological Survey of Western India.]

REPORTS OF THE AMARAVATI AND JAGGAYPVAETA BUDDHIST STUPAS, containing numerous collotype and other illustrations of Buddhist sculpture and architecture, &c., in South-eastern India ; facsimiles of inscrip-tions, &c., with descriptive and explanatory text ; together with transcriptions, translations, and elucidations of the Dhauli and Jaugada inscriptions of Asoka. With numerous plates and woodcuts. Royal 4to, half-bound, £4. 4s. [Archæological Survey of Southern India.]

BURNELL, A. C., ELEMENTS OF SOUTH INDIAN PALÆOGRAPHY, from the 4th to the 17th century : an introduction to the study of South Indian inscriptions and MSS. Enlarged edition, with map and 35 plates. 4to, £2. 12s. 6d.

CLASSIFIED INDEX TO THE SANSKRIT MSS. IN THE PALACE AT TANJORE, prepared for the Madras Government. 3 parts, 4to, 10s. each.

BURTON, Lady, INNER LIFE OF SYRIA, PALESTINE, AND THE HOLY LAND. Post 8vo, 6s.

BURY, Richard de, PHILOBIBLON, edited by E. C. THOMAS. Crown 8vo. 10s. 6d.

BUTLER, F., SPANISH TEACHER AND COLLOQUIAL PHRASE-BOOK. 18mo, half-roan, 2s. 6d.

BUXTON, Major, ELEMENTS OF MILITARY ADMINISTRATION. First part : Permanent System of Administration. Small crown 8vo, 7s. 6d.

BYRNE, James, GENERAL PRINCIPLES OF THE STRUCTURE OF LANGUAGE. 2 vols. 8vo, 36s.

ORIGIN OF GREEK, LATIN, AND GOTHIC ROOTS. 8vo, 18s.

CABLE, G. W., STRANGE TRUE STORIES OF LOUISIANA. 8vo, 7s. 6d.

CAIRD, Mona, THE WING OF AZRAEL. Crown 8vo, 6s.

CALDWELL, Bishop R., COMPARATIVE GRAMMAR OF THE DRAVIDIAN OR SOUTH INDIAN FAMILY OF LANGUAGES. Enlarged edition, 8vo, 28s.

CALLEJA, Camilo, PRINCIPLES OF UNIVERSAL PHYSIOLOGY. **Crown 8vo,** 3s. 6d.

GENERAL PHYSIOLOGY, OR PHYSIOLOGICAL THEORY OF COSMOS. Crown 8vo, 6s.

THEORY OF PHYSICS : a rectification of the theories of molar mechanics, heat, chemistry, sound, light, and electricity. Crown 8vo, 5s.

CAMERINI, E., L'Eco Italiano : a guide to Italian conversation, with vocabulary. 12mo, 4*s.* 6*d.*

CAMERON, Miss, Soups and Stews and Choice Ragouts. 1*s.* 6*d.* ; paper, 1*s.*

Campaign of Fredericksburg, November–December 1862 : a study for officers of Volunteers, by a Line Officer, with 5 maps and plans. 2nd edition, crown 8vo, 5*s.*

CAMPBELL, Prof. Lewis, Æschylus : the seven plays in English verse. Crown 8vo, 7*s.* 6*d.*

Sophocles : the seven plays in English verse. Crown 8vo, 7*s.* 6*d.*

CAMPBELL, Wm., Account of Missionary Success in the Island of Formosa, first published in 1650, and now reprinted with copious appendices, illustrations and map. 2 vols, crown 8vo, 10*s.*

The Gospel of St. Matthew in Formosan (Sinkang Dialect), with corresponding versions in Dutch and English. Edited from Gravius's edition of 1661. Fcap. 4to, 10*s.* 6*d.*

Candid Examination of Theism, by Physicus. 2nd edition, post 8vo, 7*s.* 6*d.* [*Philosophical Library.*

CANDLER, C., Prevention of Consumption : a new theory of the nature of the tubercle-bacillus. 8vo, 10*s.* 6*d.*

Prevention of Measles. Crown 8vo, 5*s.*

CANDOLLE, Alphonse de, Origin of Cultivated Plants. 2nd edition, crown 8vo, 5*s.* [I.S.S.

CARLYLE, Thomas, Sartor Resartus. Elzevir 8vo (*Parchment Library*), vellum, 7*s.* 6*d.* ; parchment or cloth, 6*s.*

CARPENTER, W. B., Principles of Mental Physiology, with their applications to the training and discipline of the mind, and the study of its morbid conditions. Illustrated. 6th edition, 8vo, 12*s.*

Nature and Man, with a memorial sketch by J. Estlin Carpenter. Portrait. Large crown 8vo, 8*s.* 6*d.*

CARREÑO, Metodo para aprender a Leer, escribir y hablar el Inglés segun el sistema de Ollendorff. 8vo, 4*s.* 6*d.* Key, 3*s.*

CASSAL, Charles, Glossary of Idioms, Gallicisms, and other Difficulties contained in the Senior Course of the 'Modern French Reader.' Crown 8vo, 2*s.* 6*d.*

CASSAL, Ch., and KARCHER, Théodore, Modern French Reader, Junior Course. 10th edition, crown 8vo, 2*s.* 6*d.*

Senior Course. 3rd edition, crown 8vo, 4*s.*

Senior Course and Glossary in 1 vol. Crown 8vo, 6*s.*

Little French Reader : extracted from the "Modern French Reader." Third edition, crown 8vo, 2*s.*

Catholic Dictionary, containing some account of the doctrine, discipline, rites, ceremonies, councils, and religious orders of the Catholic Church. Edited by Thomas Arnold. 3rd edition, demy 8vo, 21*s.*

CATLIN, George, O-Kee-Pa, a religious ceremony ; and other customs of the Mandans. With 13 coloured illustrations. Small 4to, 14*s.*

The Lifted and Subsided Rocks of America, with their influence on the oceanic, atmospheric, and land currents, and the distribution of races. With 2 maps. Crown 8vo, 6*s.* 6*d.*

Shut your Mouth and Save your Life, with 29 illustrations 8th edition, crown 8vo, 2*s.* 6*d.*

CHALMERS, J., Structure of Chinese Characters, under 300 primary forms, after the Shwoh-wan, 100 A.D. 8vo, 12s. 6d.

CHAMBERLAIN, Basil, Classical Poetry of the Japanese. Post 8vo (*Trübner's Oriental Series*), 7s. 6d.

Simplified Japanese Grammar. Crown 8vo, 5s.

Romanised Japanese Reader, consisting of Japanese anecdotes and maxims, with English translations and notes. 12mo, 6s.

Handbook of Colloquial Japanese. 8vo, 12s. 6d.

Things Japanese. Crown 8vo, 7s. 6d.

CHAMBERS, J. D., Theological and Philosophical Works of Hermes Trismegistus, Christian Neoplatonist. Translated from the Greek. 8vo, 7s. 6d.

CHARNOCK, R. S., Nuces Etymologicæ. Crown 8vo, 10s.

Prœnomina, or The etymology of the principal Christian names of Great Britain and Ireland. Crown 8vo, 6s.

CHATTERJI, Mohini, Bhagavad Gîtâ, or The Lord's Lay. Translated from the Sanskrit, with commentary and notes. 2nd edition, royal 8vo, 10s. 6d.

CHAUCER, G., Canterbury Tales, edited by A. W. Pollard. 2 vols. elzevir 8vo (*Parchment Library*), vellum, 15s. ; parchment or cloth, 12s.

Chaucer Society. Subscription, two guineas per annum. List of publications on application.

CHEYNE, Canon, The Prophecies of Isaiah, with notes and dissertations. 2 vols. 5th edition, 8vo, 25s.

Job and Solomon, or The wisdom of the Old Testament. 8vo, 12s. 6d.

The Psalms, or Book of the praises of Israel, with commentary. 8vo, 16s. Elzevir 8vo (*Parchment Library*), vellum, 7s. 6d. ; parchment or cloth, 6s.

CHILDERS, R. C., Pali-English Dictionary, with Sanskrit equivalents. Imperial 8vo, £3. 3s.

CLAPPERTON, Jane Hume, Scientific Meliorism and the Evolution of Happiness. Large crown 8vo, 8s. 6d.

CLARKE, Henry IV., History of Tithes, from Abraham to Queen Victoria. Crown 8vo, 5s.

CLARKE, James Freeman, Ten Great Religions : an essay in comparative theology. 8vo, 10s. 6d.

Ten Great Religions. Part II. A Comparison of all Religions. 8vo, 10s. 6d.

CLAUSEWITZ, General Carl von, On War, translated by Colonel Graham. Fcap. 4to, 10s. 6d.

CLEMENT, C. E., and HUTTON, L., Artists of the Nineteenth Century and their Works. Two thousand and fifty biographical sketches. 3rd edition, revised, crown 8vo, 15s.

CLERY, Col. C. Francis, Minor Tactics, with 26 maps and plans. 13th edition, revised, crown 8vo, 9s.

CLIFFORD, W. K., COMMON SENSE OF THE EXACT SCIENCES. 2nd edition, with 100 figures, crown 8vo, 5*s*. [I.S.S.

CLODD, Edward, CHILDHOOD OF THE WORLD : a simple account of man in early times. 8th edition, crown 8vo, 3*s*. Special edition for schools, 1*s*.

CHILDHOOD OF RELIGIONS, including a simple account of the birth and growth of myths and legends. 8th thousand, crown 8vo, 5*s*. Special edition for schools, 1*s*. 6*d*.

JESUS OF NAZARETH, with a brief sketch of Jewish history to the time of His birth. 2nd edition, small crown 8vo, 6*s*. Special edition for schools, in 2 parts, each 1*s*. 6*d*.

COCKLE, Mrs. Moss, THE GOLDEN QUEST : and other poems. Small crown 8vo, 2*s*. 6*d*.

CODD, John, LEGEND OF THE MIDDLE AGES, and other songs of the past and present. Crown 8vo, 4*s*.

COGHILL, Mrs. H., OAK AND MAPLE : poems. Crown 8vo, 3*s*. 6*d*.

COKE, Henry, CREEDS OF THE DAY, or Collated opinions of reputable thinkers. 2 vols. 8vo, 21*s*.

COLEBROOKE, H. T., MISCELLANEOUS ESSAYS, with biography by his son, Sir T. E. COLEBROOKE. 3 vols. 8vo, 42s.

COLERIDGE, Hon. Stephen, THE SANCTITY OF CONFESSION : a romance. Crown 8vo, 5*s*.

COLLETTE, C. H., LIFE, TIMES, AND WRITINGS OF THOMAS CRANMER, D.D., THE FIRST REFORMING ARCHBISHOP OF CANTERBURY. 8vo, 7*s*. 6*d*.

POPE JOAN : an historical study, from the Greek of Rhoïdis. 12mo, 2*s*. 6*d*.

COLLINS, Mabel, THROUGH THE GATES OF GOLD: a fragment of thought. Small 8vo, 4*s*. 6*d*.

COLVILLE, Lieut.-Col. C. F., MILITARY TRIBUNALS. Crown 8vo, sewed, 2*s*. 6*d*.

COMPTON, C. G., SCOT FREE : a novel. Crown 8vo, 6*s*.

COMTE, Auguste, CATECHISM OF POSITIVE RELIGION, from the French by R. CONGREVE. 2nd edition, crown 8vo, 2*s*. 6*d*.

EIGHT CIRCULARS OF AUGUSTE COMTE. Fcap. 8vo, 1*s*. 6*d*.

APPEAL TO CONSERVATIVES. Crown 8vo, 2*s*. 6*d*.

POSITIVE PHILOSOPHY OF AUGUSTE COMTE, translated and condensed by HARRIET MARTINEAU. 2 vols. 2nd edition, post 8vo, 25*s*.

CONCISE HANDBOOK TO MADEIRA, with plan and map. 2nd edition, fcap. 8vo, 1*s*. 6*d*.

CONTE, Joseph le, SIGHT : an exposition of the principles of monocular and binocular vision. 2nd edition, with 132 illustrations, crown 8vo, 5*s*. [I.S.S.

CONTOPOULOS, N., LEXICON OF MODERN GREEK-ENGLISH AND ENGLISH-MODERN GREEK. 2 vols. 8vo, 27*s*.

CONWAY, M. D., EMERSON AT HOME AND ABROAD, with portrait. Post 8vo, 10*s*. 6*d*. [*Philosophical Library.*

. SACRED ANTHOLOGY : a book of ethnical scriptures. New edition, crown 8vo, 5*s*.

CONWAY, R. S., VERNER'S LAW IN ITALY: an essay in the history of the Indo-European sibilants. 8vo, 5*s.*

COOK, Louisa S., GEOMETRICAL PSYCHOLOGY, or The science of representation. An abstract of the theories and diagrams of B. W. Betts. 16 plates. 8vo, 7*s.* 6*d.*

COOKE, Prof. J. P., NEW CHEMISTRY, with 31 illustrations. 9th edition, crown 8vo, 5*s.* [I.S.S.

COOKE, M. C., FUNGI: their nature, influences, and uses, edited by M. J. BERKELEY, with numerous illustrations. 4th edition. crown 8vo, 5*s.* [I.S.S.

INTRODUCTION TO FRESH-WATER ALGÆ, with an enumeration of all the British species, with 13 plates. Crown 8vo, 5*s.* [I.S.S.

COOMARA SIVAMY, Mutu, THE DATHAVANSA, or The history of the tooth relic of Getama Buddha. Pali text. 8vo, 10*s.* 6*d.* English translation, 6*s.*

SUTTA NIPATA, cr Dialogues and discourses of Gotama Buddha, translated from the original Pali. Crown 8vo, 6*s.*

CORPUS INSCRIPTIONUM INDICARUM. Vol. I. Inscriptions of Asoka, by A. CUNNINGHAM, 4to, with 31 plates, 32*s.* Vol. II. [Not yet published.] Vol. III. Inscriptions of the Early Gupta Kings and their Successors, by J. F. FLEET, 4to, 50*s.*

COTTON, H. J. S., NEW INDIA, or India in transition. 3rd edition, crown 8vo, 4*s.* 6*d.* ; cheap edition, paper covers, 1*s.*

COTTON, Louise, PALMISTRY AND ITS PRACTICAL USES. 12 plates, crown 8vo, 2*s.* 6*d.*

COWELL, E. B., SHORT INTRODUCTION TO THE ORDINARY PRAKRIT OF THE SANSKRIT DRAMAS. Crown 8vo, 3*s.* 6*d.*

PRAKRITA-PRAKASA, or The Prakrit Grammar of Vararuchi, with the Commentary (Manorama) of Bhamaha. 8vo, 14*s.*

COWELL, E. B., and GOUGH, A. E., SARVA-DARSANA-SAMGRAHA, or Review of the different systems of Hindu philosophy. Post 8vo (*Trübner's Oriental Series*), 10*s.* 6*d.*

COX, Sir George W., MYTHOLOGY OF THE ARYAN NATIONS. New edition, 8vo, 16*s.*

TALES OF ANCIENT GREECE. New edition, small crown 8vo, 6*s.*

MANUAL OF MYTHOLOGY IN THE FORM OF QUESTION AND ANSWER. New edition, fcap. 8vo, 3*s.*

INTRODUCTION TO THE SCIENCE OF COMPARATIVE MYTHOLOGY AND FOLK-LORE. 2nd edition, crown 8vo, 7*s.* 6*d.*

COX, Sir G. W., and JONES, E. H., POPULAR ROMANCES OF THE MIDDLE AGES. 3rd edition, crown 8vo, 6*s.*

COX, Samuel, D.D., COMMENTARY ON THE BOOK OF JOB, with a translation. 2nd edition, 8vo, 15*s.*

SALVATOR MUNDI, or Is Christ the saviour of all men ? 12th edition, crown 8vo, 2*s.* 6*d.*

THE LARGER HOPE: a sequel to 'Salvator Mundi.' 2nd edition, 16mo, 1*s.*

THE GENESIS OF EVIL, and other sermons, mainly expository. 4th edition, crown 8vo, 6*s.*

BALAAM: an exposition and a study. Crown 8vo, 5*s.*

MIRACLES: an argument and a challenge. Crown 8vo, 2*s.* 6*d.*

COXHEAD, Ethel, BIRDS AND BABIES, with 33 illustrations. 2nd edition, imp. 16mo, cloth, 1s.

CRANBROOK, James, FOUNDERS OF CHRISTIANITY, or Discourses upon the origin of the Christian religion. Post 8vo, 6s.

CRAVEN, T., ENGLISH-HINDUSTANI AND HINDUSTANI-ENGLISH DICTIONARY. 18mo, 3s. 6d.

CRAWFURD, Oswald, SYLVIA ARDEN, with frontispiece. Crown 8vo, 1s.

CRUISE, F. R., NOTES OF A VISIT TO THE SCENES IN WHICH THE LIFE OF THOMAS À KEMPIS WAS SPENT, with numerous illustrations. 8vo, 12s.

CUNNINGHAM, Major-General Alex., ANCIENT GEOGRAPHY OF INDIA.
    I. The Buddhist period, including the campaigns of Alexander and the travels of Hwen-Thsang, with 13 maps. 8vo, £1. 8s.

    ARCHÆOLOGICAL SURVEY OF INDIA, reports, with numerous plates. Vols. I. to XXIII. royal 8vo, 10s. and 12s. each.
        General Index, royal 8vo, 12s. (*India Office*).

    INSCRIPTIONS OF ASOKA, with 31 plates. (Corpus Inscriptionum Indicarum, Vol. I.) 4to, 32s.

CURR, Edward M., THE AUSTRALIAN RACE: its origin, languages, customs, &c., with map and illustrations. 3 vols. 8vo, 1 vol. 4to, £2. 2s.

CURTEIS, Canon, BISHOP SELWYN OF NEW ZEALAND AND OF LICHFIELD: a sketch of his life and work, with further gleanings from his letters, sermons, and speeches. Large crown 8vo, 7s. 6d.

CUST, R., MODERN LANGUAGES OF THE EAST INDIES, with 2 language maps. Post 8vo (*Trübner's Oriental Series*), 7s. 6d.

    LINGUISTIC AND ORIENTAL ESSAYS. Post 8vo (*Trübner's Oriental Series*), first series, 10s. 6d.; second series, with 6 maps, 21s.

    SKETCH OF THE MODERN LANGUAGES OF AFRICA, with language map and 31 portraits. 2 vols. post 8vo (*Trübner's Oriental Series*), 18s.

    PICTURES OF INDIAN LIFE, sketched with the pen from 1852 to 1381, with maps. Crown 8vo, 7s. 6d.

DANA, E. S., TEXT-BOOK OF MINERALOGY, with treatise on crystallography and physical mineralogy. 3rd edition, with 800 woodcuts and plate, 8vo, 15s.

DANA, James D., TEXT-BOOK OF GEOLOGY, for schools, illustrated. Crown 8vo, 10s.

    MANUAL OF GEOLOGY, illustrated by a chart of the world, and over 1,000 figures. 8vo, 21s.

    THE GEOLOGICAL STORY BRIEFLY TOLD, illustrated. 12mo, 7s. 6d.

DANA, J. D., and BRUSH, G. J., SYSTEM OF MINERALOGY. 5th edition, royal 8vo, £2. 2s.

    MANUAL OF MINERALOGY AND PETROGRAPHY. 4th edition, numerous woodcuts, crown 8vo, 8s. 6d.

DANIELL, C. J., INDUSTRIAL COMPETITION OF ASIA: an inquiry into the influence of currency on commerce in the East, 12s.

DANTE'S TREATISE "DE VULGARI ELOQUENTIÂ," translated with notes by A. G. F. HOWELL, 3s. 6d.

DASH, Blancor, DREAMING. Small crown 8vo, 5s.

    TALES OF A TENNIS PARTY. Small 8vo, 5s.

D'ASSIER, Adolphe, POSTHUMOUS HUMANITY : a study of phantoms, from the French by II. S. OLCOTT, with appendix. Crown 8vo, 7*s.* 6*d.*

DAVIES, G. Christopher, RAMBLES AND ADVENTURES OF OUR SCHOOL FIELD CLUB, with 4 illustrations. New and cheaper edition, crown 8vo, 3*s.* 6*d.*

DAVIES, F., SÁNKHYA KÁRIKÁ OF ISWARA KRISHNA : an exposition of the system of Kapila. Post 8vo (*Trübner's Oriental Series*), 6*s.*

TH ᷑ BHAGAVAD GÎTÂ, or The Sacred Lay, translated from the Sanskrit. Post 8vo (*Trübner's Oriental Series*), 8*s.* 6*d.*

DAVITT, Michael, SPEECH BEFORE THE SPECIAL COMMISSION. Crown 8vo, 5*s.*

DAIVE, William, SKETCHES IN VERSE. Small 8vo, 3*s.* 6*d.*

DAWSON, C. A., SAPPHO. Small 8vo, 5*s.*

DAWSON, George, PRAYERS, first series, edited by his wife. 10th edition, small 8vo, 3*s.* 6*d.*

> PRAYERS, second series, edited by GEORGE ST. CLAIR. Small 8vo, 3*s.* 6*d.*

> SERMONS ON DISPUTED POINTS AND SPECIAL OCCASIONS, edited by his wife. 5th edition, small 8vo, 3*s.* 6*d.*

> SERMONS ON DAILY LIFE AND DUTY, edited by his wife. 5th edition, small 8vo, 3*s.* 6*d.*

> THE AUTHENTIC GOSPEL, and other sermons, edited by GEORGE ST. CLAIR. 4th edition, small 8vo, 3*s.* 6*d.*

> EVERY-DAY COUNSELS, edited by GEORGE ST. CLAIR. Crown 8vo, 6*s.*

> BIOGRAPHICAL LECTURES, edited by GEORGE ST. CLAIR. 3rd edition large crown 8vo, 7*s.* 6*d.*

> SHAKESPEARE, and other lectures, edited by GEORGE ST. CLAIR. Large crown 8vo, 7*s.* 6*d.*

DAWSON, Sir J. W., GEOLOGICAL HISTORY OF PLANTS, with 80 figures. Crown 8vo, 5*s.*   [I.S.S.

DEAN, Teresa H., HOW TO BE BEAUTIFUL : Nature unmasked. A book for every woman. Fcap. 8vo, 2*s.* 6*d.*

DEICHMANN, Baroness, LIFE OF CARMEN SYLVA, Queen of Roumania, with 5 illustrations. 8vo, 12*s.*

DE JONCOURT, Madame Marie, WHOLESOME COOKERY. 5th edition, crown 8vo, 1*s.* 6*d.* ; paper covers, 1*s.*

DELBRUCK, B., INTRODUCTION TO THE STUDY OF LANGUAGE : the history and methods of comparative philology of the Indo-European languages. 8vo, 5*s.*

DOUBTER'S DOUBT ABOUT SCIENCE AND RELIGION. Crown 8vo, 3*s.* 6*d.*

DENMAN, Hon. G., THE STORY OF THE KINGS OF ROME, in verse. 16mo, parchment, 1*s.* 6*d.*

DENNYS, N. B., FOLK-LORE OF CHINA, AND ITS AFFINITIES WITH THAT OF THE ARYAN AND SEMITIC RACES. 8vo, 10*s.* 6*d.*

DE QUINCEY. CONFESSIONS OF AN ENGLISH OPIUM EATER, edited by RICHARD GARNETT. Elzevir 8vo (*Parchment Library*), vellum, 7*s.* 6*d.* ; parchment or cloth, 6*s.*

DEWEY, J. H., The Way, the Truth, and the Life: a handbook of Christian theosophy, healing and psychic culture, 10s. 6d.

DERING, R. G., Giraldi, or The curse of love : a tale of the sects. 2 vols. crown 8vo, 12s.

DE VERE, Aubrey, Poetical Works. Small 8vo.
- I. The Search after Proserpine, 3s. 6d.
- II. The Legends of St. Patrick, 3s. 6d.
- III. Alexander the Great, 3s. 6d.

The Foray of Queen Meave, and other legends of Ireland's heroic age. Small 8vo, 3s. 6d.

Legends of the Saxon Saints. Small 8vo, 3s. 6d.

Legends and Records of the Church and the Empire. Small 8vo, 3s. 6d.

DILLON, W., Life of John Mitchel, with portrait. 2 vols. 8vo, 21s.

DOBSON, Austin, Old World Idylls, and other verses. Elzevir 8vo, gilt top, 6s.

At the Sign of the Lyre. Elzevir 8vo, gilt top, 6s.

DONOVAN, J., From Lyre to Muse : a history of the aboriginal union of music and poetry. Crown 8vo, 3s. 6d.

Music and Action, or The elective affinity between rhythm and pitch. Crown 8vo, 3s. 6d.

D'ORSEY, A. J. D., Grammar of Portuguese and English, adapted to Ollendorff's system. 4th edition, 12mo, 7s.

Colloquial Portuguese, or The words and phrases of everyday life. 4th edition, crown 8vo, 3s. 6d.

DOUGLAS, Prof., R. K., Chinese Language and Literature. Crown 8vo, 5s.

The Life of Jenghiz Khan, translated from the Chinese. Crown 8vo, 5s.

DOWDEN, Edward, Shakspere : a critical study of his mind and art. 9th edition, large post 8vo, 12s.

Shakspere's Sonnets, with introduction and notes. Large post 8vo, 7s. 6d.

Studies in Literature, 1789–1877. 4th edition, large post 8vo, 6s.

Transcripts and Studies. Large post 8vo, 12s.

Life of Percy Bysshe Shelley, with portraits. 2 vols. 8vo, 36s.

DOWSETT, F. C., Striking Events in Irish History. Crown 8vo, 2s. 6d.

DOWSON, John, Grammar of the Urdū or Hindūstānī Language. 2nd edition, crown 8vo, 10s. 6d.

Hindūstānī Exercise Book : passages and extracts for translation into Hindūstānī. Crown 8vo, 2s. 6d.

Classical Dictionary of Hindu Mythology and History, Geography and Literature. Post 8vo (*Trübner's Oriental Series*), 16s.

DOYLE, J.; Cause. Small 8vo, 6s.

DRAPER, J. W., THE CONFLICT BETWEEN RELIGION AND SCIENCE. 21st edition, crown 8vo, 5*s.* [I.S.S.

DRAYSON, Major-General, UNTRODDEN GROUND IN ASTRONOMY AND GEOLOGY, with numerous figures. 8vo, 14*s.*

DREAM OF PILATE'S WIFE: a poem suggested by Doré's famous picture. Small crown 8vo, 2*s.*

DREAMLAND AND GHOSTLAND: an original collection of tales and warnings from the Borderland of Substance and Shadow. 3 vols. 6*s.* each.

DUCKETT, Sir G. F., VISITATIONS OF ENGLISH CLUNIAC FOUNDATIONS, translated from the original records, 7*s.* 6*d.*

DUFFY, Sir C. Gavan, THOMAS DAVIS : the memoirs of an Irish patriot, 1840-46. 8vo, 12*s.*

DUKA, Theodore, ESSAY ON THE BRĀHŪĪ GRAMMAR. 8vo, 3*s.* 6*d.*
LIFE AND WORKS OF ALEXANDER CSOMA DE KÖRÖS between 1819 and 1842, with a short notice of all his works and essays, from original documents. Post 8vo (*Trübner's Oriental Series*), 9*s.*

DU MONCEL, Count, THE TELEPHONE, THE MICROPHONE, AND THE PHONOGRAPH, with 74 illustrations. 3rd edition, small 8vo, 5*s.*

DU PREL, Carl, PHILOSOPHY OF MYSTICISM, translated from the German by C. C. MASSEY. 2 vols. 8vo, cloth, 25*s.*

DURANT, Héloïse, DANTE: a dramatic poem. Small 8vo, 5*s.*

DUSAR, P. Friedrich, GRAMMAR OF THE GERMAN LANGUAGE, with exercises. 2nd edition, crown 8vo, 4*s.* 6*d.*
GRAMMATICAL COURSE OF THE GERMAN LANGUAGE. 3rd edition, crown 8vo, 3*s.* 6*d.*

DUTT, Romesh Chunder, HISTORY OF CIVILISATION IN ANCIENT INDIA, based on Sanskrit literature. Crown 8vo. Vol. I. Vedic and Epic Ages, 8*s.* Vol. II. Rationalistic Age, 8*s.* Vol. III. Buddhist and Pauranik Ages, 8*s.*

DUTT, Toru, A SHEAF GLEANED IN FRENCH FIELDS. 8vo, 10*s.* 6*d.*
ANCIENT BALLADS AND LEGENDS OF HINDUSTAN, with an introductory memoir by EDMUND GOSSE. 18mo, cloth extra, gilt top, 5*s.*

DYMOCK, W., VEGETABLE MATERIA MEDICA OF WESTERN INDIA. 4 parts, 8vo, 5*s.*

EARLE, May, COSMO VENUCCI, SINGER : and other poems. Small 8vo, 3*s.* 6*d.*

EARLY ENGLISH TEXT SOCIETY. Subscription, one guinea per annum. List of publications on application.

EASTWICK, E. B., THE GULISTAN, or Rose Garden of Shekh Mushliu-'d-Din Sadi of Shiraz, translated from the Atish Kadah. 2nd edition. post 8vo (*Trübner's Oriental Series*), 10*s.* 6*d.*

EBERS, Georg, MARGERY: a tale of Old Nuremberg, translated from the German by CLARA BELL. 2 vols. 8*s.* ; paper, 5*s.*

ECKSTEIN, Ernst, NERO: a romance, translated from the German by CLARA BELL and MARY J. SAFFORD. 2 vols. paper, 5*s.* ; cloth, 8*s.*

EDGREN, H., COMPENDIOUS SANSKRIT GRAMMAR, with a brief sketch of Scenic Prakrit. Crown 8vo, 10*s.* 6*d.*

B 2

EDKINS, J., D.D., RELIGION IN CHINA, containing a brief account of the three religions of the Chinese. 3rd edition, post 8vo (*Trübner's Oriental Series*), 7s. 6d.

> *₊* This work is also issued as a volume of the *Philosophical Library.*

CHINESE BUDDHISM: sketches historical and critical. Post 8vo (*Trübner's Oriental Series*), 18s.

CHINA'S PLACE IN PHILOLOGY: an attempt to show that the languages of Europe and Asia have a common origin. Crown 8vo, 10s. 6d.

EVOLUTION OF THE CHINESE LANGUAGE. 8vo, 4s. 6d.

EVOLUTION OF THE HEBREW LANGUAGE. 8vo, 5s.

INTRODUCTION TO THE STUDY OF THE CHINESE CHARACTERS. Royal 8vo, 18s.

EDMONDS, Herbert, WELL-SPENT LIVES: a series of modern biographies. New and cheaper edition, crown 8vo, 3s. 6d.

EDMUNDSON, George, MILTON AND VONDEL: a curiosity of literature. Crown 8vo, 6s.

EDWARDS, Edward, MEMOIRS OF LIBRARIES, together with a practical handbook of library economy. Numerous illustrations. 2 vols. royal 8vo, £2. 8s.

LIBRARIES AND FOUNDERS OF LIBRARIES. 8vo, 18s.

FREE TOWN LIBRARIES: their formation, management, and history, with brief notices of book collectors. 8vo, 21s.

EGER, Gustav, TECHNOLOGICAL DICTIONARY IN THE ENGLISH AND GERMAN LANGUAGES. 2 vols. royal 8vo, £1. 7s.

EIGHTEENTH CENTURY ESSAYS, edited by AUSTIN DOBSON, with frontispiece. Elzevir 8vo (*Parchment Library*), vellum, 7s. 6d.; parchment or cloth, 6s.; cheap edition, fcap. 8vo, 1s. 6d.

EITEL, E. J., BUDDHISM: its historical, theoretical, and popular aspects. 3rd edition, revised, 8vo, 5s.

HANDBOOK FOR THE STUDENT OF CHINESE BUDDHISM. 2nd edition, crown 8vo, 18s.

ELECTRICITY IN DAILY LIFE: a popular account of its application to everyday uses, with 125 illustrations. Square 8vo, 9s.

ELEGIES AND MEMORIALS, by A. and L. Fcap. 8vo, 2s. 6d.

ELLIOT, Sir W., COINS OF SOUTHERN INDIA, with map and plates. Royal 4to, 25s. [*Numismata Orient.*

ELLIOT, Sir H. M., HISTORY, FOLK-LORE, AND DISTRIBUTION OF THE RACES OF THE NORTH-WESTERN PROVINCES OF INDIA, edited by J. BEAMES. With 3 coloured maps. 2 vols, 8vo. £1. 16s.

HISTORY OF INDIA, as told by its own historians: the Muhammadan period. From the posthumous papers of the late Sir H. M. ELLIOT, revised and continued by Professor JOHN DOWSON. 8 vols. 8vo, £8. 8s.

ELLIOTT, Ebenezer, POEMS, edited by his son, the Rev. EDWIN ELLIOTT, of St. John's, Antigua. 2 vols. crown 8vo, 18s.

ELLIS, Robert, SOURCES OF THE ETRUSCAN AND BASQUE LANGUAGES. 8vo, 7s. 6d.

EMERSON, Ellen R., INDIAN MYTHS ; or Legends, traditions, and symbols of the aborigines of America. 2nd edition, illustrated, post 8vo, £1. 1s.

ENCYCLOPÆDIA AMERICANA, 4 vols. 4to, £8 8s.

ENGLISH DIALECT SOCIETY. Subscription, 10s. 6d. per annum. List of publications on application.

ENGLISH COMIC DRAMATISTS, edited by OSWALD CRAWFURD. Elzevir 8vo (*Parchment Library*), vellum, 7s. 6d. ; parchment or cloth, 6s.

ENGLISH LYRICS. Elzevir 8vo (*Parchment Library*), vellum, 7s. 6d. ; parchment or cloth, 6s.

ENGLISH ODES, edited by E. GOSSE, with frontispiece. Elzevir 8vo (*Parchment Library*), vellum, 7s. 6d. ; parchment or cloth, 6s.

ENGLISH SACRED LYRICS. Elzevir 8vo (*Parchment Library*), vellum, 7s. 6d. ; parchment or cloth, 6s.

ENGLISH POETS (LIVING), with frontispiece by WALTER CRANE. 2nd edition, large crown 8vo, printed on hand-made paper, vellum, 15s. ; cloth, 12s.

ENGLISH VERSE, edited by W. J. LINTON and R. H. STODDARD. 5 vols. crown 8vo, 5s. each.

CHAUCER TO BURNS. TRANSLATIONS. LYRICS OF THE NINETEENTH CENTURY. DRAMATIC SCENES AND CHARACTERS. BALLADS AND ROMANCES.

EYTON, Robert, THE APOSTLES' CREED : sermons. Crown 8vo, 3s. 6d. THE TRUE LIFE, and other sermons. Crown 8vo, 7s. 6d.

FAUSBOLL, V., THE JATAKA, together with its COMMENTARY, being tales of the anterior birth of Gotama Buddha, now first published in Pali. 4 vols. 8vo, 28s. each.

FEATHERMAN, A., SOCIAL HISTORY OF THE RACES OF MANKIND. 8vo. The Nigritians, £1. 11s. 6d.; Papuo and Malayo Melanesians, £1. 5s. ; Oceano-Melanesians, £1. 5s.; Aoneo-Maranonians, £1. 5s. ; Chiapo and Guazano Maranonians, £1. 8s. ; The Aramæans, £1. 1s. ; Turanian Stock, £1. 1s.

FERGUSSON, T., CHINESE RESEARCHES, Chinese Chronology and Cycles. Crown 8vo, 10s. 6d.

FEUERBACH, L., ESSENCE OF CHRISTIANITY, from the German by MARIAN EVANS. 2nd edition, post 8vo, 7s. 6d. [*Philosophical Library.*

FICHTE, J. Gottlieb, CHARACTERISTICS OF THE PRESENT AGE, translated by W. SMITH. Post 8vo, 6s.

MEMOIR OF JOHANN GOTTLIEB FICHTE, by W. SMITH. 2nd edition, post 8vo, 4s.

ON THE NATURE OF THE SCHOLAR, AND ITS MANIFESTATIONS, translated by W. SMITH. 2nd edition, post 8vo, 3s.

NEW EXPOSITION OF THE SCIENCE OF KNOWLEDGE, translated by A. E. KROEGER. 8vo, 6s.

SCIENCE OF KNOWLEDGE, from the German by A. E. KROEGER, with an introduction by Prof. W. T. HARRIS. (*Philosophical Library.*) 10s. 6d.

SCIENCE OF RIGHTS, from the German by A. E. KROEGER, with an introduction by Prof. W. T. HARRIS. (*Philosophical Library.*) 12s. 6d.

POPULAR WORKS : The Nature of the Scholar ; The Vocation of the Scholar ; The Vocation of Man ; The Doctrine of Religion ; Characteristics of the Present Age ; Outlines of the Doctrine of Knowledge. With a memoir by W. SMITH. (*Philosophical Library.*) 2 vols. 21s.

FIELD, D. D., OUTLINES OF AN INTERNATIONAL CODE. 2nd edition, royal 8vo, £2. 2s.

FIFE-COOKSON, *Lieut.-Colonel*, MAN AND THE DEITY : an essay in verse. Small 8vo, 2s.

THE EMPIRE OF MAN. Small 8vo, 2s. 6d.

FINN, Alexander, PERSIAN FOR TRAVELLERS. Oblong 32mo, 5s.

FITZGERALD, Mrs. P. F., A PROTEST AGAINST AGNOSTICISM : introduction to a new theory of Idealism. 8vo, 3s. 6d.

ESSAY ON THE PHILOSOPHY OF SELF-CONSCIOUSNESS, comprising an analysis of reason and the rationale of love. 8vo, 5s.

TREATISE ON THE PRINCIPLE OF SUFFICIENT REASON: a psychological theory of reasoning, showing the relativity of thought to the thinker, of recognition to cognition, &c. 8vo, 6s.

FITZGERALD, R. D., AUSTRALIAN ORCHIDS. Part I. 7 plates ; part II. 10 plates ; part III. 10 plates ; part IV. 10 plates ; part V. 10 plates ; part VI. 10 plates. Each part, coloured. 21s.; plain, 10s. 6d. Part VII. 10 plates. Vol. II. part I. 10 plates. Each, coloured, 25s.

FIVE-O'CLOCK TEA, containing receipts for cakes, savoury sandwiches, &c. 8th thousand. Fcp. 8vo, 1s. 6d.; paper covers, 1s.

FITZPATRICK, W. J., LIFE OF THE VERY REV. T. N. BURKE, with portrait. 2 vols. 8vo, 30s.

FLEET, J. F., INSCRIPTIONS OF THE EARLY GUPTA KINGS AND THEIR SUCCESSORS. (Corpus Inscriptionum Indicarum, Vol. III.) 4to, 50s.

FLETCHER, J. S., ANDREWLINA. Crown 8vo, 1s. 6d.; paper covers, 1s.
THE WINDING WAY. Crown 8vo, 6s.

FORNANDER, A., ACCOUNT OF THE POLYNESIAN RACE: its origin and migrations, and the ancient history of the Hawaiian people. Post 8vo. Vol. I. 7s. 6d. Vol. II. 10s. 6d. Vol. III. 9s. [*Philosophical Library.*]

FOTHERINGHAM, James, STUDIES IN THE POETRY OF ROBERT BROWNING. 2nd edition, crown 8vo, 6s.

FOX, Charles, THE PILGRIMS : an allegory of the soul's progress from the earthly to the heavenly state. Crown 8vo, 5s.

FOX, J. A., KEY TO THE IRISH QUESTION. Crown 8vo, 7s. 6d.

FRANCIS, Frances, MOSQUITO : a tale of the Mexican frontier. Crown 8vo, 3s. 6d.

FRANKLYN, H. B., THE GREAT BATTLES OF 1870, and BLOCKADE OF METZ, with large map, sketch map, and frontispiece. 8vo, 15s.

FREEBOROUGH, E., and RANKEN, C. E., CHESS OPENINGS, ancient and modern, revised and corrected up to the present time from the best authorities. Large post 8vo, 7s. 6d.

FREEMAN, E. A., LECTURES TO AMERICAN AUDIENCES. I. The English People in its Three Homes ; II. Practical Bearings of General European History. Post 8vo, 8s. 6d.

FRENCH LYRICS, edited by GEORGE SAINTSBURY, with frontispiece. Elzevir 8vo (*Parchment Library*), vellum, 7s. 6d. ; parchment or cloth, 6s.

FRIEDRICH, P., PROGRESSIVE GERMAN READER, with copious notes. Crown 8vo, 4s. 6d.

FRIEDLÄNDER, M., Text-book of Jewish Religion. Crown 8vo, 1s. 6d.

FRITH, J., Life of Giordano Bruno, the Nolan, revised by Prof. Moriz Carriere, with portrait. Post 8vo, 14s.

FRŒMBLING, F. Otto, Graduated German Reader : a selection from the most popular writers, with a vocabulary. 10th edition, 12mo, 3s. 6d.

Graduated Exercises for Translation into German : extracts from the best English authors, with idiomatic notes. Crown 8vo, 4s. 6d.; without notes, 4s.

GALDOS, B. Perez, Leon Roche, a romance, from the Spanish by Clara Bell. 2 vols. 16mo, cloth, 8s.; paper, 5s.

GALLOWAY, Robert, Treatise on Fuel, scientific and practical, with illustrations. Post 8vo, 6s.

Education, Scientific and Technical, or How the inductive sciences are taught, and how they ought to be taught. 8vo, 10s. 6d.

GALLWEY, P., Apostolic Succession : a handbook. 8vo, 1s.

GAMBLE, J. S., Manual of Indian Timbers. 8vo, 10s. [*India Office.*

GARDINER, Linda, His Heritage, with frontispiece. Crown 8vo, 6s.

GARLANDA, Federico, The Fortunes of Words. Crown 8vo, 5s.

The Philosophy of Words : a popular introduction to the science of language. Crown 8vo, 5s.

GARRICK, H. B. W., India : a descriptive poem. Crown 8vo, 7s. 6d.

GASTER, M., Greeko-Slavonic Literature, and its Relation to the Folk-lore of Europe during the Middle Ages. Large post 8vo, 7s. 6d.

GAY, John, Fables, edited by Austin Dobson, with portrait. Elzevir 8vo (*Parchment Library*), vellum, 7s. 6d. ; parchment or cloth, 6s.

GEIGER, Lazarus, Contributions to the History of the Development of the Human Race, from the German by D. Asher. Post 8vo, 6s. [Philosophical Library.

GELDART, E. M., Guide to Modern Greek. Post 8vo, 7s. 6d. Key, 2s. 6d.

Simplified Grammar of Modern Greek. Crown 8vo, 2s. 6d.

GEORGE, Henry, Progress and Poverty : an inquiry into the causes of industrial depressions, and of increase of want with increase of wealth ; the remedy. 5th edition, post 8vo, 7s. 6d. Cabinet edition, crown 8vo, 2s. 6d. Cheap edition, limp cloth, 1s. 6d. ; paper covers, 1s.

Protection, or Free Trade : an examination of the tariff question, with especial regard to the interests of labour. 2nd edition, crown 8vo, 5s. Cheap edition, limp cloth, 1s. 6d.; paper covers, 1s.

Social Problems. 4th thousand, crown 8vo, 5s. Cheap edition, limp cloth, 1s. 6d.; paper covers, 1s.

GERARD, E. and D., A Sensitive Plant, a novel. 3 vols., crown 8vo, £1 11s. 6d.

GHOSE, Loke N., Modern History of the Indian Chiefs, Rajas, &c. 2 vols. post 8vo, 21s.

GIBB, E. J. W., THE HISTORY OF THE FORTY VEZIRS, or The Story of the Forty Morns and Eves, translated from the Turkish. Crown 8vo, 10s. 6d.

GILBERT, Mrs., AUTOBIOGRAPHY, AND OTHER MEMORIALS, edited by JOSIAH GILBERT. 5th edition, crown 8vo, 7s. 6d.

GOETHE'S FAUST, translated from the German by JOHN ANSTER, with an introduction by BURDETT MASON. With illustrations (18 in black and white, 10 in colour) by FRANK M. GREGORY. Grand folio, £3. 3s.

GOLDSMITH, O., VICAR OF WAKEFIELD, edited by AUSTIN DOBSON. Elzevir 8vo (*Parchment Library*), vellum, 7s. 6d. ; parchment or cloth, 6s.

GOODCHILD, J. A., MY FRIENDS AT SANT' AMPELIO. Crown 8vo, 7s. 6d.

GORDON, Major-General C. G., HIS JOURNALS AT KHARTOUM. Printed from the original MS., with introduction and notes by A. EGMONT HAKE. Portrait, 2 maps, and 30 illustrations. 2 vols. 8vo, 21s. Cheap edition, 6s.

GORDON'S LAST JOURNAL : a facsimile of the last journal received in England from General Gordon, reproduced by photo-lithography. Imperial 4to, £3. 3s.

GORDON, Sir H. W., EVENTS IN THE LIFE OF GENERAL GORDON, from the day of his birth to the day of his death, with maps and illustrations. 2nd edition, 8vo, 7s. 6d.

GOSPEL ACCORDING TO MATTHEW, MARK, AND LUKE (The). Elzevir 8vo (*Parchment Library*), vellum, 7s. 6d. ; parchment or cloth, 6s.

GOSSE, Edmund, SEVENTEENTH CENTURY STUDIES : a contribution to the history of English poetry. 8vo, 10s. 6d.

NEW POEMS. Crown 8vo, 7s. 6d.

FIRDAUSI IN EXILE, and other poems. 2nd edition. Elzevir 8vo, gilt top, 6s.

ON VIOL AND FLUTE : lyrical poems, with frontispiece by L. ALMA TADEMA, and tailpiece by HAMO THORNYCROFT. Elzevir 8vo, 6s.

LIFE OF PHILIP HENRY GOSSE, by his son. 8vo, 15s.

GOSSIP, G. H. D., THE CHESS-PLAYER'S TEXT-BOOK : an elementary treatise on the game of chess. Numerous diagrams. 16mo, 2s.

GOUGH, A. E., PHILOSOPHY OF THE UPANISHADS. Post 8vo (*Trübner's Oriental Series*), 9s.

GOUGH, Edward, THE BIBLE TRUE FROM THE BEGINNING : a commentary on all those portions of Scripture that are most questioned and assailed. Vols. 1 to 4, 8vo, 16s. each.

GOVER, C. E., FOLK-SONGS OF SOUTHERN INDIA, containing Canarese, Badaga, Coorg, Tamil, Malayalam, and Telugu songs. 8vo, 10s. 6d.

GOWER, Lord Ronald, MY REMINISCENCES. Miniature edition, printed on hand-made paper, limp parchment antique, 10s. 6d.

BRIC-À-BRAC : being some photoprints illustrating art objects at Gower Lodge, Windsor, with letterpress descriptions. Super royal 8vo, 15s. ; extra binding, 21s.

LAST DAYS OF MARIE ANTOINETTE : an historical sketch, with portrait and facsimiles. Fcap. 4to, 10s. 6d.

NOTES OF A TOUR FROM BRINDISI TO YOKOHAMA, 1883-1884. Fcap. 8vo, 2s. 6d.

RUPERT OF THE RHINE : a biographical sketch of the life of Prince Rupert, with 3 portraits. Crown 8vo, buckram, 6s.

GRAHAM, William, The Creed of Science: religious, moral, and social. 2nd edition, revised, crown 8vo, 6s.

The Social Problem, in its Economic, Moral and Political Aspects. 8vo, 14s.

Socialism New and Old. Crown 8vo, 5s. [I.S.S.

Grammaire Albanaise, à l'usage de ceux qui désirent apprendre cette langue sans l'aide d'un maître, par P. W. Crown 8vo, 7s. 6d.

GRAY, J., Ancient Proverbs and Maxims from Burmese Sources, or The Niti literature of Burma. Post 8vo (*Trübner's Oriental Series*), 6s.

GRAY, Maxwell, The Reproach of Annesley, with frontispiece. Crown 8vo, 6s.

Silence of Dean Maitland, with frontispiece. Crown 8vo, 6s.

Westminster Chimes, and other poems. Small 8vo, 5s.

GREG, W. R., Literary and Social Judgments. 4th edition, 2 vols. crown 8vo, 15s.

The Creed of Christendom, 8th edition. (*Philosophical Library.*) 2 vols. post 8vo, 15s.

Enigmas of Life, 17th edition. (*Philosophical Library.*) Post 8vo, 10s. 6d.

Political Problems for our Age and Country. 8vo, 10s. 6d.

Miscellaneous Essays. Two series. Crown 8vo, 7s. 6d. each.

GREY, Rowland, In Sunny Switzerland: a tale of six weeks. 2nd edition, small 8vo, 5s.

Lindenblumen, and other stories. Small 8vo, 5s.

By Virtue of His Office. Crown 8vo, 6s.

Jacob's Letter, and other stories. Crown 8vo, 6s.

GRIFFIN, Sir Lepel, The Rajas of the Punjab: history of the principal states in the Punjab, and their political relations with the British Government. Royal 8vo, 21s.

GRIFFIS, W. E., The Mikado's Empire. Book I. History of Japan from B.C. 660 to A.D. 1872. Book II. Personal Experiences, Observations, and Studies in Japan, 1870-1874. 2nd edition, illustrated, 8vo, 20s.

Japanese Fairy World: stories from the wonder-lore of Japan with 12 plates. Square 16mo, 3s. 6d.

GRIFFITH, F. Ll., and PETRIE, W. M. F., Two Hieroglyphic Papyri from Tanis, with 15 plates. 4to, boards, 5s.

GRIFFITH, F. L., The Inscriptions of Siut and Der Rifeh, with 21 plates. 4to, 10s.

GRIFFITH, R. T. H., Birth of the War-God: a poem from the Sanskrit of Kálidásá. 2nd edition, post 8vo (*Trübner's Oriental Series*), 5s.

Yúsuf and Zulaika: a poem by Jami, translated from the Persian into English verse. Post 8vo (*Trübner's Oriental Series*), 8s. 6d.

GRIMLEY, H. N., The Prayer of Humanity: sermons on the Lord's Prayer. Crown 8vo, 3s. 6d.

Tremadoc Sermons, chiefly on the Spiritual Body, the Unseen World, and the Divine Humanity. 4th edition, crown 8vo, 6s.

The Temple of Humanity, and other sermons. Crown 8vo, 6s.

GUBBINS, J. H., Dictionary of Chinese-Japanese Words in the Japanese Language. Part I (A to J). Crown 8vo, 7s. 6d.

GUBERNATIS, Angelo de, Zoological Mythology, or the legends of animals. 2 vols. 8vo, £1. 8s. ,

GUICCIARDINI, Counsels and Reflections, translated by N. H. Thomson. Crown 8vo, 6s.

GURNEY, Alfred, The Vision of the Eucharist, and other poems. Crown 8vo, 5s.

A Christmas Faggot. Small 8vo, 5s.

Voices from the Holy Sepulchre, and other poems. Crown 8vo, 5s.

Wagner's Parsifal : a study. Fcap. 8vo, 1s. 6d.

Our Catholic Inheritance in the Larger Hope. Crown 8vo, 1s. 6d.

GURNEY, Edmund, MYERS, F. W. H., and PODMORE, F., Phantasms of the Living. 2 vols. 8vo, 21s.

HADDON, Caroline, The Larger Life : studies in Hinton's ethics. Crown 8vo, 5s.

HAECKEL, Prof. Ernst, The History of Creation, translation revised by Professor E. Ray Lankester, with coloured plates and genealogical trees of the various groups of both plants and animals. 3rd edition, 2 vols. post 8vo, 32s.

The History of the Evolution of Man, with numerous illustrations. 2 vols. post 8vo, 32s.

A Visit to Ceylon. Post 8vo, 7s. 6d.

Freedom in Science and Teaching, with a prefatory note by Prof. T. H. Huxley. Crown 8vo, 5s.

HAGGARD, H. Rider, Cetywayo and his White Neighbours, or Remarks on recent events in Zululand, Natal, and the Transvaal. 3rd edition, crown 8vo, 6s.

HAGGARD, W. H., and LE STRANGE, G., The Vazir of Lankuran : a Persian play, with a grammatical introduction, translation, notes, and vocabulary. Crown 8vo, 10s. 6d.

HAHN, T., Tsuni- ‖ Goam, the Supreme Being of the Khoi-Khoi. Post 8vo (*Trübner's Oriental Series*), 7s. 6d.

HAINES, C. R., Christianity and Islam in Spain, A.D. 756-1031. Crown 8vo, 2s. 6d.

HALDEMAN, S. S., Pennsylvania Dutch : a dialect of South Germany with an infusion of English. 8vo, 3s. 6d.

HALL, F. T., The Pedigree of the Devil, with 7 autotype illustrations from designs by the Author. 8vo, 7s. 6d.

HALLOCK, Charles, The Sportsman's Gazetteer and General Guide to the game animals, birds, and fishes of North America. Maps and portrait. Crown 8vo, 15s.

HALTZOCH, E., South Indian Inscriptions : Tamil and Sanskrit, Vol. I. 12s. (*Arch. Survey of India.*)

HAMILTON. Memoirs of Arthur Hamilton, B.A., of Trinity College, Cambridge. Crown 8vo, 6s.

HAMILTON, Capt. Ian, THE FIGHTING OF THE FUTURE. Crown 8vo, 1*s.*

HARRIS, C., LAURENCE : a poem. Small 8vo, 2*s.* 6*d.*

HARRIS, Emily M., NARRATIVE OF THE HOLY BIBLE. Crown 8vo, 5*s.*
LADY DOBBS : a novel. 2 vols. crown 8vo, 21*s.*

HARRISON, Clifford, IN HOURS OF LEISURE. 2nd edition, crown 8vo 5*s.*

HARRISON, Col. R., OFFICER'S MEMORANDUM BOOK FOR PEACE AND WAR. 4th edition, revised, oblong 32mo, red basil, with pencil, 3*s.* 6*d.*

HARTMANN, Eduard von, PHILOSOPHY OF THE UNCONSCIOUS, translated by W. C. COUPLAND. 3 vols. post 8vo, 31*s.* 6*d.* [*Philosophical Library.*

HARTMANN, Franz, MAGIC, WHITE AND BLACK, or The science of finite and infinite life. Crown 8vo, 7*s.* 6*d.*

THE LIFE OF PARACELSUS, AND THE SUBSTANCE OF HIS TEACHINGS. Post 8vo, 10*s.* 6*d.*

LIFE AND DOCTRINES OF JACOB BOEHME : an introduction to the study of his works. Post 8vo, 10*s.* 6*d.*

HARTMANN, R., ANTHROPOID APES, with 63 illustrations. Crown 8vo, 2nd edition, 5*s.* [I.S.S

HARVEY, W. F., SIMPLIFIED GRAMMAR OF THE SPANISH LANGUAGE. Crown 8vo, 3*s.* 6*d.*

HAUG, M., ESSAYS ON THE SACRED LANGUAGE, WRITINGS, AND RELIGION OF THE PARSIS. 3rd edition, edited and enlarged by E. W. WEST, post 8vo (*Trübner's Oriental Series*), 16*s.*

HAWEIS, H. R., CURRENT COIN. Materialism—The Devil—Crime— Drunkenness—Pauperism—Emotion—Recreation—The Sabbath. 6th edition, crown 8vo, 5*s.*

ARROWS IN THE AIR. 5th edition, crown 8vo, 5*s.*

SPEECH IN SEASON. 6th edition, crown 8vo, 5*s.*

THOUGHTS FOR THE TIMES. 14th edition, crown 8vo, 5*s.*

UNSECTARIAN FAMILY PRAYERS. New edition, fcap. 8vo, 1*s.* 6*d.*

HAWTHORNE, Nathaniel, WORKS. Complete in 12 vols. large post 8vo, 7*s.* 6*d.* each.

HEATH, Richard, EDGAR QUINET : his early life and writings, with portraits, illustrations, and an autograph letter. Post 8vo, 12*s.* 6*d.*
[*Philosophical Library.*

HEBREW LITERATURE SOCIETY. Lists on application.

HECKER, J. F. C., THE EPIDEMICS OF THE MIDDLE AGES, translated by G. B. BABINGTON. 3rd edition, 8vo, 9*s.* 6*d.*

HEIDENHAIN, Rudolph, HYPNOTISM, OR ANIMAL MAGNETISM, with preface by G. J. ROMANES. 2nd edition, small 8vo, 2*s.* 6*d.*

HEILPRIN, A., BERMUDA ISLANDS, 8vo, 18*s.*

HEILPRIN, Prof. A., GEOGRAPHICAL AND GEOLOGICAL DISTRIBUTION OF ANIMALS, with frontispiece. Crown 8vo, 5*s.* [I.S.S.

HEINE, H., RELIGION AND PHILOSOPHY IN GERMANY, translated by J. SNODGRASS. Post 8vo, 6*s.* [*Philosophical Library.*

THE LOVE-SONGS OF HEINE, englished by H. B. BRIGGS. Post 8vo, parchment, 3*s.* 6*d.*

HENDRIKS, Dom Lawrence, THE LONDON CHARTERHOUSE: its monks and its martyrs. Illustrated, 8vo. 14*s.*

HENSLOW, Prof. G., ORIGIN OF FLORAL STRUCTURES THROUGH INSECT AND OTHER AGENCIES, with 88 illustrations. Crown 8vo, 5*s.*

HEPBURN, J. C., JAPANESE AND ENGLISH DICTIONARY. 2nd edition, imperial 8vo, half-roan, 18*s.*

JAPANESE-ENGLISH AND ENGLISH-JAPANESE DICTIONARY. 3rd edition, 8vo, half-morocco, cloth sides, 30*s.* Pocket edition, square 16mo, 14*s.*

HERMES TRISMEGISTUS, WORKS, translated by J. D. CHAMBERS. Post 8vo, 7*s. 6d.*

THE VIRGIN OF THE WORLD, translated and edited by the Authors of 'The Perfect Way.' Illustrations. 4to, imitation parchment, 10*s. 6d.*

HERSHON, P. J., TALMUDIC MISCELLANY, or One thousand and one extracts from the Talmud, the Midrashim, and the Kabbalah. Post 8vo (*Trübner's Oriental Series*), 14*s.*

HILLEBRAND, Karl, FRANCE AND THE FRENCH IN THE SECOND HALF OF THE 19TH CENTURY, from the third German edition. Post 8vo, 10*s. 6d.*

HILMY, H. H. Prince Ibrahim, THE LITERATURE OF EGYPT AND THE SOUDAN, a bibliography; comprising printed books, periodical writings and papers of learned societies, maps and charts, ancient papyri manuscripts, drawings, &c. 2 vols. demy 4to, £3. 3*s.*

HINTON. LIFE AND LETTERS OF JAMES HINTON, with an introduction by Sir W. W. GULL, and portrait engraved on steel by C. H. JEENS. 6th edition, crown 8vo, 8*s. 6d.*

PHILOSOPHY AND RELIGION : selections from the manuscripts of the late James Hinton, edited by CAROLINE HADDON. 2nd edition, crown 8vo, 5*s.*

THE LAW-BREAKER, and THE COMING OF THE LAW, edited by MARGARET HINTON. Crown 8vo, 6*s.*

THE MYSTERY OF PAIN. New edition, fcap. 8vo, 1*s.*

HODGSON. B. H., ESSAYS ON THE LANGUAGES, LITERATURE, AND RELIGION OF NEPAL AND TIBET. Royal 8vo, 14*s.*

ESSAYS RELATING TO INDIAN SUBJECTS. 2 vols. post 8vo (*Trübner's Oriental Series*), 28*s.*

HODGSON, J. E., ACADEMY LECTURES. Crown 8vo, 7*s. 6d.*

HODGSON, W. B., THE EDUCATION OF GIRLS ; and THE EMPLOYMENT OF WOMEN OF THE UPPER CLASSES EDUCATIONALLY CONSIDERED. 2nd edition, crown 8vo, 3*s. 6d.*

HOLBEIN SOCIETY. Subscription, one guinea per annum. List of publications on application.

HOLMES-FORBES, A. W., THE SCIENCE OF BEAUTY : an analytical inquiry into the laws of æsthetics. 2nd edition, post 8vo, 3*s. 6d.*

HOLMES, Oliver Wendell, JOHN LOTHROP MOTLEY : a memoir. Crown 8vo, 6*s.*

LIFE OF RALPH WALDO EMERSON, with portrait. English copyright edition, crown 8vo, 6*s.*

HOLYOAKE, G. J., HISTORY OF CO-OPERATION IN ENGLAND : its literature and its advocates. 2 vols. crown 8vo, 14*s.*

SELF-HELP BY THE PEOPLE : thirty-three years of co-operation in Rochdale. 9th edition, crown 8vo, 2*s. 6d.*

HOME, Mme. Dunglas, D. D. HOME : his life and mission, with portrait. 8vo, 12*s. 6d.*

GIFT OF D. D. HOME. 8vo, 10*s.*

HOMER'S ILIAD. Greek text, with translation by J. G. CORDERY. 2 vols. 8vo, 14*s.* Cheap edition (translation only), crown 8vo, 5*s.*

HOOLE Henry, SCIENCE AND ART OF TRAINING : a handbook for athletes. 8vo, 3*s. 6d.*

HOOPER, Mary, LITTLE DINNERS : how to serve them with elegance and economy. 21st edition, crown 8vo, 2*s. 6d.*

COOKERY FOR INVALIDS, PERSONS OF DELICATE DIGESTION, AND CHILDREN. 5th edition, crown 8vo, 2*s. 6d.*

EVERY-DAY MEALS : being economical and wholesome recipes for breakfast, luncheon, and supper. 7th edition, crown 8vo, 2*s. 6d.*

HOPKINS, Ellice, WORK AMONGST WORKING MEN. 6th edition, crown 8vo, 3*s. 6d.*

HOPKINS, E. W., ORDINANCES OF MANU, translated from the Sanskrit, with an introduction by the late A. C. BURNELL. Post 8vo (*Trübner's Oriental Series*), 12*s.*

HOPKINS, F. L., ELEMENTARY GRAMMAR OF THE TURKISH LANGUAGE, with a few easy exercises. Crown 8vo, 3*s. 6d.*

HORATIUS FLACCUS, Q., OPERA, edited by F. A. CORNISH, with frontispiece. Elzevir 8vo (*Parchment Library*), vellum, 7*s. 6d.* ; parchment or cloth, 6*s.*

HORNADAY, W. T., TWO YEARS IN A JUNGLE, with illustrations. 8vo, 21*s.*

HOSPITALIER, E., THE MODERN APPLICATIONS OF ELECTRICITY, translated and enlarged by JULIUS MAIER. 2nd edition, revised, with many additions and numerous illustrations, 2 vols. 8vo, 25*s.*

HOWELLS, W. D., A LITTLE GIRL AMONG THE OLD MASTERS, with 54 plates. Oblong crown 8vo, 10*s.*

HUES, Ivan, HEART TO HEART. Small 8vo, 5*s.*

HUGHES, H., PRINCIPLES OF NATURAL AND SUPERNATURAL MORALS. Vol. I. Natural Morals. 8vo, 12*s.*

HUGHES, Walter, LYRA MANCUNIENSIS. Small 8vo, 1*s. 6d.*

HULME, F. Edward, MATHEMATICAL DRAWING INSTRUMENTS, AND HOW TO USE THEM, with illustrations. 3rd edition, imperial 16mo, 3*s. 6d.*

HUMBOLDT, Baron W. von, THE SPHERE AND DUTIES OF GOVERNMENT, from the German by J. COULTHARD. Post 8vo, 5*s.*

HUNTER, Capt. F. M., ACCOUNT OF THE BRITISH SETTLEMENT OF ADEN, IN ARABIA. 8vo, cloth, 7*s. 6d.* [*India Office.*

HUNTER, Hay, and WHYTE, Walter, MY DUCATS AND MY DAUGHTER, with frontispiece. Crown 8vo, 6*s.*

HUNTER, Sir W. W., Imperial Gazetteer of India. New edition, with maps. 1886–87. 14 vols. half-morocco, £3. 3s.

The Indian Empire: its people, history, and products. 2nd edition, revised, with map, 8vo, £1. 1s.

Brief History of the Indian People. 4th edition, with map, crown 8vo, 3s. 6d.

The Indian Musalmans. 3rd edition, 8vo, 10s. 6d.

Statistical Account of Bengal. 20 vols. 8vo, half-morocco, £5. (*India Office.*)

Statistical Account of Assam, with 2 maps. 2 vols. 8vo, half-morocco, 10s. (*India Office.*)

HUTCHINSON, A. B., The Mind of Mencius, or Political Economy founded upon Moral Philosophy. A systematic digest of the doctrines of the Chinese philosopher Mencius, translated from the German of Faber, with additional notes. Post 8vo (*Trübner's Oriental Series*), 10s. 6d.

HUTCHINSON, Colonel, and MACGREGOR, Major, Military Sketching and Reconnaissance. 5th edition, with 16 plates, small crown 8vo, 4s.

HUXLEY, Prof. T. H., The Crayfish : an introduction to the study of zoology, with 82 illustrations. 5th edition, crown 8vo, 5s. [I.S.S.

HYNDMAN, H. M., Historical Basis of Socialism in England. Large crown 8vo, 8s. 6d.

IHNE, W., Latin Grammar for Beginners, on Ahn's system. 12mo, 3s.

IM THURN, Everard F., Among the Indians of Guiana : sketches, chiefly anthropologic, from the interior of British Guiana, with 53 illustrations and a map. 8vo, 18s.

India.—Gazetteer of the Bombay Presidency. 8vo, half-bound. Vols. II. to XXV. 8s. to 16s. per vol.

Statistical, Descriptive, and Historical Account of the North-Western Provinces of India. 8vo, half-bound. Vols. I. to XIV. 10s. and 12s. per volume.

Geographical Department of the India Office, London. List of publications on application.

Geological Survey of India. List of publications on application.

INGELOW, Jean, Off the Skelligs : a novel, with frontispiece. Crown 8vo, 6s.

INGLEBY, Clement M., Essays, edited by his Son. Crown 8vo, 7s. 6d.

INGLEBY, Holcombe, Echoes from Naples, and other poems, with illustrations by his Wife. Crown 8vo, 3s. 6d.

INMAN, James, Nautical Tables, designed for the use of British seamen. New edition, revised and enlarged, 8vo, 16s.

Irresponsibility and its Recognition, by a Graduate of Oxford. Crown 8vo, 3s. 6d.

IVANOFF'S Russian Grammar, 16th edition, translated, enlarged, and arranged for use of students by Major W. E. Gowan. 8vo, 6s.

JACOB, G. A., Manual of Hindu Pantheism : the Vedantasara. 2nd edition, post 8vo (*Trübner's Oriental Series*), 6s.

JAPP, Alexander H., DAYS WITH INDUSTRIALS : adventures and experiences among curious industries, with illustrations. Crown 8vo, 6*s.*

JÄSCHKE, H. A., A TIBETAN-ENGLISH DICTIONARY, with special reference to the prevailing dialects, to which is added an English-Tibetan vocabulary. Imperial 8vo, £1. 10*s.* (*India Office.*)

TIBETAN GRAMMAR, prepared by Dr. H. WENZEL. 2nd edition, crown 8vo, 5*s.*

JENKINS, E., and RAYMOND, J., ARCHITECT'S LEGAL HANDBOOK. 4th edition, revised, crown 8vo, 6*s.*

JENKINS, E., A MODERN PALADIN : contemporary manners. Crown 8vo, 5*s.*

JENKINS, Jabez, VEST-POCKET LEXICON : an English dictionary of all except familiar words, including the principal scientific and technical terms. 64mo, roan, 1*s.* 6*d.*; cloth, 1*s.*

JENKINS, R. C., HERALDRY, ENGLISH AND FOREIGN, with a dictionary of heraldic terms and 156 illustrations. Small 8vo, 3*s.* 6*d.*

JENNINGS, Hargrave, THE INDIAN RELIGIONS, or Results of the mysterious Buddhism. 8vo, 10*s.* 6*d.*

JESUS THE CARPENTER OF NAZARETH, by a Layman. Crown 8vo, 7*s.* 6*d.*

JEVONS, W. Stanley, MONEY AND THE MECHANISM OF EXCHANGE. 8th edition, crown 8vo, 5*s.* [I.S.S.

JOHNSON, C. P., HINTS TO COLLECTORS OF ORIGINAL EDITIONS OF THE WORKS OF DICKENS. Crown 8vo, vellum, 6*s.*

HINTS TO COLLECTORS OF ORIGINAL EDITIONS OF THE WORKS OF THACKERAY. Crown 8vo, vellum, 6*s.*

JOHNSON, Edwin, THE RISE OF CHRISTENDOM. 8vo, 14*s.*

JOHNSON, J. B., THINGS PRESENT AND THINGS TO COME. Crown 8vo, 4*s.* 6*d.*

JOHNSON, Samuel, ORIENTAL RELIGIONS AND THEIR RELATION TO UNIVERSAL RELIGION. PERSIA. 8vo, 18*s.*

ORIENTAL RELIGIONS AND THEIR RELATION to UNIVERSAL RELIGION. INDIA. 2 vols. 21*s.* (*Philosophical Library.*)

JOHNSTON, H. H., THE KILIMA-NJARO EXPEDITION : a record of scientific exploration in Eastern Equatorial Africa, with 6 maps and 80 illustrations. 8vo, 21*s.*

HISTORY OF A SLAVE, with 47 illustrations. Square 8vo, 6*s.*

JOLY, N., MAN BEFORE METALS, with 148 illustrations. 4th edition, crown 8vo, 5*s.* [I.S.S.

JOLLY, J., MANAVA-DHARMA-CASTRA : the Code of Manu. Original Sanskrit text, with critical notes. Post 8vo (*Trübner's Oriental Series*), 10*s.* 6*d.*

JORDAN, F., CHARACTER AS SEEN IN BODY AND PARENTAGE. Crown 8vo, paper boards, 2*s.*

JOSEPH, N. S., RELIGION, NATURAL AND REVEALED : a series of progressive lessons for Jewish youth. Crown 8vo, 3*s.*

JUDD, Prof. J. W., VOLCANOES : what they are and what they teach, with 96 illustrations on wood. 4th edition, crown 8vo, 5*s.* [I.S.S.

JUVENALIS SATIRÆ, with a literal English prose translation and notes by J. D. LEWIS. 2nd edition, 2 vols. 8vo, 12*s.*

KARCHER, *Théodore,* QUESTIONNAIRE FRANCAIS : questions on French grammar, idiomatic difficulties, and military expressions. 4th edition, crown 8vo, 4s. 6d. ; interleaved with writing paper, 5s. 6d.

KARDEC, *Allen,* THE SPIRIT'S BOOK : the principles of Spiritist doctrine on the immortality of the soul, &c., translated by ANNA BLACKWELL. Crown 8vo, 7s. 6d.

THE MEDIUM'S BOOK, or Guide for mediums and for evocations, translated by ANNA BLACKWELL. Crown 8vo, 7s. 6d.

HEAVEN AND HELL, or The Divine justice vindicated in the plurality of existences, translated by ANNA BLACKWELL. Crown 8vo, 7s. 6d.

KARMARSCH, *Karl,* TECHNOLOGICAL DICTIONARY, 4th edition, revised, imperial 8vo, 3 vols.
　　　　Vol. 1.—German-English-French, 12s.
　　　　Vol. 2.—English-German-French, 12s.
　　　　Vol. 3.—French-German-English, 15s.

KAUFMANN, *M.,* SOCIALISM : its nature, its dangers, and its remedies considered. Crown 8vo, 7s. 6d.

UTOPIAS, or Schemes of social improvement from Sir Thomas More to Karl Marx. Crown 8vo, 5s.

CHRISTIAN SOCIALISM. Crown 8vo, 4s. 6d.

KEATS, *John,* POETICAL WORKS, edited by W. T. ARNOLD. Large crown 8vo, choicely printed on hand-made paper, with etched portrait, vellum, 15s. ; parchment or cloth, 12s. New edition, crown 8vo, cloth, 3s. 6d.

KEBLE, *J.,* CHRISTIAN YEAR, with portrait. Elzevir 8vo (*Parchment Library*), vellum, 7s. 6d. ; parchment or cloth, 6s.

KEMPIS, *Thomas à,* THE IMITATION OF CHRIST, revised translation. Elzevir 8vo. (*Parchment Library*), vellum, 7s. 6d. ; parchment or cloth, 6s. Red line edition, fcap. 8vo, 2s. 6d. Cabinet edition, small 8vo, 1s. 6d. ; cloth limp, 1s. Miniature edition, 32mo, with red lines, 1s. 6d. ; without red lines, 1s.

THE IMITATION OF CHRIST : a metrical version, by HENRY CARRINGTON. Crown 8vo. 5s.

KERRISON, *Lady Caroline,* A COMMONPLACE BOOK OF THE FIFTEENTH CENTURY, containing a religious play and poetry, legal forms, and local accounts. From the original M.S. at Brome Hall, Suffolk. Edited by LUCY TOULMIN SMITH. With 2 facsimiles, 8vo, 7s. 6d.

KEYS OF THE CREEDS. Third edition, revised, crown 8vo, 2s. 6d.

KINAHAN, *G. H.,* VALLEYS AND THEIR RELATION TO FISSURES, FRACTURES, AND FAULTS. Crown 8vo, 7s. 6d.

KING, *Mrs. Hamilton,* THE DISCIPLES. 10th edition, elzevir 8vo, 6s. ; small 8vo, 5s.

A BOOK OF DREAMS. 3rd edition, crown 8vo, 3s. 6d.

SERMON IN THE HOSPITAL (from 'The Disciples '). Fcap. 8vo, 1s. Cheap edition, 3d.

BALLADS OF THE NORTH, and other poems. Crown 8vo, 5s.

KINGSFORD, *Anna,* THE PERFECT WAY IN DIET : a treatise advocating a return to the natural and ancient food of our race. 3rd edition, small 8vo, 2s.

SPIRITUAL HERMENEUTICS OF ASTROLOGY AND HOLY WRIT, illustrated. 4to, parchment, 10s. 6d.

KINGSFORD, Anna, and MAITLAND, Edward, THE VIRGIN OF THE WORLD OF HERMES MERCURIUS TRISMEGISTUS, rendered into English. 4to, imit. parchment, 10s. 6d.

THE PERFECT WAY, or The finding of Christ. 3rd edition, revised, square 16mo, 7s. 6d.

KINGSFORD, W., HISTORY OF CANADA. 8vo.
Vol. I. 1608–1682. 15s.
Vol. II. 1679–1725. 15s.
Vol. III. 1726–1756, with 3 maps. 15s.
Vol. IV. 1757– 15s.

KINGSLEY, J. S., NATURAL HISTORY. 'Riverside' edition. 6 vols. with 2,200 illustrations, 4to, £6. 6s.

KISTNER, Otto, BUDDHA AND HIS DOCTRINES : a bibliographical essay. 4to, 2s. 6d.

KITTON, Fred. G., JOHN LEECH, ARTIST AND HUMOURIST : a biographical sketch. 18mo, 1s.

KLEIN, Felix, LECTURES ON THE IKOSAHEDRON, and the solution of equations of the fifth degree, translated by G. G. MORRICE. 8vo, 10s. 6d.

KNOWLES, J. H., FOLK-TALES OF KASHMIR. Post 8vo, 16s.

FOLK-TALES OF KASHMIR. Post 8vo (*Trübner's Oriental Series*), 16s.

KOLBE, F. W., A LANGUAGE-STUDY BASED ON BANTU, an inquiry into the laws of root-formation. 8vo, 6s.

KRAPF, L., DICTIONARY OF THE SUAHILI LANGUAGE. 8vo, 30s.

KRAUS, J., CARLSBAD AND ITS NATURAL HEALING AGENTS, with notes by JOHN T. WALLERS. 3rd edition, crown 8vo, 6s. 6d.

LAGRANGE, F., PHYSIOLOGY OF BODILY EXERCISE. 2nd edition, crown 8vo, 5s. [I.S.S.

LAMB, Charles, BEAUTY AND THE BEAST, or A rough outside with a gentle heart. A poem. Fcap. 8vo, vellum, 10s. 6d.

LANDON, Joseph, SCHOOL MANAGEMENT ; including a general view of the work of education, organisation, and discipline. 7th edition, crown 8vo, 6s. (*Education Library.*)

LANE, E. W., SELECTIONS FROM THE KORAN. New edition, with introduction by STANLEY LANE-POOLE. Post 8vo (*Trübner's Oriental Series*), 9s.

LANG, Andrew, IN THE WRONG PARADISE, and other stories. Crown 8vo, 6s.

BALLADES IN BLUE CHINA. Elzevir 8vo, 5s.

RHYMES À LA MODE, with frontispiece by E. A. ABBEY. 2nd edition, Elzevir 8vo, 5s.

LOST LEADERS. Crown 8vo, 5s.

LANGE, Prof. F. A., HISTORY OF MATERIALISM, and Criticism of its present importance. Authorised translation by ERNEST C. THOMAS. 3 vols. post 8vo, 10s. 6d. each. [*Philosophical Library.*

LANGE, F. K. W., GERMAN GRAMMAR PRACTICE. Crown 8vo, 1s. 6d.

COLLOQUIAL GERMAN GRAMMAR. Crown 8vo, 4s. 6d.

GERMANIA : a German reading-book. Part I. Anthology of Prose and Poetry, with vocabulary. Part II. Essays on German History and Institutions. 8vo, 2 vols. 5s. 6d. ; separately, 3s. 6d. each.

LANGSTROTH ON THE HIVE AND HONEY BEE. Revised and enlarged edition, with numerous illustrations. 8vo, 9s.

LARMOYER, M. de, PRACTICAL FRENCH GRAMMAR. Part I. crown 8vo, 3s. 6d.

LATHE (THE) AND ITS USES, or Instruction in the art of turning wood and metal. 6th edition, illustrated, 8vo, 10s. 6d.

LE-BRUN, L., MATERIALS FOR TRANSLATING ENGLISH INTO FRENCH. 7th edition, post 8vo, 4s. 6d.

LEE, G., MANUAL OF POLITICS. Small crown 8vo, 2s. 6d.

LEFEVRE, Right Hon. G. Shaw, PEEL AND O'CONNELL. 8vo, 10s. 6d.

INCIDENTS OF COERCION : a journal of visits to Ireland. 3rd edition, crown 8vo, limp cloth, 1s. 6d. ; paper covers, 1s.

IRISH MEMBERS AND ENGLISH GAOLERS. Crown 8vo, limp cloth, 1s. 6d. ; paper covers, 1s.

COMBINATION AND COERCION IN IRELAND : sequel to 'Incidents of Coercion.' Crown 8vo, cloth, 1s. 6d. ; paper covers, 1s.

LEGGE, James, CHINESE CLASSICS, with a translation, critical and exegetical. 8 parts published. Royal 8vo, £2. 2s. each.

CHINESE CLASSICS, translated into English. Popular edition, crown 8vo.
Vol. I. Life and Teachings of Confucius. 6th edition, 10s. 6d.
Vol. II. Works of Mencius, 12s.
Vol. III. She-King, or Book of Poetry, 12s.

LELAND, C. G., BREITMANN BALLADS. The only authorised edition, including nineteen original ballads, illustrating his travels in Europe. Crown 8vo, 6s. Another edition (*Lotos Series*), 3s. 6d.

GAUDEAMUS : humorous poems from the German of JOSEPH VICTOR SCHEFFEL and others. 16mo, 3s. 6d.

ENGLISH GIPSIES AND THEIR LANGUAGE. 2nd edition, crown 8vo, 7s. 6d.

FU-SANG ; or The discovery of America by Chinese Buddhist priests in the 5th century. Crown 8vo, 7s. 6d.

PIDGIN-ENGLISH SING-SONG, or Songs and stories in the China-English dialect. 2nd edition, crown 8vo, 5s.

THE GYPSIES. Crown 8vo, 10s. 6d.

LENDENFELD, R. von, MONOGRAPH OF THE HORNY SPONGES, with 50 plates. Issued by direction of the Royal Society. 4to, £3.

LEOPARDI, Giacomo, ESSAYS AND DIALOGUES OF, translated by CHARLES EDWARDES, with biographical sketch. Post 8vo, 7s. 6d.
[*Philosophical Library.*

LESLEY, J. P., MAN'S ORIGIN AND DESTINY, sketched from the platform of the Physical Sciences. 2nd edition, crown 8vo, 7s. 6d.

LESSING, Gotthold E., EDUCATION OF THE HUMAN RACE, from the German by F. W. Robertson. Fcap. 8vo, 2s. 6d.

LEVI, Prof. Leone, INTERNATIONAL LAW, with materials for a code of international law. Crown 8vo, 5s. [I.S.S.

LEWES, George Henry, PROBLEMS OF LIFE AND MIND. 8vo.
Series i. Foundations of a Creed. 2 vols. 28s.
Series ii. Physical Basis of Mind. With illustrations, 16s.
Series iii. 2 vols. 22s. 6d.

LIGHT ON THE PATH, for the personal use of those who are ignorant of the Eastern Wisdom. Written down by M. C. Fcap. 8vo, 1s. 6d.

LILLIE, Arthur, POPULAR LIFE OF BUDDHA, containing an answer to the Hibbert Lectures of 1881. With illustrations. Crown 8vo, 6s.

BUDDHISM IN CHRISTENDOM, or Jesus the Essene, with illustrations. 8vo, 15s.

LILLY, W. S., CHARACTERISTICS FROM THE WRITINGS OF CARDINAL NEWMAN: selections from his various works. 8th edition, with portrait, crown 8vo, 6s.

LINDSAY, Lady, LYRICS, AND OTHER POEMS. Elzevir 8vo, 5s.

LINTON, W. J., RARE POEMS OF THE 16TH AND 17TH CENTURIES. Crown 8vo, 5s.

LINTON, W. J., and STODDARD, R. H., ENGLISH VERSE. 5 vols. crown 8vo, 5s. each.
    CHAUCER TO BURNS—TRANSLATIONS—LYRICS OF THE NINETEENTH CENTURY— DRAMATIC SCENES AND CHARACTERS—BALLADS AND ROMANCES.

LIVERSIDGE, A., MINERALS OF NEW SOUTH WALES, &c., with large coloured map. Royal 8vo, 18s.

LOCHER, Carl, EXPLANATION OF ORGAN STOPS, with hints for effective combinations. 8vo, 5s.

LOCKER, F., LONDON LYRICS. 10th edition, with portrait, elzevir 8vo, cloth extra, gilt top, 5s.

LOCKHART, W., LIFE OF ANTONIO ROSMINI SERBATI, with portraits 2 vols. crown 8vo, 12s.

LOCKYER, J. Norman, STUDIES IN SPECTRUM ANALYSIS, with 6 photographic illustrations of spectra, and numerous engravings on wood. 4th edition, crown 8vo, 6s. 6d.   [I.S.S.

LOMMEL, Dr. Eugene, NATURE OF LIGHT, with a general acconut of Physical Optics, with 188 illustrations and a table of spectra in chromo-lithography. 5th edition, crown 8vo, 5s.   [I.S.S.

LONG, J., EASTERN PROVERBS AND EMBLEMS ILLUSTRATING OLD TRUTHS Post 8vo (*Trübner's Oriental Series*), 6s.

LONGFELLOW, Samuel, LIFE OF H. WADSWORTH LONGFELLOW, by his brother, with portraits and illustrations. 3 vols. 8vo, 42s.

LONSDALE, Margaret, SISTER DORA : a biography, with portrait. 30th edition, small 8vo, 2s. 6d.

GEORGE ELIOT : thoughts upon her life, her books, and herself. 2nd edition, small 8vo, 1s. 6d.

LOTI, Pierre, RARAHU ; OR, THE MARRIAGE OF LOTI. 4s. ; paper, 2s. 6d.

LOWDER. CHARLES LOWDER : a biography, by the author of ' St. Teresa.' 12th edition, with portrait, crown 8vo, 3s. 6d.

LOWE, R. W., THOMAS BETTERTON. Crown 8vo, 2s. 6d. [*Eminent Actors.*

LOWELL, James Russell, BIGLOW PAPERS, edited by THOMAS HUGHES, Q.C. Fcap. 8vo, 2s. 6d.

LOWSLEY, Major B., GLOSSARY OF BERKSHIRE WORDS AND PHRASES. Crown 8vo, half-calf, gilt edges, interleaved, 12s. 6d.

LUBBOCK, Sir John, ANTS, BEES, AND WASPS : a record of observations on the habits of the social hymenoptera, with 5 chromo-lithographic illustrations. 10th edition, crown 8vo, 5s.   [I.S.S.

ON THE SENSES, INSTINCTS, AND INTELLIGENCE OF ANIMALS, with special reference to insects, with 100 illustrations. 3rd edition, crown 8vo, 5s.
[I.S.S.

LÜCKES, Eva C. E., LECTURES ON GENERAL NURSING, delivered to the Probationers of the London Hospital Training School for Nurses. 3rd edition, crown 8vo, 2s. 6d.

LUKIN, J., AMONGST MACHINES : a description of various mechanical appliances used in the manufacture of wood, metal, &c. A book for boys. 2nd edition, with 64 engravings, crown 8vo, 3s. 6d.

THE BOY ENGINEERS : what they did, and how they did it. A book for boys. With 30 engravings. Imperial 16mo, 3s. 6d.

THE YOUNG MECHANIC : a book for boys, containing directions for the use of all kinds of tools, and for the construction of steam-engines and mechanical models. 6th edition, with 70 engravings, crown 8vo, 3s. 6d.

LULWORTH, Eric, SUNSHINE AND SHOWER, and other poems. Small 8vo, 5s.

LUMLEY, E., ART OF JUDGING THE CHARACTER OF INDIVIDUALS FROM THEIR HANDWRITING AND STYLE, with 35 plates. Square 16mo, 5s.

LUYS, J., THE BRAIN AND ITS FUNCTIONS, with illustrations. 3rd edition, crown 8vo, 5s.   [I.S.S.

LYALL, Sir Alfred, VERSES WRITTEN IN INDIA. Elzevir 8vo, gilt top, 5s.

LYSCHINSKA, M.J., and MONTEFIORE, T. G., FROEBEL'S ETHICAL TEACHING : two essays. Fcap. 8vo, 2s. 6d.

LYTTON, Earl of, LIFE, LETTERS, AND LITERARY REMAINS OF EDWARD BULWER, LORD LYTTON, with portraits, illustrations, and fac-similes. 8vo. Vols. I. and II. 32s.

MACAULAYS ESSAYS ON MEN AND BOOKS : Lord Clive, Milton, Earl of Chatham, Lord Byron, edited by ALEX. H. JAPP (*Lotos Series*), 3s. 6d.

MACDONALD, George, DONAL GRANT, with frontispiece. Crown 8vo, 6s.

HOME AGAIN, with frontispiece. Crown 8vo, 6s.

CASTLE WARLOCK, with frontispiece. Crown 8vo, 6s.

MALCOLM, with portrait of the author engraved on steel. Crown 8vo, 6s.

THE MARQUIS OF LOSSIE, with frontispiece. Crown 8vo, 6s.

ST. GEORGE AND ST. MICHAEL, with frontispiece. Crown 8vo, 6s.

WHAT'S MINE'S MINE, with frontispiece. Crown 8vo, 6s.

ANNALS OF A QUIET NEIGHBOURHOOD, with frontispiece. Crown 8vo, 6s.

THE SEABOARD PARISH : a sequel to 'Annals of a Quiet Neighbour-hood,' with frontispiece. Crown 8vo, 6s.

WILFRED CUMBERMEDE : an autobiographical story, with frontispiece. Crown 8vo, 6s.

THOMAS WINGFOLD, CURATE, with frontispiece. Crown 8vo, 6s.

PAUL FABER, SURGEON, with frontispiece. Crown 8vo, 6s.

THE ELECT LADY, with frontispiece. Crown 8vo, 6s.

MACDONALD, W. A., HUMANITISM : the scientific solution of the social problem. Large post 8vo, 7*s.* 6*d.*

MACHIAVELLI, Niccolò, DISCOURSES ON THE FIRST DECADE OF TITUS LIVIUS, from the Italian by N. HILL THOMPSON. Large crown 8vo, 12*s.*

THE PRINCE, from the Italian by N. H. T. Small 8vo, printed on hand-made paper, 6*s.*

MACKAY, Eric, A LOVER'S LITANIES, and other poems, with portrait of author (*Lotos Series*), 3*s.* 6*d.*

MACKAY, Donald J., BISHOP FORBES : a memoir, with portrait and map. Crown 8vo, 7*s.* 6*d.*

MAC KENNA, S. J., PLUCKY FELLOWS : a book for boys, with 6 illustrations. 5th edition, crown 8vo, 3*s.* 6*d.*

MACKONOCHIE. ALEXANDER HERIOT MACKONOCHIE : a memoir by E. A. T., edited, with preface, by E. F. RUSSELL, with portrait and views. Large crown 8vo, 7*s.* 6*d.*

MACRITCHIE, David, THE TESTIMONY OF TRADITION, with 20 illustrations, 8vo, 7*s.* 6*d.*

MADDEN, F. W., COINS OF THE JEWS, with 279 woodcuts, &c. Royal 4to, 40*s.* [*Numismata Orient.*

MAGNUS, Sir Philip, INDUSTRIAL EDUCATION. 6*s.* [*Education Library*

MAGUIRE, W. R., DOMESTIC SANITARY DRAINAGE AND PLUMBING. 8vo, 12*s.*

MAHAFFY, Prof., OLD GREEK EDUCATION. 2nd edition, 3*s.* 6*d* [*Education Library.*

MAIDEN, J. H., USEFUL NATIVE PLANTS OF AUSTRALIA (including Tasmania). 8vo, 12*s.* 6*d.*

MAIMONIDES, GUIDE OF THE PERPLEXED, from the original text, and annotated by M. FRIEDLÄNDER. 3 vols. post 8vo, 31*s.* 6*d.* [*Philosophical Library.*

MALET, Lucas, LITTLE PETER: a Christmas morality for children of any age, with numerous illustrations. 4th thousand, 5*s.*

COLONEL ENDERBY'S WIFE, with frontispiece. Crown 8vo, 6*s.*

A COUNSEL OF PERFECTION, with frontispiece. Crown 8vo, 6*s.*

MANNING, TOWARDS EVENING : selections from the writings of Cardinal Manning. 3rd edition, 16mo, 2*s.*

MARCHANT, W. T., IN PRAISE OF ALE : songs, ballads, epigrams, and anecdotes. Crown 8vo, 10*s.* 6*d.*

MAREY, Prof. E. J., ANIMAL MECHANISM : a treatise on terrestrial and aërial locomotion, with 117 illustrations. 3rd edition, crown 8vo, 5*s.* '[I.S.S.

MARIETTE-BEY, Auguste, MONUMENTS OF UPPER EGYPT. A translation of the ' Itinéraire de la Haute Egypt,' by ALPHONSE MARIETTE. Crown 8vo, 7*s.* 6*d.*

MARKHAM, Capt. Albert Hastings, R.N., THE GREAT FROZEN SEA : a personal narrative of the voyage of the *Alert* during the Arctic Expedition of 1875-6, with illustrations and maps. 6th and cheaper edition, crown 8vo, 6*s.*

MARSDEN, William, NUMISMATA ORIENTALIA ILLUSTRATA : 57 plates of Oriental coins, ancient and modern, from the collection of the late WILLIAM MARSDEN, F.R.S., engraved from drawings made under his directions. 4to, 31*s.* 6*d.*

MARTIN, G. A., THE FAMILY HORSE : its stabling, care, and feeding. Crown 8vo. 3s. 6d.

MARTINEAU, Harriet, THE POSITIVE PHILOSOPHY OF AUGUSTE COMTE, translated and condensed. 2nd edition, 2 vols. post 8vo, 25s.

MARTINEAU, James, ESSAYS, PHILOSOPHICAL AND THEOLOGICAL. 2 vols. crown 8vo, £1. 4s.

MASON, Charlotte M., HOME EDUCATION : a course of lectures to ladies. Crown 8vo, 3s. 6d.

MASON, Capt. F. H., LIFE AND PUBLIC SERVICE OF JAMES A. GARFIELD, PRESIDENT U.S.A., with a preface by BRET HARTE. Portrait. Crown 8vo, 2s. 6d.

MASON, F., BURMA : its people and productions ; geology, mineralogy, zoology, and botany, rewritten by W. THEOBALD. 2 vols. royal 8vo, £3.

MASSEY, Gerald, MY LYRICAL LIFE : poems old and new. Two Series. 2nd edition, with additions, fcap. 8vo, 3s. 6d. each.

MATHER, G., and BLAGG, C. J., BISHOP RAWLE : a memoir. Large crown 8vo, 7s. 6d.

MATHERS, S. L. M., THE KEY OF SOLOMON THE KING, translated from ancient MSS. in the British Museum, with plates. Crown 4to, 25s.

THE KABBALAH UNVEILED, · containing the three books of the Zohar, translated from the Chaldee and Hebrew text. Post 8vo, 10s. 6d.

, THE TAROT : its occult signification, use in fortune-telling, and method of play. With pack of 78 tarot cards, 5s. ; without the cards, 1s. 6d.

MAUDSLEY, H., BODY AND WILL: an essay concerning will, in its metaphysical, physiological, and pathological aspects. 8vo, 12s.

NATURAL CAUSES AND SUPERNATURAL SEEMINGS. 2nd edition, crown 8vo, 6s.

RESPONSIBILITY IN MENTAL DISEASE. 4th edition, crown 8vo, 5s. [I.S.S.

MAXWELL, W. E., MANUAL OF THE MALAY LANGUAGE. 2nd edition, crown 8vo, 7s. 6d.

MAYERS, W. F., CHINESE GOVERNMENT : a manual of Chinese titles. 2nd edition, royal 8vo, 15s.

MEAD, C. M., D.D., SUPERNATURAL REVELATION : an essay concerning the basis of the Christian faith. Royal 8vo, 14s.

MEARS, A. G., IDYLLS, LEGENDS, AND LYRICS. Crown 8vo, 7s. 6d.

MECHANIC'S WORKSHOP (AMATEUR): plain and concise directions for the manipulation of wood and metals. By the author of 'The Lathe and its Uses.' 6th edition, illustrated, 8vo, 6s.

MEDITATIONS ON DEATH AND ETERNITY, translated from the German by FREDERICA ROWAN. Published by Her Majesty's gracious permission. Crown 8vo, 6s.

MEDITATIONS ON LIFE AND ITS RELIGIOUS DUTIES, translated from the German by FREDERICA ROWAN. Published by Her Majesty's gracious permission. Crown 8vo, 6s.

MENDELSSOHN'S LETTERS TO IGNAZ AND CHARLOTTE MOSCHELES, translated by FELIX MOSCHELES. Numerous illustrations and facsimiles. 8vo, 12s.

MEYER, G. Hermann *von*, Organs of Speech and their Application in the Formation of Articulate Sounds, with 47 woodcuts. Crown 8vo, 5*s*. [I.S.S.

MEYNELL, Wilfrid, John Henry Newman, the Founder of Modern Anglicanism and a Cardinal of the Roman Church. Crown 8vo, 2*s*. 6*d*.

MILL, John Stuart, Auguste Comte and Positivism. 3rd edition, post 8vo, 3*s*. 6*d*. [*Philosophical Library.*

MILLHOUSE, John, English and Italian Dictionary. 2 vols. 8vo, 12*s*.
Manual of Italian Conversation. 18mo, 2*s*.

MILNE, Prof. J., Earthquakes and other Earth Movements, with 38 figures. 2nd edition, crown 8vo, 5*s*. [I.S.S.

MILTON, John, Prose Writings, edited by E. Myers. Elzevir 8vo (*Parchment Library*), vellum, 7*s*. 6*d*. ; parchment or cloth, 6*s*.
Poetical Works. 2 vols. elzevir 8vo (*Parchment Library*), vellum, 7*s*. 6*d*. ; parchment or cloth, 6*s*.
Sonnets, edited by Mark Pattison, with portrait. Elzevir 8vo (*Parchment Library*), vellum, 7*s*. 6*d*. ; parchment or cloth, 6*s*.

MINTON, Francis, Capital and Wages. 8vo, 15*s*.
Welfare of the Millions. Crown 8vo, limp cloth, 1*s*. 6*d*. ; paper covers, 1*s*.

MITCHELL, E. H., Forty Days in the Holy Land, with 6 illustrations. Crown 8vo, 6*s*.

MITCHELL, Lucy M., History of Ancient Sculpture, with numerous illustrations. Super-royal 8vo, 42*s*.

MIVART, St. George, On Truth. 8vo, 16*s*.
Origin of Human Reason. 8vo, 10*s*. 6*d*.

MOCKLER, E., Grammar of the Baloochee Language, as it is spoken in Makran (ancient Gedrosia), in the Persia-Arabic and Roman characters. Fcap. 8vo, 5*s*.

MONIER-WILLIAMS, Sir M., Modern India and the Indians: a series of impressions, notes, and essays. 5th edition, post 8vo (*Trübner's Oriental Series*), 14*s*.

MOODIE, D. C. F., History of the Battles and Adventures of the British, the Boers, the Zulus, &c., in South Africa, with illustrations and coloured maps. 2 vols. crown 8vo, 36*s*.

MORFILL, W. R., Simplified Grammar of the Polish Language. Crown 8vo, 3*s*. 6*d*.
Simplified Serbian Grammar. Crown 8vo, 4*s*. 6*d*.

MORFIT, Campbell, Manufacture of Soaps, with illustrations 8vo, £2. 12*s*. 6*d*.
Pure Fertilizers, and the chemical conversion of rock guanos, &c., into various valuable products, with 28 plates. 8vo, £4. 4*s*.

MOORE, Aubrey L., Essays, scientific and philosophical, with memoir of the author. Crown 8vo, 6*s*.
Lectures and Papers on the History of the Reformation in England and on the Continent. 8vo, 16*s*.

MOORE, Aubrey L., SCIENCE AND THE FAITH : essays on apologetic subjects. Crown 8vo, 6s.

MORISON, J. Cotter, THE SERVICE OF MAN : an essay towards the religion of the future. Crown 8vo, 5s.

MORRIS, Charles, ARYAN SUN-MYTHS THE ORIGIN OF RELIGIONS. Introduction by CHARLES MORRIS. Crown 8vo, 6s.

MORRIS, Anne C., DIARY AND LETTERS OF GOUVERNEUR MORRIS Minister of the U.S. to France, with portraits. 2 vols. 8vo, 30s.

MORRIS, Lewis, POETICAL WORKS. New and cheaper edition, 5 vols. fcap. 8vo, 5s. each.

SONGS OF TWO WORLDS, 13th edition.

THE EPIC OF HADES, 23rd edition.

GWEN and THE ODE OF LIFE, 7th edition.

SONGS UNSUNG and GYCIA, 5th edition.

SONGS OF BRITAIN, 3rd edition.

POETICAL WORKS. In 1 vol. crown 8vo, 6s. Cloth extra, gilt leaves, 7s. 6d.

THE EPIC OF HADES, with 16 autotype illustrations, after the drawings of the late GEORGE R. CHAPMAN. 4to, cloth extra, gilt leaves, 21s.

THE EPIC OF HADES. Presentation edition, 4to, cloth extra, gilt leaves, 10s. 6d.

BIRTHDAY BOOK, edited by S. S. COPEMAN, with frontispiece. 32mo, cloth extra, gilt edges, 2s. ; cloth limp, 1s. 6d.

A VISION OF SAINTS. Fcap. 8vo, 6s.

MORSELLI, Prof. H., SUICIDE : an essay on comparative moral statistics. 2nd edition, with diagrams, crown 8vo, 5s. [I.S.S.

MOSENTHAL, J. de, and HARTING, James E., OSTRICHES AND OSTRICH FARMING. 2nd edition, with 8 full-page illustrations and 20 woodcuts, royal 8vo, 10s. 6d.

MUELLER, F. von, SELECT PLANTS FOR EXTRA TROPICAL COUNTRIES. 8vo, 8s. [India Office.

MUIR, John, ORIGINAL SANSKRIT TEXTS, on the origin and history of the people of India. 5 vols. 8vo.

MYTHICAL AND LEGENDARY ACCOUNTS OF THE ORIGIN OF CASTE. 3rd edition, £1. 1s.

₊ This work is also issued as a volume of *Trübner's Oriental Series,* at the same price.

THE TRANS-HIMALAYAN ORIGIN OF THE HINDUS. 2nd edition, £1. 1s.

THE VEDAS. 2nd edition, 16s.

THE PRINCIPAL INDIAN DEITIES. 2nd edition, £1. 1s.

COSMOGONY, MYTHOLOGY, &c., OF THE INDIANS IN THE VEDIC AGE. 3rd edition, £1. 1s.

METRICAL TRANSLATIONS FROM SANSKRIT WRITERS. Post 8vo (*Trübner's Oriental Series*), 14s.

MULHALL, M. G. and E. T., HANDBOOK OF THE RIVER PLATE, comprising the Argentine Republic, Uruguay, and Paraguay, with 6 maps. 5th edition, crown 8vo, 7s. 6d.

MULHOLLAND, Rosa, MARCELLA GRACE : an Irish novel. Crown 8vo,6s.

A FAIR EMIGRANT, with frontispiece. Crown 8vo, 6s.

MÜLLER, F. Max, OUTLINE DICTIONARY, for the use of missionaries, explorers, and students of language. 12mo, morocco, 7s. 6d.

SACRED HYMNS OF THE BRAHMINS, as preserved in the oldest collection of religious poetry, the Rig-Veda-Sanhita. Vol. I. Hymns to the Maruts, or the Storm-Gods. 8vo, 12s. 6d.

HYMNS OF THE RIG-VEDA, in the Sanhita and Pada texts. 2 vols. 2nd edition, 8vo, £1. 12s.

MÜLLER, E., SIMPLIFIED GRAMMAR OF THE PALI LANGUAGE. Crown 8vo, 7s. 6d.

MUNCHAUSEN'S TRAVELS AND SURPRISING ADVENTURES, illustrated by ALFRED CROWQUILL. (*Lotos Series*), 3s. 6d.

MURPHY, J. J., SONNETS : and other poems. Small 8vo, 5s.

NAVILLE, E., STORE CITY OF PITHOM, and Route of the Exodus, with 15 plates and maps. 3rd edition, royal 4to, 25s.

GOSHEN, with 11 plates. Royal 4to, 25s.

NAVILLE, E., and GRIFFITH, F. Ll., THE MOUND OF THE JEW, &c., with 26 plates, 25s. [*Egypt Exploration Fund.*

"*NEMO,*" WHAT IS TRUTH ? A consideration of the doubts as to the efficacy of prayer, raised by evolutionists, materialists, and others. Crown 8vo, 5s.

NEVILL, F., RETROGRESSION OR DEVELOPMENT. Crown 8vo, 3s. 6d.

THE VICTORY OF LOVE. Crown 8vo, 3s. 6d.

NEVILL, J. H. N., BIOLOGY OF DAILY LIFE. Post 8vo, 3s. 6d.

NEWMAN. CHARACTERISTICS FROM THE WRITINGS OF CARDINAL NEWMAN. Selections from his various works, arranged by W. S. LILLY. 8th edition, with portrait, crown 8vo, 6s.

⁎⁎ Portrait of the late Cardinal Newman, mounted for framing, 2s. 6d.

NEWMAN, Francis William, ESSAYS ON DIET. Small 8vo, cloth limp, 2s.

MISCELLANIES. Essays, tracts, and addresses, moral and religious. 8vo. Vol. I. 10s. 6d. Vols. II. and III. 12s. each. Vol. IV. 10s. 6d.

CONTRIBUTIONS CHIEFLY TO THE EARLY HISTORY OF THE LATE CARDINAL NEWMAN. Crown 8vo, 3s. 6d.

REMINISCENCES OF TWO EXILES AND TWO WARS. Crown 8vo, 3s. 6d.

PHASES OF FAITH, or Passages from the history of my Creed. Crown 8vo, 3s. 6d.

THE SOUL : her sorrows and her aspirations. 10th edition, post 8vo, 3s. 6d.

HEBREW THEISM. Royal 8vo, 4s. 6d.

ANGLO-SAXON ABOLITION OF NEGRO SLAVERY. 8vo, 5s.

A HANDBOOK OF MODERN ARABIC. Post 8vo, 6s.

DICTIONARY OF MODERN ARABIC (Anglo-Arabic and Arabo-English). 2 vols. crown 8vo, £1. 1s.

NEWTON-ROBINSON, C., TINTINNABULA : poems. Elzevir 8vo, 3s. 6d.

NICHOLS, J. B., and **DYMOND, C. W.,** PRACTICAL VALUE OF CHRISTIANITY, two prize essays. Crown 8vo, 3s. 6d.

NICOLS, Arthur, CHAPTERS FROM THE PHYSICAL HISTORY OF THE EARTH : an introduction to geology and palæontology, with numerous illustrations. Crown 8vo, 5s.

NOTES ON CAVALRY TACTICS, ORGANISATION, &c., by a Cavalry Officer, with diagrams. 8vo, 12s.

NUGENT'S FRENCH-ENGLISH AND ENGLISH-FRENCH POCKET DICTIONARY. 24mo, 3s.

NUMISMATA ORIENTALIA (The). Royal 4to, in paper wrapper. Part I. Ancient Indian Weights, by E. THOMAS, with a plate and map, 9s. 6d. Part II. Coins of the Urtuki Turkumáns, by S. LANE POOLE, with 6 plates, 9s. Part III. Coinage of Lydia and Persia, by BARCLAY V. HEAD, with 3 plates, 10s. 6d. Part IV. Coins of the Tuluni Dynasty, by E. T. ROGERS, with 1 plate, 5s. Part V. Parthian Coinage, by PERCY GARDNER, with 8 plates, 18s. Part VI. Ancient Coins and Measures of Ceylon, by T. W. RHYS DAVIDS, with 1 plate, 10s.

Vol. I. containing the first six parts, as specified above. Royal half-bound, £3. 13s. 6d.

Vol. II. COINS OF THE JEWS : being a history of the Jewish coinage in the Old and New Testaments, by F. W. MADDEN, with 279 woodcuts and plate. Royal 4to, £2.

Vol. III. part I. THE COINS OF ARAKAN, OF PEGU, AND OF BURMA, by Lieut.-General Sir ARTHUR PHAYRE. Also contains the Indian Balhara, and the Arabian Intercourse with India in the Ninth and following Centuries, by EDWARD THOMAS, with 5 illustrations. Royal 4to, 8s. 6d.

Vol. III. part II. THE COINS OF SOUTHERN INDIA, by Sir W. ELLIOT with map and plates. Royal 4to, 25s.

OATES, Frank, MATABELE LAND AND THE VICTORIA FALLS : a naturalist's wanderings in the interior of South Africa, edited by C. G. OATES, with numerous illustrations and 4 maps. 8vo, 21s.

O'BRIEN, R. Barry, IRISH WRONGS AND ENGLISH REMEDIES, with other essays. Crown 8vo, 5s.

HOME RULER'S MANUAL. Crown 8vo, cloth, 1s. 6d. ; paper covers, 1s.

LIFE AND LETTERS OF THOMAS DRUMMOND, Under-Secretary in Ireland, 1835-40. 8vo, 14s.

O'CONNOR, E., INDEX TO SHAKESPEARE'S WORKS. Crown 8vo, 5s.

OGLE, Anna C., A LOST LOVE. Small crown 8vo, 2s. 6d.

OLCOTT, Colonel, POSTHUMOUS HUMANITY : a study of phantoms, from the French of Adolphe D'Assier, with appendix and notes. Crown 8vo, 7s. 6d.

THEOSOPHY, RELIGION, AND OCCULT SCIENCE, with glossary of Eastern words. Crown 8vo, 7s. 6d.

OTTÉ, E. C., DANO-NORWEGIAN GRAMMAR : a manual for students of Danish, based on the Ollendorffian system. 3rd edition, crown 8vo, 7s. 6d. Key, 3s.

SIMPLIFIED GRAMMAR OF THE DANISH LANGUAGE. Crown 8vo, 2s. 6d.

SIMPLIFIED GRAMMAR OF THE SWEDISH LANGUAGE. Crown 8vo, 2s. 6d.

OWEN, John, Verse Musings on Nature : Faith and Freedom. Crown Svo, 7*s.* 6*d.*

OWEN, Robert Dale, Footfalls on the Boundary of Another World, with narrative illustrations. Post Svo, 7*s.* 6*d.*

Debatable Land between this World and the Next, with illustrative narrations. 2nd edition, crown 8vo, 7*s.* 6*d.*

Threading my Way : twenty-seven years of autobiography. Crown Svo, 7*s.* 6*d.*

PALMER, E. H., English-Persian Dictionary, with simplified grammar of the Persian language. Royal 16mo, 10*s.* 6*d.*

Persian-English Dictionary. 2nd edition, royal 16mo, 10*s.* 6*d.*

Simplified Grammar of Hindustani, Persian, and Arabic. 2nd edition, crown Svo, 5*s.*

Papers relating to Indo-China, reprinted from Dalrymple's Oriental Repertory, Asiatick Researches, and the Journal of the Asiatic Society of Bengal. Post Svo (*Trübner's Oriental Series*), 2 vols. 21*s.* ; second series, 2 vols. 25*s.*

PARKER, G. W., Concise Grammar of the Malagasy Language. Crown Svo, 5*s.*

PARKER, Theodore, Discourse on Matters pertaining to Religion. People's edition, crown 8vo, 2*s.* ; 1*s.* 6*d.*

Collected Works of Theodore Parker, Minister of the Twenty-eighth Congregational Society at Boston, U.S. 14 vols. 8vo, 6*s.* each.

Vol. I. Discourse on Matters pertaining to Religion. II. Ten Sermons and Prayers. III. Discourses on Theology. IV. Discourses on Politics. V. and VI. Discourses on Slavery. VII. Discourses on Social Science. VIII. Miscellaneous Discourses. IX. and X. Critical Writings. XI. Sermons on Theism, Atheism, and Popular Theology. XII. Autobiographical and Miscellaneous Pieces. XIII. Historic Americans. XIV. Lessons from the World of Matter and the World of Man.

PARR, Col. H. Hallam, Dress, Horses, and Equipment of Infantry and Staff Officers. Crown 8vo, 1*s.*

Further Training and Equipment of Mounted Infantry. Crown Svo, 1*s.*

PARRY, E. Gambier, Biography of Reynell Taylor, C.B., C.S.I., with portrait and map. 8vo, 14*s.*

PARSLOE, Joseph, Our Railways : sketches, historical and descriptive, with information as to fares and rates, &c. Crown 8vo, 6*s.*

PASCAL, Blaise, Thoughts, translated by C. Kegan Paul. Fcap. 8vo, parchment, 12*s.* New edition, crown Svo, 6*s.*

PATON, A. A., History of the Egyptian Revolution, from the period of the Mamelukes to the death of Mohammed Ali. 2nd edition, 2 vols. 8vo, 7*s.* 6*d.*

PAUL, C. Kegan, Biographical Sketches. Crown 8vo, 7*s.* 6*d.*

PAULI, Reinhold, Simon de Montfort, Earl of Leicester, the creator of the House of Commons. Crown 8vo, 6*s.*

Paul of Tarsus, by the author of 'Rabbi Jeshua.' Crown 8vo, 4*s.* 6*d.*

PEMBERTON, T. Edgar, Charles Dickens and the Stage : a record of his connection with the drama. Crown 8vo, 6*s.*

PFEIFFER, Emily, WOMEN AND WORK : an essay on the higher education of girls. Crown 8vo, 6s.

FLOWERS OF THE NIGHT. Crown 8vo, 6s.

PETRIE, W. M. Flinders, TANIS, with 83 plates and plans. Royal 4to, 2 parts, 25s. each.

     ** Part II. by Messrs. Petrie and Griffith.

NAUKRATIS, with 69 plates. Royal 4to, 2 parts, 25s. each

     ** Part I. by Messrs. Petrie, Smith, Gardner, and Head.
     Part II. by Messrs. Gardner and Griffith.

KAHUN GUROB AND HAWARA, with 28 plates. 16s.

PETTIGREW, J. B., ANIMAL LOCOMOTION, or Walking, swimming, and flying, with 130 illustrations. 3rd edition, crown 8vo, 5s.   [I.S.S.

PHAYRE, Gen. Sir A., HISTORY OF BURMA, including Burma Proper Pegu, Taungu, Tenasserim, and Arakan, from the earliest time to the end of the first war with British India. Post 8vo (*Trübner's Oriental Series*), 14s.

PHAYRE, Gen. Sir A., and THOMAS, E., COINS OF ARAKAN, OF PEGU, AND OF BURMA, with 5 illustrations. Royal 4to, 8s. 6d. [*Numismata Orient.*

PHILLIPS, W., MANUAL OF BRITISH DISCOMYCETES, with descriptions of all the species of Fungi hitherto found in Britain included in the family, and illustrations of the genera. Crown 8vo, 5s.   [I.S.S.

"*PHYSICUS,*" CANDID EXAMINATION OF THEISM. 2nd edition, post 8vo, 7s. 6d. (*Philosophical Library.*)

PICCIOTTO, James, SKETCHES OF ANGLO-JEWISH HISTORY. 8vo, 12s.

PICKFORD, John, MAHÁ-VIRA-CHARITA, or The adventures of the great hero Rama, from the Sanskrit of BHAVABHÚTI. Crown 8vo, 5s.

PIERCE, J., IN CLOUD AND SUNSHINE : poems. Fcap. 8vo, 3s. 6d.

PIERCE, Jas. and W. T., CHESS PAPERS AND PROBLEMS. Crown 8vo, 6s. 6d.

PIESSE, C. H., CHEMISTRY IN THE BREWING ROOM: a course of lessons to practical brewers. Fcap, 5s.

PLEA FOR TRUTH IN RELIGION. Crown 8vo, 2s. 6d.

PLIMSOLL, Samuel, CATTLE SHIPS : being the fifth chapter of "An Appeal for our Seamen," with 46 illustrations. 5s. ; cheap edition, 1s.

PLINY. THE LETTERS OF PLINY THE YOUNGER, translated by J. D. LEWIS. Post 8vo, 15s.

PLUMPTRE, C. J., LECTURES ON ELOCUTION, delivered at King's College. 4th edition, post 8vo, 15s.

POE, Edgar Allan, POEMS, edited by ANDREW LANG, with frontispiece. Elzevir 8vo (*Parchment Library*), vellum, 7s. 6d. ; parchment or cloth. 6s.

THE RAVEN, with commentary by JOHN H. INGRAM. Crown 8vo, parchment, 6s.

POLE, W., PHILOSOPHY OF MUSIC: lectures delivered at the Royal Institution. 2nd edition, post 8vo, 7s. 6d.   [*Philosophical Library.*

PONSARD, F., CHARLOTTE CORDAY: a tragedy, edited by Professor C. CASSAL. 3rd edition, 12mo, 2s. 6d.

L'HONNEUR ET L'ARGENT : a comedy, edited by Professor C. CASSAL. 2nd edition, 12mo, 3s. 6d.

PONTOPIDDAN, Henrik, THE APOTHECARY'S DAUGHTERS, translated from the Danish by GORDIUS NIELSEN. Crown 8vo, 3*s.* 6*d.*

POOLE, W. F., INDEX TO PERIODICAL LITERATURE. 3rd edition, royal 8vo, £3. 13*s.* 6*d.*

POOLE, W. F., and FLETCHER, W. I., INDEX TO PERIODICAL LITERATURE, first supplement, 1882 to 1887. Royal 8vo, £1. 16*s.*

POSNETT, H. M., COMPARATIVE LITERATURE. Crown 8vo, 5*s.* [I.S.S.

POULTON, E. B., COLOURS OF ANIMALS : their meaning and use, especially considered in the case of insects, with coloured frontispiece and 66 illustrations in text. Crown 8vo, 5*s.* [I.S.S.

PRACTICAL GUIDES, to see all that ought to be seen in the shortest period and at the least expense. 113th thousand, illustrated, small 8vo, paper covers. France, Belgium, Holland, and the Rhine, 1*s.* Italian Lakes, 1*s.* Wintering Places of the South, 2*s.* Switzerland, Savoy, and North Italy, 2*s.* 6*d.* General Continental Guide, 5*s.* Geneva, 1*s.* Paris, 1*s.* Bernese Oberland, 1*s.* Italy, 4*s.*

PRATT, George, GRAMMAR AND DICTIONARY OF THE SAMOAN LANGUAGE. 2nd edition, crown 8vo, 18*s.*

PRATT, Lieut.-Colonel, FIELD ARTILLERY : its equipment, organisation, and tactics. 4th edition, small crown 8vo, 6*s.*

MILITARY LAW : its procedure and practice. 5th revised edition, small crown 8vo, 4*s.* 6*d.*

PRIG, The, BLACK IS WHITE ; or, Continuity continued. 3*s.* 6*d.*

THE PRIGMENT : 'The Life of a Prig,' 'Prig's Bede,' 'How to Make a Saint,' 'The Churgress.' In 1 vol. crown 8vo, 6*s.*

A ROMANCE OF THE RECUSANTS. Crown 8vo, 5*s.*

PRIOR, Matthew, SELECTED POEMS, edited by AUSTIN DOBSON. Elzevir 8vo (*Parchment Library*), vellum, 7*s.* 6*d.* ; parchment or cloth, 6*s.*

PROTHERO, G. W., HENRY BRADSHAW : a memoir, with portrait and facsimile. 8vo, 16*s.*

PSALMS OF THE WEST. Small 8vo, 5*s.*

PULPIT COMMENTARY, THE (*Old Testament Series*). Edited by the Rev. J. S. EXELL and the Very Rev. Dean H. D. M. SPENCE, D.D. Super royal 8vo.

GENESIS, by the Rev. T. WHITELAW, D.D., homilies by the Very Rev. J. F. MONTGOMERY, D.D., Rev. Prof. R. A. REDFORD, Rev. F. HASTINGS, Rev. W. ROBERTS ; introduction to the study of the Old Testament by Archdeacon FARRAR, D.D. ; introductions to the Pentateuch by the Right Rev. H. COTTERILL, D.D., and Rev. T. WHITELAW, D.D., 9th edition, 15*s.*

EXODUS, by the Rev. Canon RAWLINSON, homilies by the Rev. J. ORR, D.D., Rev. D. YOUNG, Rev. C. A. GOODHART, Rev. J. URQUHART, and the Rev. H. T. ROBJOHNS, 4th edition, 2 vols. 9*s.* each.

LEVITICUS, by the Rev. Prebendary MEYRICK, introductions by the Rev. R. COLLINS, Rev. Professor A. CAVE, homilies by the Rev. Prof. REDFORD, Rev. J. A. MACDONALD, Rev. W. CLARKSON, Rev. S. R. ALDRIDGE, and Rev. McCHEYNE EDGAR, 4th edition, 15*s.*

NUMBERS, by the Rev. R. WINTERBOTHAM, homilies by the Rev. Prof. W. BINNIE, D.D., Rev. E. S. PROUT, Rev. D. YOUNG, Rev. J. WAITE, introduction by the Rev. THOMAS WHITELAW, D.D., 5th edition, 15*s.*

DEUTERONOMY, by the Rev. W. L. ALEXANDER, D.D., homilies by the Rev. C. CLEMANCE, D.D., Rev. J. ORR, D.D., Rev. R. M. EDGAR, Rev. D. DAVIES, 4th edition, 15*s.*

PULPIT COMMENTARY—*cont.*

JOSHUA, by the Rev. J. J. LIAS, homilies by the Rev. S. R. ALDRIDGE, Rev. R. GLOVER, Rev. E. DE PRESSENSÉ, D.D., Rev. J. WAITE, Rev. W. F. ADENEY, introduction by the Rev. A. PLUMMER, D.D., 6th edition., 12s. 6d.

JUDGES and RUTH, by the Bishop of BATH and WELLS, and Rev. J. MORISON, D.D., homilies by the Rev. A. F. MUIR, Rev. W. F. ADENEY, Rev. W. M. STATHAM, and Rev. Prof. J. THOMSON, 5th edition, 10s. 6d.

1 *and* 2 *SAMUEL*, by the Very Rev. R. P. SMITH, D.D., homilies by the Rev. DONALD FRASER, D.D., Rev. Prof. CHAPMAN, Rev. B. DALE, and Rev. G. WOOD, 7th edition, 2 vols. 15s. each.

1 *KINGS*, by the Rev. JOSEPH HAMMOND, homilies by the Rev. E. DE PRESSENSÉ, D.D., Rev. J. WAITE, Rev. A. ROWLAND, Rev. J. A. MACDONALD, and Rev. J. URQUHART, 5th edition, 15s.

2 *KINGS*, by the Rev. Canon RAWLINSON, homilies by the Rev. J. ORR, D.D., Rev. D. THOMAS, and Rev. C. H. IRWIN, 15s.

1 *CHRONICLES*, by the Rev. Prof. P. C. BARKER, homilies by the Rev. Prof. J. R. THOMSON, Rev. R. TUCK, Rev. W. CLARKSON, Rev. F. WHITFIELD, and Rev. RICHARD GLOVER, 2nd edition, 15s.

2 *CHRONICLES*, by the Rev. PHILIP C. BARKER; homilies by the Rev. W. CLARKSON and Rev. T. WHITELAW, D.D., 15s.

EZRA, NEHEMIAH, and ESTHER, by the Rev. Canon G. RAWLINSON, homilies by the Rev. Prof. J. R. THOMSON, Rev. Prof. R. A. REDFORD, Rev. W. S. LEWIS, Rev. J. A. MACDONALD, Rev. A. MACKENNAL, Rev. W. CLARKSON, Rev. F. HASTINGS, Rev. W. DINWIDDIE, Rev. Prof. ROWLANDS, Rev. G. WOOD, Rev. Prof. P. C. BARKER, and the Rev. J. S. EXELL, 7th edition, 12s. 6d.

ISAIAH, by the Rev. Canon G. RAWLINSON, homilies by the Rev. Prof. E. JOHNSON, Rev. W. CLARKSON, Rev. W. M. STATHAM, and Rev. R. TUCK, 2nd edition, 2 vols. 15s. each.

JEREMIAH (Vol. I.), by the Rev. Canon T. K. CHEYNE, D.D., homilies by the Rev. W. F. ADENEY, Rev. A. F. MUIR, Rev. S. CONWAY, Rev. J. WAITE, and Rev. D. YOUNG, 3rd edition, 15s.

JEREMIAH (Vol. II.) *and LAMENTATIONS*, by the Rev. Canon T. K. CHEYNE, D.D., homilies by the Rev. Prof. J. R. THOMSON, Rev. W. F. ADENEY, Rev. A. F. MUIR, Rev. S. CONWAY, Rev. D. YOUNG, 3rd edition, 15s.

HOSEA and JOEL, by the Rev. Prof. J. J. GIVEN, D.D., homilies by the Rev. Prof. J. R. THOMSON, Rev. A. ROWLAND, Rev. C. JERDAN, Rev. J. ORR, D.D., and Rev. D. THOMAS, D.D., 15s.

PULPIT COMMENTARY, THE (*New Testament Series*). Edited by the Very Rev. H. D. M. SPENCE, D.D., and Rev. JOSEPH S. EXELL.

ST. MARK, by the Very Rev. Dean E. BICKERSTETH, D.D., homilies by the Rev. Prof. THOMSON, Rev. Prof. J. J. GIVEN, D.D., Rev. Prof. JOHNSON, Rev. A. ROWLAND, Rev. A. MUIR, and Rev. R. GREEN, 6th edition, 2 vols. 10s. 6d. each.

ST. LUKE, by the Very Rev. H. D. M. SPENCE, homilies by the Rev. J. MARSHALL LANG, D.D., Rev. W. CLARKSON, and Rev. R. M. EDGAR, 2 vols. 10s. 6d. each.

ST. JOHN, by the Rev. Prof. H. R. REYNOLDS, D.D., homilies by the Rev. Prof. T. CROSKERY, D.D., Rev. Prof. J. R. THOMSON, Rev. D. YOUNG, Rev. B. THOMAS, and Rev. G. BROWN, 3rd edition, 2 vols. 15s. each.

THE ACTS of the APOSTLES, by the Bishop of BATH and WELLS, homilies by the Rev. Prof. P. C. BARKER, Rev. Prof. E. JOHNSON, Rev. Prof. R. A. REDFORD, Rev. R. TUCK, Rev. W. CLARKSON, 4th edition, 2 vols. 10s. 6d. each.

PULPIT COMMENTARY—*cont.*

ROMANS, by the Rev. J. BARMBY ; homiletics by Rev. Prof. J. R. THOMSON; homilies by Rev. C. H. IRWIN, Rev. T. F. LOCKYER, Rev. S. R. ALDRIDGE, and Rev. R. M. EDGAR, 15*s.*

1 *CORINTHIANS*, by the Ven. Archdeacon FARRAR, D.D, homilies by the Rev. Ex-Chancellor LIPSCOMB, Rev. DAVID THOMAS, D.D., Rev. D. FRASER, D.D., Rev. Prof. J. R. THOMSON, Rev. J. WAITE, Rev. R. TUCK, Rev. E. HURNDALL, and Rev. H. BREMNER, 4th edition, 15*s.*

2 *CORINTHIANS and GALATIANS*, by the Ven. Archdeacon FARRAR, D.D. and Rev. Prebendary E. HUXTABLE, homilies by the Rev. Ex-Chancellor LIPSCOMB, Rev. DAVID THOMAS, D.D., Rev. DONALD FRASER, D.D., Rev. R. TUCK, Rev. E. HURNDALL, Rev. Prof. J. R. THOMSON, Rev. R. FINLAYSON, Rev. W. F. ADENEY, Rev. R. M. EDGAR, and Rev. T. CROSKERY, D.D., 2nd edition, 21*s.*

EPHESIANS, PHILIPPIANS, and COLOSSIANS, by the Rev. Prof. W. G. BLAIKIE, D.D., Rev. B. C. CAFFIN, and Rev. G. G. FINDLAY, homilies by the Rev. D. THOMAS, D.D., Rev. R. M. EDGAR, Rev. R. FINLAYSON, Rev. W. F. ADENEY, Rev. Prof. T. CROSKERY, D.D., Rev. E. S. PROUT, Rev. Canon VERNON HUTTON, and Rev. U. R. THOMAS, D.D., 3rd edition, 21*s.*

THESSALONIANS, TIMOTHY, TITUS, and PHILEMON, by the Bishop of BATH and WELLS, Rev. Dr. GLOAG, and Rev. Dr. EALES, homilies by the Rev. B. C. CAFFIN, Rev. R. FINLAYSON, Rev. Prof. T. CROSKERY, D.D., Rev. W. F. ADENEY, Rev. W. M. STATHAM, and Rev. D. THOMAS, D.D., 2nd edition, 15*s.*

HEBREWS and JAMES, by the Rev. J. BARMBY, D.D., and Rev. Prebendary E. C. S. GIBSON, homiletics by the Rev. C. JERDAN and Rev. Prebendary E. C. S. GIBSON, homilies by the Rev. W. JONES, Rev. C. NEW, Rev. D. YOUNG, Rev. J. S. BRIGHT, Rev. T. F. LOCKYER, and Rev. C. JERDAN, 3rd edition, 15*s.*

PETER, JOHN, and JUDE, by the Rev. B. C. CAFFIN, Rev. A. PLUMMER, D.D., and Rev. S. D. F. SALMOND, D.D., homilies by the Rev. A. MAC-LAREN, D.D., Rev. C. CLEMANCE, D.D., Rev. Prof. J. R. THOMSON, Rev. C. NEW, Rev. U. R. THOMAS, Rev. R. FINLAYSON, Rev. W. JONES, Rev. Prof. T. CROSKERY, D.D., and Rev. J. S. BRIGHT, D.D., 2nd edition, 15*s.*

REVELATION, introduction by the Rev. T. RANDELL, principal of Bede College, Durham ; exposition by the Rev. T. RANDELL, assisted by the Rev. A. PLUMMER, D.D., principal of University College, Durham, and A. T. BOTT, homilies by the Rev. C. CLEMANCE, D.D., Rev. S. CONWAY, Rev. R. GREEN, and Rev. D. THOMAS, D.D., 15*s.*

PURITZ, Ludwig, CODE-BOOK OF GYMNASTIC EXERCISES, translated by O. KNOFE and J. W. MACQUEEN. 32mo, boards, 1*s. 6d.*

PUSEY. SERMONS FOR THE CHURCH'S SEASONS FROM ADVENT TO TRINITY, selected from the published sermons of the late EDWARD BOUVERIE PUSEY, D.D. Crown 8vo, 5*s.*

PYE'S SURGICAL HANDICRAFT : a manual of surgical manipulations, with 233 illustrations. 2nd edition, crown 8vo, 10*s. 6d.*

ELEMENTARY BANDAGING AND SURGICAL DRESSING, for the use of dressers and nurses. 18mo, 2*s.*

PUBLIC SCHOOLS (OUR) : Eton, Harrow, Winchester, Rugby, West-minster, Marlborough, and The Charterhouse. Crown 8vo, 6*s.*

QUATREFAGES, Prof. A. de, THE HUMAN SPECIES. 5th edition, crown 8vo, 5*s.* [I.S.S

RALSTON, W. R. S., TIBETAN TALES, derived from Indian sources, done into English from the German of F. ANTON VON SCHIEFNER. Post 8vo (*Trübner's Oriental Series*), 14s.

RAMSAY, E. P., TABULAR LIST OF ALL THE AUSTRALIAN BIRDS AT PRESENT KNOWN TO THE AUTHOR. Crown 4to, 12s. 6d.

RAPSON, Edward J., STRUGGLE BETWEEN ENGLAND AND FRANCE FOR SUPREMACY IN INDIA. Crown 8vo, 4s. 6d.

RARE POEMS OF THE 16TH AND 17TH CENTURIES, edited by W. J. LINTON. Crown 8vo, 5s.

RASK, Erasmus, GRAMMAR OF THE ANGLO-SAXON TONGUE, from the Danish by B. THORPE. 3rd edition, post 8vo, 5s. 6d.

RAVENSTEIN, E. G., and HULLEY, John, THE GYMNASIUM AND ITS FITTINGS, with illustrations. 8vo, 2s. 6d.

READE, Winwood, THE MARTYRDOM OF MAN. 13th edition, 8vo, 7s. 6d.

REANEY, Mrs. G. S., WAKING AND WORKING, or From girlhood to womanhood. New and cheaper edition, with frontispiece, crown 8vo, 3s. 6d.

BLESSING AND BLESSED : a sketch of girl life. New and cheaper edition, crown 8vo, 3s. 6d.

ROSE GURNEY'S DISCOVERY : a story for girls, dedicated to their mothers. Crown 8vo, 3s. 6d.

ENGLISH GIRLS : their place and power, with preface by the Rev. R. W. DALE. 5th edition, fcap. 8vo, 2s. 6d.

JUST ANYONE, and other stories, with 3 illustrations. 16mo, 1s. 6d.

SUNBEAM WILLIE, and other stories, with 3 illustrations. 16mo, 1s. 6d.

SUNSHINE JENNY, and other stories, with 3 illustrations. 16mo, 1s. 6d.

REDHOUSE. J. W., SIMPLIFIED GRAMMAR OF THE OTTOMAN-TURKISH. Crown 8vo, 10s. 6d.

TURKISH VADE-MECUM OF OTTOMAN COLLOQUIAL LANGUAGE, English-Turkish and Turkish-English, the whole in English characters, the pronunciation being fully indicated. 3rd edition, 32mo, 6s.

THE MESNEVI (usually known as the Mesneviyi Sherif, or Holy Mesnevi) of Mevlānā (Our Lord) Jelālu-'d-Din Muhammed, Er-Rūmi. Illustrated by a selection of characteristic anecdotes. Post 8vo (*Trübner's Oriental Series*), £1. 1s.

HISTORY, SYSTEM, AND VARIETIES OF TURKISH POETRY, illustrated by selections in the original English paraphrase. 8vo, 2s. 6d.

TENTATIVE CHRONOLOGICAL SYNOPSIS OF THE HISTORY OF ARABIA AND ITS NEIGHBOURS, from B.C. 500,000 (?) to A.D. 679. 8vo, 2s.

REEVES, B., CASSIOPE : and other poems. Small 8vo, 5s.

RENAN, Ernest, PHILOSOPHICAL DIALOGUES AND FRAGMENTS. Post 8vo, 7s. 6d.

AGE AND ANTIQUITY OF THE BOOK OF NABATHÆAN AGRICULTURE. Crown 8vo, 3s. 6d.

LIFE OF JESUS. Crown 8vo, 1s. 6d. ; paper covers, 1s.

THE APOSTLES. Crown 8vo, 1s. 6d. ; paper covers, 1s.

RENDELL, J. M., HANDBOOK OF THE ISLAND OF MADEIRA, with plan and map. 2nd edition, fcap. 8vo, 1*s.* 6*d.*

REYNOLDS, J. W., THE SUPERNATURAL IN NATURE : a verification by free use of science. 3rd edition, revised and enlarged, 8vo, 14*s.*

MYSTERY OF THE UNIVERSE OUR COMMON FAITH. 8vo, 14*s.*

MYSTERY OF MIRACLES. 3rd edition, enlarged, crown 8vo, 6*s.*

THE WORLD TO COME : immortality a physical fact. Crown 8vo, 6*s.*

REYNOLDS, Sir Joshua, DISCOURSES, edited by E. GOSSE. Elzevir 8vo (*Parchment Library*), vellum, 7*s.* 6*d.* ; parchment or cloth, 6*s.*

RHOIDIS, Emmanuel, POPE JOAN, an historical study, from the Greek by C. H. COLLÉTTE. 12mo, 2*s.* 6*d.*

RHYS, John, LECTURES ON WELSH PHILOLOGY. 2nd edition, crown 8vo, 15*s.*

RHYS DAVIDS, T. W., BUDDHIST BIRTH-STORIES, or Jataka tales, the oldest collection of Folk-lore extant : being the Jātakatthavannanā, translated from the Pali text of V. FAUSBOLL. Post 8vo (*Trübner's Oriental Series*), 18*s.*

RIBOT, Prof. Th., DISEASES OF MEMORY : an essay in the positive psychology. 3rd edition, crown 8vo, 5*s.* [I.S.S.]

HEREDITY : a psychological study of its phonomena, laws, causes, and consequences. 2nd edition, large crown 8vo, 9*s.*

ENGLISH PSYCHOLOGY. Crown 8vo, 7*s.* 6*d.*

RICHARD, Ap, MARRIAGE AND DIVORCE, including the religious, practical, and political aspects of the question. Crown 8vo, 5*s.*

RICHARDSON, Austin, 'WHAT ARE THE CATHOLIC CLAIMS ?' Introduction by Rev. LUKE RIVINGTON. Crown 8vo, 3*s.* 6*d.*

RICHARDSON, M. T., PRACTICAL BLACKSMITHING, with 400 illustrations. 3 vols. crown 8vo, 5*s.* each.

PRACTICAL HORSESHOER, with 170 illustrations, crown 8vo, 5*s.*

RIDEAL, C. F., WELLERISMS, FROM ' PICKWICK ' AND ' MASTER HUMPHREY'S CLOCK,' edited by CHARLES KENT. 18mo, 2*s.*

RIOLA, Henry, HOW TO LEARN RUSSIAN : a manual for students, based upon the Ollendorffian system. 4th edition, crown 8vo, 12*s.* Key, 5*s.*

RUSSIAN READER, with vocabulary. Crown 8vo, 10*s.* 6*d.*

RIVINGTON, Luke, AUTHORITY, or A plain reason for joining the Church of Rome. 5th edition, crown 8vo, 3*s.* 6*d.*

DEPENDENCE, or The insecurity of the Anglican position. Crown 8vo. 5*s.*

ROBERTSON. LIFE AND LETTERS OF F. W. ROBERTSON, edited by STOPFORD BROOKE.
    I. Library edition, with portrait. 8vo, 12*s.*
    II. With portrait. 2 vols. crown 8vo, 7*s.* 6*d.*
    III. Popular edition. Crown 8vo, 6*s.*

ROBERTSON, F. W., SERMONS. Five series. Small 8vo, 3*s.* 6*d.* each.

NOTES ON GENESIS. New and cheaper edition, small 8vo, 3*s.* 6*d.*

ST. PAUL'S EPISTLES TO THE CORINTHIANS : expository lectures. New edition, small 8vo, 5*s.*

LECTURES AND ADDRESSES, with other literary remains. New edition, small 8vo, 5*s.*

ANALYSIS OF TENNYSON'S 'IN MEMORIAM' (dedicated by permission to the Poet-Laureate). Fcap. 8vo, 2*s.*

EDUCATION OF THE HUMAN RACE, translated from the German of GOTTHOLD EPHRAIM LESSING. Fcap. 8vo, 2*s.* 6*d.*

*** Portrait of the late Rev. F. W. Robertson, mounted for framing, 2*s.* 6*d.*

ROBINSON, Sir J. C., THE DEAD SAILOR, and other stories. Crown 6vo, 5*s.*

ROBINSON, A. Mary F., THE FORTUNATE LOVERS : 27 novels of the Queen of Navarre. Frontispiece by G. P. JACOMB HOOD. Large crown 8vo, 10*s.* 6*d.*

ROCHE, A., FRENCH GRAMMAR, adopted by the Imperial Council of Public Instruction. Crown 8vo, 3*s.*

PROSE AND POETRY, from English authors, for reading, composition, and translation. 2nd edition, fcap. 8vo, 2*s.* 6*d.*

ROCKHILL, W. W., LIFE OF THE BUDDHA, AND THE EARLY HISTORY OF HIS ORDER, derived from Tibetan works in the Bkah-Hgyur and the Bstan-Hgyur. Post 8vo (*Trübner's Oriental Series*), 10*s.* 6*d.*

UDANAVARGA : a collection of verses from the Buddhist Canon, compiled by DHARMATRÂTA and translated from the Tibetan. Post 8vo (*Trübner's Oriental Series*), 9*s.*

RODD, E. H., BIRDS OF CORNWALL AND THE SCILLY ISLANDS, edited by J. E. HARTING, with portrait and map. 8vo, 14*s.*

ROOD, Ogden N, MODERN CHROMATICS, with applications to art and industry, with 130 original illustrations. 3rd edition, crown 8vo, 5*s.* [I.S.S.

ROLFE, E. N., and INGLEBY, H., NAPLES IN 1888, with illustrations. Crown 8vo, 6*s.*

ROMANES, G. J., MENTAL EVOLUTION IN ANIMALS, with posthumous essay on instinct by CHARLES DARWIN. 8vo, 12*s.*

MENTAL EVOLUTION IN MAN : origin of the human faculty. 8vo. 14*s.*

ANIMAL INTELLIGENCE. 4th edition, crown 8vo, 5*s.* [I.S.S.

JELLY-FISH, STAR-FISH, AND SEA-URCHINS : being a research on primitive nervous systems, with illustrations. 2nd edition, crown 8vo, 5*s.* [I.S.S.

ROSENTHAL, Prof. J., GENERAL PHYSIOLOGY OF MUSCLES AND NERVES. 3rd edition, with 75 illustrations, crown 8vo, 5*s.* [I.S.S.

ROSING, S., ENGLISH-DANISH DICTIONARY. Crown 8vo, 8*s.* 6*d.*

ROSMINI. LIFE OF ANTONIO ROSMINI, by W. LOCKHART, with portraits. 2 vols. crown 8vo. 12*s.*

ROSS, Percy, A PROFESSOR OF ALCHEMY. Crown 8vo, 3*s.* 6*d.*

ROSS, Lieut.-Col. W. A., ALPHABETICAL MANUAL OF BLOWPIPE ANALYSIS. Crown 8vo, 5*s.*

PYROLOGY, OR FIRE CHEMISTRY. Small 4to, 36*s.*

ROTH, H. Ling, GUIDE TO THE LITERATURE OF SUGAR. 8vo, 7*s.* 6*d.*

ROUTLEDGE, James, ENGLISH RULE AND NATIVE OPINION IN INDIA. 8vo, 10*s.* 6*d.*

ROWBOTHAM, J. F., THE HUMAN EPIC, canto i. Crown 8vo, 1*s.* 6*d.*

HISTORY OF MUSIC. 3 vols. 8vo, each 18*s.*

ROWING AT WESTMINSTER, 1813–1883 : extracted from the school water-ledgers. Crown 8vo, 5*s.*

RULE, Martin, LIFE AND TIMES OF ST. ANSELM, ARCHBISHOP OF CANTERBURY AND PRIMATE OF THE BRITAINS. 2 vols. 8vo, 32*s.*

RUSSELL, E. F., MEMOIR OF A. H. MACKONOCHIE, with portrait and views. Large crown 8vo, 7*s.* 6*d.*

RUTHERFORD, Mark, AUTOBIOGRAPHY OF MARK RUTHERFORD AND MARK RUTHERFORD'S DELIVERANCE, edited by REUBEN SHAPCOTT. 3rd edition, crown 8vo, 7*s.* 6*d.*

REVOLUTION IN TANNER'S LANE, edited by REUBEN SHAPCOTT. Crown 8vo, 7*s.* 6*d.*

MIRIAM'S SCHOOLING, and other papers, edited by REUBEN SHAP-COTT. Crown 8vo, 6*s.*

SALMONÉ, H. A., ARABIC-ENGLISH DICTIONARY, comprising about 120,000 Arabic words, with English index of about 50,000 words. 2 vols. post 8vo, 36*s.*

SAMUELSON, James, INDIA, PAST AND PRESENT : historical, social, and political, with map, woodcuts, views, portraits, &c. 8vo, 21*s.*

HISTORY OF DRINK, social, scientific, and political. 2nd edition, 8vo, 6*s.*

BULGARIA, PAST AND PRESENT : historical, political, and descriptive, with map and numerous illustrations. 8vo, 10*s.* 6*d.*

SANDWITH, F. M., EGYPT AS A WINTER RESORT. Crown 8vo, 3*s.* 6*d.*

SANTIAGOE, Daniel, CURRY COOK'S ASSISTANT. Fcap. 8vo, 1*s.* 6*d.* ; paper covers, 1*s.*

SATOW, E. M., ENGLISH-JAPANESE DICTIONARY OF THE SPOKEN LANGUAGE. 2nd edition, imp. 32mo, 12*s.* 6*d.*

SAYCE, A. H., INTRODUCTION TO THE SCIENCE OF LANGUAGE. New and cheaper edition. 2 vols. crown 8vo, 9*s.*

ASSYRIAN GRAMMAR, for comparative purposes. Crown 8vo, 7*s.* 6*d.*

PRINCIPLES OF COMPARATIVE PHILOLOGY. 3rd edition, crown 8vo, 10*s.* 6*d.*

SAYWELL, J. L., HANDBOOK OF COUNTY DIALECTS. Crown 8vo, 5*s.*

SCANNELL, Thomas B., and WILHELM, Joseph, D.D., MANUAL OF CATHOLIC THEOLOGY, based on SCHEEBEN'S 'Dogmatik.' 2 vols. 8vo Vol. I. 15*s.*

SCHAIBLE, C. H., SYSTEMATIC TRAINING OF THE BODY. Crown 8vo, 5*s.*

SCHAW, Col. H., DEFENCE AND ATTACK OF POSITIONS AND LOCALITIES. 4th edition, crown 8vo, 3*s.* 6*d.*

SCHEFFEL, J. V., GAUDEAMUS, translated by C. G. LELAND. 16mo, 3*s.* 6*d.*

SCHLAGINTWEIT, Emil, BUDDHISM IN TIBET, illustrated by literary documents and objects of religious worship, with 20 plates. 2 vols. royal 8vo and folio, £2. 2*s.*

D 2

SCHLEICHER, *August*, COMPARATIVE GRAMMAR OF THE INDO-EUROPEAN, SANSKRIT, GREEK, AND LATIN LANGUAGES, from the 3rd German edition, by H. BENDALL. 8vo, 13s. 6d.

SCHMIDT, *Prof. O.*, DOCTRINE OF DESCENT AND DARWINISM, with 26 illustrations. 7th edition, crown 8vo, 5s. [I.S.S.

MAMMALIA IN THEIR RELATION TO PRIMEVAL TIMES, with 51 woodcuts. Crown 8vo, 5s. [I.S.S.

SCHOPENHAUER, A., THE WORLD AS WILL AND IDEA, from the German by R. B. HALDANE and J. KEMP. 3 vols. post 8vo, £2. 10s.
[Philosophical Library.

SCHÜTZENBERGER, Prof., ON FERMENTATION, with 28 illustrations. 4th edition, crown 8vo, 5s. [I.S.S.

SCHWAAB, E. F., THE SECRETS OF CANNING, a complete exposition of the theory and art of this industry. Crown 8vo, 25s.

SCHWENDLER, Louis, INSTRUCTIONS FOR TESTING TELEGRAPH LINES. 2 vols. 8vo, 21s.

SCOONES, W. B., FOUR CENTURIES OF ENGLISH LETTERS : a selection of 350 letters by 150 writers, from the period of the Paston letters to the present time. 3rd edition, large crown 8vo, 6s.

SCOTT, Benjamin, A STATE INIQUITY : its rise, extension, and overthrow. 8vo, gilt, 5s. ; plain, 3s. 6d.

SCOTT, G. F. E., SURSUM CORDA, or Songs and service. Small 8vo, 5s.

SCOTT, James George, BURMA AS IT WAS, AS IT IS, AND AS IT WILL BE. Cheap edition, crown 8vo, 2s. 6d.

SCOTT, Robert H., ELEMENTARY METEOROLOGY. 4th edition, with numerous illustrations, crown 8vo, 5s. [I.S.S.

SEARELLE, Luscombe, THE DAWN OF DEATH. Crown 8vo, 4s. 6d.

SELBY, H. M., SHAKESPEARE CLASSICAL DICTIONARY, or Mythological allusions in the plays of Shakespeare explained. Fcap. 8vo, 1s.

SEMPER, Karl, NATURAL CONDITIONS OF EXISTENCE AS THEY AFFECT ANIMAL LIFE, with 2 maps and 106 woodcuts. 3rd edition, crown 8vo, 5s. [I.S.S.

SERJEANT, W. C. Eldon, THE ASTROLOGER'S GUIDE (ANIMA ASTROLOGIÆ). 8vo, 7s. 6d.

SEVERNE, Florence, THE PILLAR HOUSE, with frontispiece. Crown 8vo, 6s.

SHAKSPERE, W., WORKS. Avon edition, 12 vols. Elzevir 8vo (*Parchment Library*), vellum, 7s. 6d. per vol. ; parchment or cloth, 6s. per vol.; cheap edition, 1s. 6d. per vol.

⁎⁎⁎ The cheap edition may also be had complete, 12 vols. in cloth box, 21s., or bound in 6 vols. 15s.

NEW VARIORUM EDITION, edited by HORACE HOWARD FURNESS. Royal 8vo. Vol. I. Romeo and Juliet, 18s. Vol. II. Macbeth, 18s. Vol. III. and IV. Hamlet, 2 vols. 36s. Vol. V. King Lear, 18s. Vol. VI. Othello, 18s.

SONNETS, edited by EDWARD DOWDEN, with frontispiece. Elzevir 8vo (*Parchment Library*), vellum, 7s. 6d. ; parchment or cloth, 6s.

SHAW, Flora L., CASTLE BLAIR : a story of youthful days. Crown 8vo, 3s. 6d.

SHAW, Lieut.-Colonel Wilkinson, ELEMENTS OF MODERN TACTICS PRACTICALLY APPLIED TO ENGLISH FORMATIONS. 7th edition, with 31 plates and maps, small crown 8vo, 9s.

SHEEPSHANKS, J., CONFIRMATION AND UNCTION OF THE SICK. Small 8vo, 3s. 6d.

SHELLEY. LIFE OF P. B. SHELLEY, by EDWARD DOWDEN, LL.D., with portraits. 2 vols. 8vo, 36s.

SHELLEY, P. B. POEMS, edited by RICHARD GARNETT, with frontispiece. Elzevir 8vo (*Parchment Library*), vellum, 7s. 6d. ; parchment or cloth, 6s.

SELECT LETTERS, edited by RICHARD GARNETT. Elzevir 8vo (*Parchment Library*), vellum, 7s. 6d. ; parchment or cloth, 6s.

SHERRING, M. A., SACRED CITY OF THE HINDUS : an account of Benares, with illustrations. 8vo, 21s.

SIBREE, James, THE GREAT AFRICAN ISLAND, MADAGASCAR : its physical geography, &c, with maps and illustrations. 8vo, 10s. 6d.

POEMS, including " Rosalie," crown 8vo, 6s.

SIDGWICK, A., FALLACIES: a view of logic from the practical side. 2nd edition, crown 8vo, 5s. [I.S.S.

SIGERSON, George, POLITICAL PRISONERS AT HOME AND ABROAD, with appendix on dietaries. Crown 8vo, 2s. 6d.

SIMCOX, Edith, EPISODES IN THE LIVES OF MEN, WOMEN, AND LOVERS. Crown 8vo. 7s. 6d.

NATURAL LAW : an essay in ethics. 2nd edition, post 8vo, 10s. 6d.
[*Philosophical Library.*

SIME, Jas., LESSING : his life and writings. 2nd edition, 2 vols. with portraits, post 8vo, 21s. [*Philosophical Library.*

SIMONNE, METODO PARA APRENDER A LEER, escribir y hablar el Frances, segun el verdadero sistema de Ollendorff. Crown 8vo, 6s. Key, 3s. 6d.

SIMPSON, M. C. M., LETTERS AND RECOLLECTIONS OF JULIUS AND MARY MOHL, with portraits and 2 illustrations. 8vo, 15s.

SINCLAIR, F., GERMAN VOCABULARY. Crown 8vo, 2s.

SINCLAIR, Thomas, ESSAYS. Crown 8vo, 1s. 6d. ; paper covers, 1s. TRAVEL SKETCH. Crown 8vo, 5s.

SINGER, I., SIMPLIFIED GRAMMAR OF THE HUNGARIAN LANGUAGE. Crown 8vo, 4s. 6d.

SINNETT, A. P., THE OCCULT WORLD. 4th edition, crown 8vo, 3s. 6d:
INCIDENTS IN THE LIFE OF MADAME BLAVATSKY, with portrait. 8vo, 10s. 6d.

SKINNER. JAMES SKINNER, A MEMOIR, by the author of 'Charles Lowder,' with preface by the Rev. Canon CARTER, and portrait. Large crown 8vo, 7s. 6d. Cheap edition, crown 8vo, 3s. 6d.

SMITH, E., FOODS, with numerous illustrations. 9th edition, crown 8vo, 5s. [I.S.S.

SMITH, H. Percy, GLOSSARY OF TERMS AND PHRASES, edited by H. PERCY SMITH and others. Cheaper edition, medium 8vo, 3s. 6d.

SMITH, Hamilton, HYDRAULICS : the flow of water through orifices, over weirs, and through open conduits and pipes, with 17 plates. Royal 4to, 30s.

SMITH, Huntington, A CENTURY OF AMERICAN LITERATURE : Benjamin Franklin to James Russell Lowell. Crown 8vo, 6s.

SMITH, M., and HORNEMAN, H., NORWEGIAN GRAMMAR, with a glossary for tourists. Post 8vo, 2s.

SMITH, S., DIVINE GOVERNMENT. 5th edition, crown 8vo, 6s.

SMYTH, R. Brough, THE ABORIGINES OF VICTORIA, compiled for the Government, with maps, plates, and woodcuts. 2 vols, royal 8vo, £3. 3s.

SOPHOCLES. THE SEVEN PLAYS, translated into English verse by LEWIS CAMPBELL. Crown 8vo, 7s. 6d.

SPECIMENS OF ENGLISH PROSE STYLE FROM MALORY TO MACAULAY, selected and annotated, with an introductory essay, by GEORGE SAINTSBURY. Large crown 8vo, printed on hand-made paper, vellum, 15s. ; parchment antique or cloth, 12s.

SPEARMAN, Major, BRITISH BURMA GAZETTEER, compiled for the Government of India, with 11 photographs. 2 vols., 8vo, £2 10s.

SPEDDING, James, LIFE AND TIMES OF FRANCIS BACON. 2 vols. post 8vo, 21s.

SPENCER, Herbert, STUDY OF SOCIOLOGY. 14th edition, crown 8vo, 5s.
[I.S.S.

SPINOZA, Benedict de, ETHIC DEMONSTRATED IN GEOMETRICAL ORDER AND DIVIDED INTO FIVE PARTS, which treat (1) of God, (2) of the nature and origin of the mind, (3) of the origin and nature of the affects, (4) of human bondage, or of the strength of the affects, (5) of the power of the intellect, or of human liberty. From the Latin by W. HALE WHITE. Post 8vo, 10s. 6d. *[Philosophical Library.*

SPINOZA. LIFE, CORRESPONDENCE, AND ETHICS OF SPINOZA, by R. WILLIS. 8vo, 21s.

SPRAGUE, Charles E., HANDBOOK OF VOLAPUK, the international language. 2nd edition, crown 8vo, 5s.

ST. HILL, Katharine, GRAMMAR of PALMISTRY, with 18 illustrations 12mo, 1s.

STACKELBERG, Baroness, LIFE OF 'CARMEN SYLVA,' Queen of Roumania, translated by Baroness DEICHMANN, with 5 illustrations. 8vo, 12s.

STALLO, J. B., CONCEPTS AND THEORIES OF MODERN PHYSICS. 3rd edition, crown 8vo, 5s. [I.S.S.

STARCKE, C. N., THE PRIMITIVE FAMILY : its origin and development. Crown 8vo, 5s. [I.S.S.

STEELE, Th., AN EASTERN LOVE-STORY : Kusa Játakaya. Crown 8vo, 6s.

STEPHEN, Caroline E., QUAKER STRONGHOLDS. Crown 8vo, 5s.

STEVENSON, A. L., RAYMOND : a story in verse. Small 8vo, 3s. 6d.

STEWART, Balfour, CONSERVATION OF ENERGY, with 14 illustrations. 7th edition, crown 8vo, 5s. [I.S.S.

STICKNEY, A., THE POLITICAL PROBLEM. Crown 8vo, 4s. 6d.

STOKES, Whitley, GOIDELICA : old and early-middle Irish glosses, prose and verse. 2nd edition, med. 8vo, 18s.

STONE, Capt. F. G., TACTICAL STUDIES FROM THE FRANCO-GERMAN WAR OF 1870-71, with 22 lithographic sketches and maps. 8vo, 10s. 6d.

STOPES, C., THE BACON-SHAKESPEARE QUESTION ANSWERED. 2nd edition, 8vo, 6s.

STORR, F., and TURNER, H., CANTERBURY CHIMES, or Chaucer tales re-told to children, with 6 illustrations from the Ellesmere manuscript. 3rd edition, fcap. 8vo, 3s. 6d.

STRACHEY, Sir John, INDIA, with map. 8vo, 15s.

STRECKER, Adolph, TEXT-BOOK OF ORGANIC CHEMISTRY, edited by Prof. WISLICENUS, translated and edited, with extensive additions, by W. R. HODGKINSON and A. J. GREENAWAY. 2nd and cheaper edition, 8vo, 12s. 6d.

STREET, J. C., THE HIDDEN WAY ACROSS THE THRESHOLD, or The mystery which hath been hidden for ages and from generations, with plates. Large 8vo, 15s.

STRETTON, Hesba, DAVID LLOYD'S LAST WILL, with 4 illustrations. New edition, royal 16mo, 2s. 6d.

THROUGH A NEEDLE'S EYE : a story, with frontispiece. Crown 8vo, 6s.

SULLY, James, ILLUSIONS : a psychological study. 3rd edition, crown 8vo, 5s. [I.S.S.

SUMNER, W. G., WHAT SOCIAL CLASSES OWE TO EACH OTHER. 18mo, 3s. 6d.

SUYEMATZ, K., GENJI MONOGATARI, the most celebrated of the classical Japanese romances, translated. Crown 8vo, 7s. 6d.

SWINBURNE, Algernon Charles, A WORD FOR THE NAVY. (Only 250 copies printed.) Imperial 16mo, paper covers, 5s.

BIBLIOGRAPHY OF SWINBURNE, 1857-87. Crown 8vo, vellum gilt, 6s.

SYME, David, ON THE MODIFICATION OF ORGANISMS. Crown 8vo, 5s.

SYMONDS, John Addington, VAGABUNDULI LIBELLUS. Crown 8vo, 6s.

SYMONS, G. J., THE ERUPTION OF KRAKATOA, AND SUBSEQUENT PHENOMENA : report of the Krakatoa Committee of the Royal Society, with 6 chromolithographs and 40 maps and diagrams. 4to, £1. 10s.

SWIFT, Jon., LETTERS AND JOURNALS, edited by STANLEY LANE-POOLE. Elzevir 8vo (*Parchment Library*), vellum, 7s. 6d. ; parchment or cloth, 6s.

PROSE WRITINGS, edited by STANLEY LANE-POOLE, with portrait. Elzevir 8vo (*Parchment Library*), vellum, 7s. 6d. ; parchment or cloth, 6s.

TARRING, C. J., ELEMENTARY TURKISH GRAMMAR. Crown 8vo, 6s.

' *TASMA,*' A SYDNEY SOVEREIGN, and other tales. Crown 8vo, cloth, 6s.

UNCLE PIPER OF PIPER'S HILL : an Australian novel. 3rd edition, crown 8vo, 6s.

IN HER EARLIEST YOUTH. Cheap edition, crown 8vo, 6s.

TAYLER, J. J., RETROSPECT OF THE RELIGIOUS LIFE OF ENGLAND, or Church, Puritanism, and free inquiry. 2nd edition, post 8vo, 7s. 6d.

TAYLOR, Col. Meadows, Seeta : a novel, with frontispiece. Crown 8vo, 6s.

Tippoo Sultaun : a tale of the Mysore war, with frontispiece. Crown 8vo, 6s.

Ralph Darnell, with frontispiece. Crown 8vo, 6s.

A Noble Queen, with frontispiece. Crown 8vo, 6s.

The Confessions of a Thug, with frontispiece. Crown 8vo, 6s.

Tara : a Mahratta tale, with frontispiece. Crown 8vo, 6s.

TAYLOR, Canon Isaac, The Alphabet : an account of the origin and development of letters, with numerous tables and facsimiles. 2 vols. 8vo, 36s.

Leaves from an Egyptian Note-Book. Crown 8vo, 5s.

TAYLOR. Reynell Taylor, C.B. C.S.I. : a biography, by E. Gambier Parry, with portrait and map. 8vo, 14s.

TAYLOR, Sir H., Works, 5 vols. Crown 8vo, 30s.

Philip Van Artevelde. Fcap. 8vo, 3s. 6d.

The Virgin Widow, &c. Fcap. 8vo, 3s. 6d.

The Statesman. Fcap. 8vo, 3s. 6d.

Technological Dictionary of the terms employed in the arts and sciences (architecture, engineering, mechanics, shipbuilding and navigation, metallurgy, mathematics, &c.), by Karl Kamarsch. 4th revised edition, 3 vols. imperial 8vo.

Vol. I. German-English-French. 12s.
Vol. II. English-German-French. 12s.
Vol. III. French-German-English. 15s.

THACKERAY, S. W., The Land and the Community. Crown 8vo, 3s. 6d.

THACKERAY, W. M., Essay on the Genius of George Cruickshank, reprinted verbatim from the *Westminster Review,* with 40 illustrations. Royal 8vo, 7s. 6d.

Sultan Stork, and other stories and sketches, 1829–44, now first collected, to which is added the bibliography of Thackeray. Large 8vo, 10s. 6d.

Theology and Piety alike Free, from the point of view of Manchester New College, Oxford : a contribution to its effort offered by an old student. 8vo, 9s.

THOMPSON, A. R., Dialogues, Russian and English. Crown 8vo, 5s.

THOMPSON, Sir H., Diet in Relation to Age and Activity. Fcap. 8vo, 1s. 6d. ; paper covers, 1s.

Modern Cremation. Crown 8vo, 2s. 6d.

THOMPSON, R. A., Thomas Becket, Martyr-Patriot. Crown 8vo, 6s.

THORNELY, J. L., Stanley : a drama. Small 8vo, 3s. 6d.

THURSTON, Prof. R. H., History of the Growth of the Steam Engine, with numerous illustrations. 4th edition, crown 8vo, 5s.   [I.S.S.

Through North Wales with a Knapsack, by Four Schoolmistresses, with a sketch map. Small 8vo, 2s. 6d.

TIELE, Prof. C. P., OUTLINES OF THE HISTORY OF RELIGION TO THE SPREAD OF THE UNIVERSAL RELIGIONS, from the Dutch by J. ESTLIN CARPENTER. 4th edition, post 8vo, 7s. 6d.
[*Philosophical Library, and Trübner's Oriental Series.*
HISTORY OF THE EGYPTIAN RELIGION, translated by J. BALLINGAL. Post 8vo (*Trübner's Oriental Series*), 7s. 6d.

TISDALL, W. St. Clair, SIMPLIFIED GRAMMAR AND READING BOOK OF THE PANJÄBĪ LANGUAGE. Crown 8vo, 7s. 6d.

TOBACCO TALK AND SMOKERS' GOSSIP. 16mo, 2s.

TORCEANU, R., SIMPLIFIED GRAMMAR OF THE ROUMANIAN LAN-GUAGE. Crown 8vo, 5s.

TOORGEYNIEFF, Ivan, THE UNFORTUNATE ONE : a novel from the Russian by A. R. THOMPSON. Crown 8vo, 3s. 6d.

TOSCANI, G., ITALIAN CONVERSATIONAL COURSE. 4th edition, 12mo, 5s.
ITALIAN READING COURSE. Fcap. 8vo, 4s. 6d.

TRANT, William, TRADE UNIONS : their origin, objects, and efficacy. Small 8vo, 1s. 6d. ; paper covers, 1s.

TREHERNE, Mrs., SUMMER IN A DUTCH COUNTRY HOUSE. Crown 8vo, 6s.

TRENCH. LETTERS AND MEMORIALS OF ARCHBISHOP TRENCH, by the author of ' Charles Lowder,' with 2 portraits. 2 vols. 8vo, 21s.

TRENCH, Archbishop, ENGLISH, PAST AND PRESENT. 13th edition, revised and improved, fcap. 8vo, 5s.
ON THE STUDY OF WORDS. 20th edition, revised, fcap. 8vo, 5s.
NOTES ON THE PARABLES OF OUR LORD. 8vo, 12s. ; cheap edition, 56th thousand, 7s. 6d.
NOTES ON THE MIRACLES OF OUR LORD. 8vo, 12s. ; cheap edition, 48th thousand, 7s. 6d.
HOUSEHOLD BOOK OF ENGLISH POETRY. 4th edition, revised, extra fcap. 8vo, 5s.
ESSAY ON THE LIFE AND GENIUS OF CALDERON, with translations from his ' Life's a Dream ' and ' Great Theatre of the World.' 2nd edition, revised and improved, extra fcap. 8vo, 5s. 6d.
GUSTAVUS ADOLPHUS IN GERMANY, and other lectures on the Thirty Years' War. 3rd edition, enlarged, fcap. 8vo, 4s.
PLUTARCH : his life, his lives, and his morals. 2nd edition, enlarged, fcap. 8vo, 3s. 6d.
REMAINS OF THE LATE MRS. RICHARD TRENCH : being selections from her journals, letters, and other papers, edited by her son, Archbishop TRENCH. New and cheaper edition, with portraits, 8vo, 6s.
LECTURES ON MEDIÆVAL CHURCH HISTORY : being the substance of lectures delivered at Queen's College, London. 2nd edition, 8vo, 12s.
POEMS. 10th edition, fcap. 8vo, 7s. 6d.
POEMS. Library edition, 2 vols. small 8vo, 10s.
PROVERBS AND THEIR LESSONS. 7th edition, enlarged, fcap. 8vo, 4s.

SACRED LATIN POETRY, chiefly lyrical. 3rd edition, corrected, and improved, fcap. 8vo, 7*s.*

SELECT GLOSSARY OF ENGLISH WORDS USED FORMERLY IN SENSES DIFFERENT FROM THE PRESENT. 7th edition, revised and enlarged, fcap. 8vo, 5*s.*

BRIEF THOUGHTS AND MEDITATIONS ON SOME PASSAGES IN HOLY SCRIPTURE. 3rd edition, crown 8vo, 3*s.* 6*d.*

COMMENTARY ON THE EPISTLES TO THE SEVEN CHURCHES IN ASIA. 4th edition, revised, 8vo, 8*s.* 6*d.*

ON THE AUTHORISED VERSION OF THE NEW TESTAMENT. 2nd edition, 8vo, 7*s.*

SERMONS NEW AND OLD. Crown 8vo, 6*s.*

WESTMINSTER AND OTHER SERMONS. Crown 8vo, 6*s*

THE SERMON ON THE MOUNT : an exposition drawn from the writings of St. Augustine. 4th edition, enlarged, 8vo, 10*s.* 6*d.*

SHIPWRECKS OF FAITH : three sermons preached before the University of Cambridge. Fcap. 8vo, 2*s.* 6*d.*

STUDIES IN THE GOSPELS. 5th edition, revised, 8vo, 10*s.* 6*d.*

SYNONYMS OF THE NEW TESTAMENT. 10th edition, enlarged, 8vo, 12*s.*

TRENCH, Major-General, CAVALRY IN MODERN WAR. Small crown 8vo, 6*s.*

TRIMEN, Roland, SOUTH AFRICAN BUTTERFLIES : a monograph of the extra-tropical species, with 12 coloured plates. 3 vols. 8vo, £2. 12*s.* 6*d.*

TRINDER, D., THE WORSHIP OF HEAVEN, and other sermons. Crown 8vo, 5*s.*

TROUESSART, E. L., MICROBES, FERMENTS, AND MOULDS, with 107 illustrations. Crown 8vo, 5*s.* [I.S S.

TRÜBNER'S BIBLIOGRAPHICAL GUIDE TO AMERICAN LITERATURE, from 1817 to 1857. 8vo, half-bound, 18*s.*

CATALOGUE OF DICTIONARIES AND GRAMMARS OF THE PRINCIPAL LANGUAGES AND DIALECTS OF THE WORLD. 2nd edition, 8vo, 5*s.*

TRUMBULL, H. Clay, THE BLOOD-COVENANT : a primitive rite and its bearings on Scripture. Post 8vo, 7*s.* 6*d.*

TURNER, C. E., COUNT TOLSTOÏ, AS NOVELIST AND THINKER : lectures delivered at the Royal Institution. Crown 8vo, 3*s.* 6*d.*

MODERN NOVELISTS OF RUSSIA : lectures delivered at the Taylor Institution, Oxford. Crown 8vo, 3*s.* 6*d.*

TWEEDIE, Mrs. Alec, OBER-AMMERGAU PASSION PLAY, 1890. Small 8vo, 2*s.* 6*d.*

TYLL OWLGLASS' MARVELLOUS AND RARE CONCEITS, translated by KENNETH MACKENZIE, illustrated by ALFRED CROWQUILL (*Lotos Series*), 3*s.* 6*d.*

TYNAN, Katherine, LOUISE DE LA VALLIERE, and other poems. Small 8vo, 3*s.* 6*d.*

SHAMROCKS. Small 8vo, 5*s.*

TYNDALL, J., FORMS OF WATER IN CLOUDS AND RIVERS, ICE AND GLACIERS, with 25 illustrations. 9th edition, crown 8vo, 5*s*. [I.S.S.

VAN LAUN, H., GRAMMAR OF THE FRENCH LANGUAGE. Crown 8vo. Accidence and syntax, 4*s*. ; exercises, 3*s*. 6*d*.

VAN EYS, IV., OUTLINES OF BASQUE GRAMMAR. Crown 8vo, 3*s*. 6*d*.

VAUGHAN, H. H., BRITISH REASON IN ENGLISH RHYME. Crown 8vo, 6*s*.

VELASQUEZ, M. de la Cadena, DICTIONARY OF THE SPANISH AND ENGLISH LANGUAGES, for the use of young learners and travellers. Crown 8vo, 6*s*.
PRONOUNCING DICTIONARY OF THE SPANISH AND ENGLISH LAN-GUAGES. Royal 8vo, £1. 4*s*.
NEW SPANISH READER : passages from the most approved authors, with vocabulary. Post 8vo, 6*s*.
INTRODUCTION TO SPANISH CONVERSATION. 12mo, 2*s*. 6*d*.

VELASQUEZ and SIMONNÉ, NEW METHOD TO READ, WRITE, AND SPEAK THE SPANISH LANGUAGE, adapted to Ollendorff's system. Revised edition. Post 8vo, 6*s*. ; key, 4*s*.

VESCELIUS-SHELDON, Louise, AN I. D. B. IN SOUTH AFRICA, illus-trated. Crown 8vo, 7*s*. 6*d*.
YANKEE GIRLS IN ZULU-LAND, illustrated. Crown 8vo, 5*s*.

VIEYRA'S POCKET DICTIONARY OF THE PORTUGUESE AND ENGLISH LANGUAGES. 2 vols. post 8vo, 10*s*.

VIGNOLI, Tito, MYTH AND SCIENCE : an essay. 3rd edition, with supplementary note, crown 8vo, 5*s*. [I.S.S.

VINCENT, Frank, AROUND AND ABOUT SOUTH AMERICA : twenty months of quest and query, with maps, plans, and 54 illustrations. Medium 8vo, 21*s*.

VOGEL, Dr. Hermann, CHEMISTRY OF LIGHT AND PHOTOGRAPHY, with 100 illustrations. 5th edition, crown 8vo, 5*s*. [I.S.S.

WADDIE, John, DIVINE PHILOSOPHY. Small 8vo, 5*s*.

WAITE, A. E., LIVES OF ALCHEMYSTICAL PHILOSOPHERS. 8vo, 10*s*. 6*d*.
MAGICAL WRITINGS OF THOMAS VAUGHAN. Small 4to, 10*s*. 6*d*.
REAL HISTORY OF THE ROSICRUCIANS, with illustrations. Crown 8vo, 7*s*. 6*d*.
MYSTERIES OF MAGIC : a digest of the writings of Eliphas Lévi, with illustrations. 8vo, 10*s*. 6*d*.

WAKE, C. S., SERPENT-WORSHIP, and other essays, with a chapter on Totemism. 8vo, 10*s*. 6*d*.
DEVELOPMENT OF MARRIAGE AND KINSHIP. 8vo, 18*s*.

WALL, George, NATURAL HISTORY OF THOUGHT IN ITS PRACTICAL ASPECT, FROM ITS ORIGIN IN INFANCY. 8vo, 12*s*. 6*d*.

WALLACE, Alfred Russell, MIRACLES AND MODERN SPIRITUALISM. 2nd edition, crown 8vo, 5*s*.

WALPOLE, C. G., SHORT HISTORY OF IRELAND, with 5 maps and appendices. 3rd edition, crown 8vo, 6*s*.

WALTERS, J. Cuming, IN TENNYSON LAND: a brief account of the home and early surroundings of the Poet-Laureate, with illustrations. 8vo, 5*s*.

WANKLYN, J. A., MILK ANALYSIS : a practical treatise on the examination of milk and its derivatives, cream, butter, and cheese. 2nd edition, crown 8vo, 5*s*.
TEA, COFFEE, AND COCOA : a practical treatise on the analysis of tea, coffee, cocoa, chocolate, and maté (Paraguay tea). Crown 8vo, 5*s*.

WANKLYN, J. A., and COOPER, W. J, BREAD ANALYSIS : a practical treatise on the examination of flour and bread. Crown 8vo, 5*s*.
AIR ANALYSIS : a practical treatise, with appendix on illuminating gas. Crown 8vo, 5*s*.

WANKLYN, J. A., and CHAPMAN, E. T., WATER ANALYSIS : a treatise on the examination of potable water. 7th edition, entirely re-written, crown 8vo, 5*s*.

WARD, Wilfrid, THE WISH TO BELIEVE : a discussion concerning the temper of mind in which a reasonable man should undertake religious inquiry. Small 8vo, 5*s*.

WARD, W. G., ESSAYS ON THE PHILOSOPHY OF THEISM, edited, with an introduction, by WILFRID WARD. 2 vols. 8vo, 21*s*.

WARING, E. J., PHARMACOPŒIA OF INDIA. Crown 8vo, 6*s*. [*India Office.*

WARNER, Prof. F., PHYSICAL EXPRESSION : its modes and principles, with 50 illustrations. Crown 8vo, 5*s*. [I.S.S.

WARTER, J. W., AN OLD SHROPSHIRE OAK. 2 vols. 8vo, 28*s*.

WATERHOUSE, Col. J., PREPARATION OF DRAWINGS FOR PHOTOGRAPHIC REPRODUCTION, with plates. Crown 8vo, 5*s*.

WATSON, John Forbes, INDEX TO THE NATIVE AND SCIENTIFIC NAMES OF INDIAN AND OTHER EASTERN ECONOMIC PLANTS AND PRODUCTS. Imperial 8vo, £1. 11*s*. 6*d*.

WATSON, R. G., SPANISH AND PORTUGUESE SOUTH AMERICA DURING THE COLONIAL PERIOD. 2 vols. post 8vo, 21*s*.

WEAVER, F. W., WELLS WILLS, arranged in parishes and annotated. 8vo, 10*s*. 6*d*.

WEBER, A., HISTORY OF INDIAN LITERATURE, from the German by J. MANN and T. ZACHARIAE. 2nd edition, post 8vo, (*Trübner's Oriental Series*), 10*s*. 6*d*.

WEDGWOOD, H., DICTIONARY OF ENGLISH ETYMOLOGY. 4th edition, revised and enlarged, 8vo, £1. 1*s*.
CONTESTED ETYMOLOGIES IN THE DICTIONARY OF THE REV. W. W. SKEAT. Crown 8vo, 5*s*.

WEDGWOOD, Julia, THE MORAL IDEAL : an historic study. 2nd edition, 8vo, 9*s*.

WEISBACH, Julius, THEORETICAL MECHANICS : a manual of the mechanics of engineering, designed as a text-book for technical schools and for the use of engineers. From the German by E. B. COXE. With 902 woodcuts. 8vo, 31*s*. 6*d*.

WELLER, E., IMPROVED DICTIONARY, English-French and French-English. Royal 8vo, 7*s*. 6*d*.

WESTROPP, Hodder M., PRIMITIVE SYMBOLISM AS ILLUSTRATED IN PHALLIC WORSHIP, or The Reproductive Principle, with introduction by Major-Gen. FORLONG. 8vo, 7*s*. 6*d*.

WHEELDON, J. P., Angling Resorts near London : the Thames and the Lea. Crown 8vo, paper, 1*s.* 6*d.*

WHEELER, J. Talboys, History of India from the Earliest Ages. 8vo. Vol. I. Containing the Vedic Period and the Mahá Bhárata, with map. Vol. II. The Ramayana, and the Brahmanic Period, with 2 maps, 21*s.* Vol. III. Hindu, Buddhist, and Brahmanical Revival, with 2 maps, 18*s.* Vol. IV. Part I. Mussulman Rule, 14*s.* Vol. IV. Part II. Completing the History of India down to the time of the Moghul Empire, 12*s.*

** Vol. III. is also published as an independent work under the title of ' History of India : Hindu, Buddhist, and Brahmanical.'

Early Records of British India : a history of the English settlements in India, as told in the Government records and other contemporary documents. Royal 8vo, 15*s.*

WHERRY, E. M., Comprehensive Commentary to the Quran, with Sale's preliminary discourse, and additional notes. Post 8vo (*Trübner's Oriental Series*), Vols. I. II. and III. 12*s.* 6*d.* each. Vol. IV. 10*s.* 6*d.*

WHIBLEY, Chas., In Cap and Gown : three centuries of Cambridge wit. 2nd edition, crown 8vo, 7*s.* 6*d.*

WHINFIELD, E. H., The Quatrains of Omar Khayyám. The Persian text, with an English verse translation. Post 8vo (*Trübner's Oriental Series*), 10*s.* 6*d.* ; translation only, 5*s.*

Masnavi I Ma'navi : the spiritual couplets of Mauláná Jalálu-'d-Din Muhammad I Rúmí, translated and abridged. Post 8vo (*Trübner's Oriental Series*), 7*s.* 6*d.*

WHITAKER, Florence, Christy's Inheritance : a London story, illustrated. Royal 16mo, 1*s.* 6*d.*

WHITMAN, Sidney, Imperial Germany : a critical study of fact and character. Crown 8vo, 7*s.* 6*d.*

WHITNEY, Prof. W. D., Life and Growth of Language. 5th edition, crown 8vo, 5*s.* [I.S.S.

Essentials of English Grammar. 2nd edition, crown 8vo. 3*s.* 6*d.*

Language and the Study of Language. 4th edition, crown 8vo, 10*s.* 6*d.*

Language and its Study, with especial reference to the Indo-European family of languages, edited by R. Morris. 2nd edition, crown 8vo, 5*s.*

Sanskrit Grammar, including both the classical language and the older dialects of Veda and Brahmana. 2nd edition, 8vo, 12*s.*

WHITWORTH, G. C., Anglo-Indian Dictionary : a glossary of Indian terms used in English, and of such English or other non-Indian terms as have obtained special meanings in India. 8vo, cloth, 12*s.*

WIGSTON, W. F. C., Hermes Stella, or Notes and jottings on the Bacon cipher. 8vo, 6*s.*

WILBERFORCE, Reginald, Life of Bishop Wilberforce of Oxford and Winchester, by his Son, Crown 8vo, 9*s.*

WILDRIDGE, T. Tyndall, The Dance of Death, in Painting and in Print, with woodcuts. Small 4to, 3*s.* 6*d.*

WILHELM, Joseph, and SCANNELL, Thomas B., Manual of Catholic Theology, based on Scheeben's 'Dogmatick.' 2 vols. 8vo. Vol. I. 15*s.*

WILKINSON, Capt. H. Spenser, CITIZEN SOLDIERS : essays towards the improvement of the Volunteer Force. Crown 8vo, 2*s.* 6*d.*

WILLIAMS, S. Wells, SYLLABIC DICTIONARY OF THE CHINESE LANGUAGE ; arranged according to the Wu-Fang Yuen Yin, with the pronunciation of the characters as heard in Pekin, Canton, Amoy, and Shanghai. 4to, £5. 5*s.*

WILLIS, R., LIFE, CORRESPONDENCE, AND ETHICS OF BENEDICT DE SPINOZA. 8vo, 21*s.*

WILSON, Crawford, PASTORALS AND POEMS. Crown 8vo, 7*s.* 6*d.*

WILSON, H. H., RIG-VEDA-SANHITA : a collection of ancient Hindu hymns, from the Sanskrit, edited by E. B. COWELL and W. F. WEBSTER. 6 vols. 8vo. Vols. I. II. III. 21*s.* each. Vol. IV. 14*s.* Vols. V. and VI. 21*s.* each.

THE MEGHA-DUTA (Cloud Messenger), translated from the Sanskrit of KALIDASA. New edition, 4to, 10*s.* 6*d.*

ESSAYS AND LECTURES, chiefly on the religion of the Hindus, collected and edited by Dr. REINHOLD ROST. 2 vols. 21*s.*

ESSAYS, analytical, critical, and philological, on subjects connected with Sanskrit literature, collected and edited by Dr. REINHOLD ROST. 3 vols. 36*s.*

VISHNU PURÁNÁ : a system of Hindu mythology and tradition, from the original Sanskrit, illustrated by notes derived chiefly from other Puránás, edited by FITZEDWARD HALL. 5 vols. £3. 4*s.* 6*d.*

SELECT SPECIMENS OF THE THEATRE OF THE HINDUS, from the original Sanskrit. 3rd edition, 2 vols. 21*s.*

WITHIN SOUND OF THE SEA, with frontispiece. Crown 8vo, 6*s.*

WISE, Clement, PURITANISM IN POWER. 8vo, 14*s.*

WOLTMANN, Alfred, and WOERMANN, Karl, HISTORY OF PAINTING, with numerous illustrations. Medium 8vo. Vol. I. Painting in Antiquity and the Middle Ages, 28*s.* Vol. II. The Painting of the Renascence, 42*s.* The two volumes may be had bound in cloth with bevelled boards and gilt leaves, price 30*s.* and 45*s.* respectively.

WOOD, M. W., DICTIONARY OF VOLAPÜK : Volapük-English and English-Volapük. Crown 8vo, 10*s.* 6*d.*

WOODBURY, Chas. J., TALKS WITH RALPH WALDO EMERSON. Crown 8vo, 5*s.*

WORDSWORTH BIRTHDAY BOOK, edited by ADELAIDE and VIOLET WORDSWORTH. 32mo, 2*s.* ; cloth limp, 1*s.* 6*d.*

WORDSWORTH, SELECTIONS FROM, by WILLIAM KNIGHT and other members of the Wordsworth Society, printed on hand-made paper. Large crown 8vo, with portrait, vellum, 15*s.* ; parchment, 12*s.* Cheap edition, crown 8vo, 4*s.* 6*d.*

WOOLFIELD'S LIFE AT CANNES, AND LORD BROUGHAM'S FIRST ARRIVAL, by J. M. 2*s.* 6*d.*

WORTHAM, B. H., SATAKAS OF BHARTRIHARI, translated from the Sanskrit. Post 8vo (*Trübner's Oriental Series*), 5*s.*

WORTHY, Charles, PRACTICAL HERALDRY, an epitome of English armory, with 124 illustrations. Crown 8vo, 7*s.* 6*d.*

WRIGHT, G. Frederick, THE ICE AGE IN NORTH AMERICA, AND ITS BEARING UPON THE ANTIQUITY OF MAN, with maps and illustrations. 8vo, 21s.

WRIGHT, Thomas, THE HOMES OF OTHER DAYS : a history of domestic manners and sentiments during the Middle Ages, with 350 illustrations, drawn and engraved by F. W. FAIRHOLT. Medium 8vo, 21s.

ANGLO-SAXON AND OLD ENGLISH VOCABULARIES. 2nd edition, edited by R. P. WULCKER. 2 vols. 8vo, 28s.

THE CELT, THE ROMAN, AND THE SAXON : a history of the early inhabitants of Britain down to the conversion of the Anglo-Saxons to Christianity. Corrected and enlarged edition, with nearly 300 engravings, crown 8vo, 9s.

WRIGHT, W., THE BOOK OF KALILAH AND DIMNAH, translated from Arabic into Syriac, with preface and glossary in English. 8vo, 21s.

WURTZ, Prof., THE ATOMIC THEORY, translated by E. CLEMINSHAW. 5th edition, crown 8vo, 5s. [I.S.S.

WYNELL-MAYOW, S. S., THE LIGHT OF REASON. Crown 8vo, 5s.

YEATS, W. B., THE WANDERINGS OF OISIN, and other poems. Small 8vo, 5s.

YELVERTON, Christopher, ONEIROS, or Some questions of the day. Crown 8vo, 5s.

YOUNG, Prof., THE SUN, with illustrations. 3rd edition, crown 8vo, 5s. [I.S.S.

YOUMANS, Eliza A., FIRST BOOK OF BOTANY, designed to cultivate the observing powers of children, with 300 engravings. New and cheaper edition, crown 8vo, 2s. 6d.

SHAKSPERE'S WORKS.

THE AVON. EDITION.

Printed on thin opaque paper, and forming 12 handy volumes, cloth, 18*s.*, or bound in 6 volumes, 15*s.*

The set of 12 volumes may also be had in a cloth box, price 21*s.*, or bound in Roan, Persian, Crushed Persian Levant, Calf, or Morocco, and enclosed in an attractive leather box, at prices from 31*s.* 6*d.* upwards.

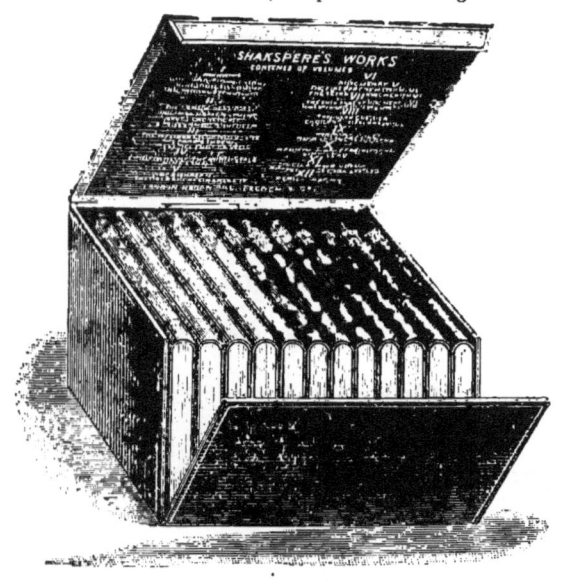

THE PARCHMENT LIBRARY EDITION.

In 12 volumes Elzevir 8vo, choicely printed on hand-made paper, and bound in parchment or cloth, price £3. 12*s.*, or in vellum, price £4. 10*s.*

The set of 12 volumes may also be had in a strong cloth box, price £3. 17*s.*, or with an oak hanging shelf, £3. 18*s.*

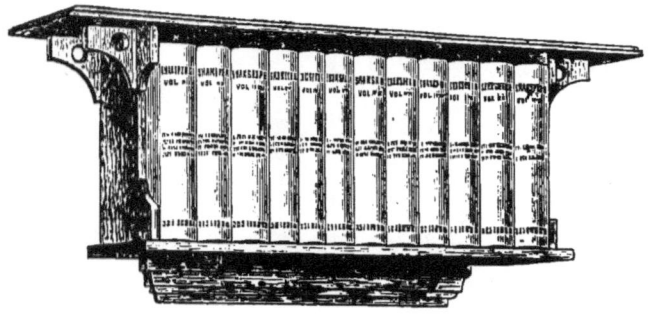

LONDON: KEGAN PAUL, TRENCH, TRÜBNER, & CO., LTᴰ.

Spottiswoode & Co. Printers, New-street Square, London.